USBORNE PUBLISHING

SHOCK HORROR HISTORY!

The Stone Age Sentinel........1

The Egyptian Echo...............33

The Greek Gazette...............65

The Roman Record...............97

STONE AGE SENTINEL

Cavemates!

Ed Zog here with four million years' worth of history, all crammed into a rock-melting 32 pages!

This here is the STONE AGE SENTINEL, and it's translated from the original Caveman for your comfort and convenience.

HOT

So what have we got? First of all we've got 18 pages of the hottest news this side of an erupting volcano. We start with

the first hominids to walk on two legs rather than four. (What's a hominid? You are, bone brain, and so are any of your ape-man predecessors!)

SWEAT

Read on and find out why bigger brains are best, why sweating is no bad thing, and why fire is the greatest thing since sliced mammoth.

Officially the Stone Age lasts from around 2,000,000 to 2,000 BC. But as we cover much more – from 4,000,000 to 2,000 BC – you're getting more years for your money than any other comparable newspaper!!!

WHAT'S THE CATCH?

And that's not all.

Want to know how to catch a mate Stone Age style?

Curious about what's cooking in the Stone Age stockpot?

Itching to find out what gets them grooving on the Stone Age dance floor?

Read our features between pages 20 and 32!

And remember, if it ain't stone, it ain't worth a bone!!!

Your pal

ed zog

Ed Zog, Editor,
Stone Age Sentinel

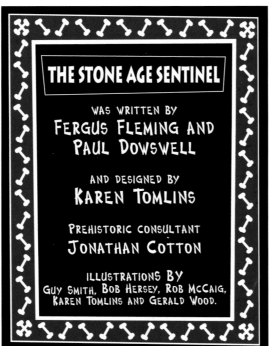

THE STONE AGE SENTINEL

WAS WRITTEN BY
FERGUS FLEMING AND
PAUL DOWSWELL

AND DESIGNED BY
KAREN TOMLINS

PREHISTORIC CONSULTANT
JONATHAN COTTON

ILLUSTRATIONS BY
GUY SMITH, BOB HERSEY, ROB McCAIG,
KAREN TOMLINS AND GERALD WOOD.

THE STONE AGE SENTINEL
ON OTHER PAGES

NEWS

Ape man in "walking" sensation 4,000,000 BC **2**

Think big! Brains matter, say experts 2,000,000 BC **4**

Cave shortage prompts hut building spree 380,000 BC **7**

Wise man wins human race 100,000 BC **8**

Cave dwellers in graffiti uproar 15,000 BC **11**

Mammoth shortage shock 12,000 BC **13**

Farming frenzy hits Fertile Crescent 7,500 BC **14**

Wheel meet again. Transportation special 3,000 BC **17**

New threat to stone 3,000 BC **19**

FEATURES

Short, sharp, shock weapons special **20-21**

Mrs. Ogg's Stone Age beauty page **22**

There's no business like snow business. Surviving in the Arctic **23**

Speech. What everyone needs to hear **24-25**

What's cooking? Get stuffed with the *SENTINEL!* **26-27**

Dazzy Dork's WHAT'S HAPPENING music column **28**

Aaaachooo! Why, bless me, it's our medical page **29**

Bite the dust in Stone Age style with our guide to prehistoric burials **30**

Meet Stagman – the priest who thinks he's a reindeer **31**

Name that tool! Pass a desperate ten minutes with our quiz on humankind's most boring implements **32**

The Stone Age Sentinel

ARE YOU A MAN OR A MOUSE?

Want to know where you come from? Look at the *Sentinel*'s easy-to-follow family tree and you'll see in a second how you fit into the evolutionary scheme of things...

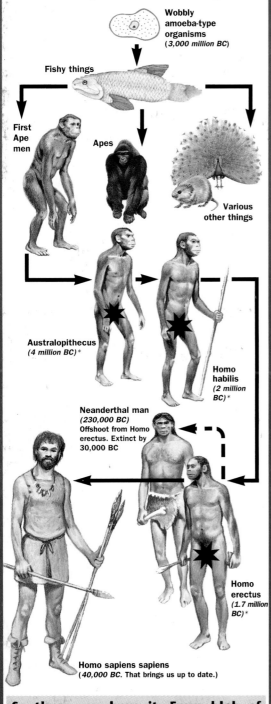

Wobbly amoeba-type organisms (*3,000 million BC*)

Fishy things

First Ape men

Apes

Various other things

Australopithecus (*4 million BC*)*

Homo habilis (*2 million BC*)*

Neanderthal man (*230,000 BC*) Offshoot from Homo erectus. Extinct by 30,000 BC

Homo erectus (*1.7 million BC*)*

Homo sapiens sapiens (*40,000 BC*. That brings us up to date.)

So there you have it. From blob of jelly to modern man in a mere 3,000 million years. So whether you're an Australopithecus or a Homo erectus (or even a mouse), just remember, the *Sentinel* is FIRST WITH THE NEWS!!

TWO LEGS BETTER THAN FOUR

Ape-man in "walking" sensation

4,000,000 BC

Is it a shoe or is it a glove? The age-old debate is over, according to evolutionary whiz-kids *Australopithecus*. From now on, say these ape-men, we don't have to go around on all fours. Instead we can walk upright.

FURROW

The brow-furrowing breakthrough came when this bunch of hominids realized the advantages of standing on two feet.

"It makes us nimbler and faster," said a two-legged spokesman. "It also makes us more versatile – we can carry things and run at the same time, for example. But above all, it gives us a very satisfying impression of height. When you walk on two feet you can peer over bushes, gaze manfully into the distance and grab things from high branches. None of this was possible on all fours."

THICK

"Naturally, we will retain some of our earlier characteristics – thick brows, massive jaws, long, strong arms, a tendency to stoop, and awkward table manners – but these will iron themselves out with the passage of time."

Standing a full 1.4m (4½ft) high, and weighing in at 27kg (60lb), *Australopithecus* (or "New Ape-Man") is more than able to cope with the demands of his environment.

Some *Australopithecus*es show off their two-legged skills. "They'll be dancing *Swan Lake* next," sneer rival species.

REELING

Apes who still walk on all four limbs are seriously worried for their future. "It's left us reeling!" said a representative of all-fours pressure group 'Can't Stand, Won't Stand.' "There we were, minding our own business, when these lanky streaks came darting past on two legs. It spoiled our day.

"We've tried copying them, but we just can't get the hang of it. They say it's like riding a bicycle: once you've learned, you never forget. What nonsense! And what's a bicycle anyway? Take it from me: two legs are downright unnatural!"

Our Getting-Around Correspondent, Larry Plunck says: "Walking is just the tip of the iceberg. Very soon we'll be able to amble, stroll, tiptoe, skip, march and dance the gavotte. The possibilities are endless."

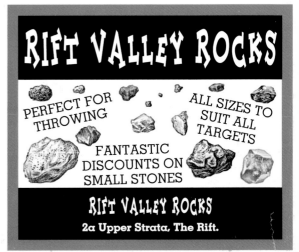

*The Sentinel is a respectable family newspaper and does not approve of nudity in any era.

ROCK ON!
IT'S THE STONE AGE!

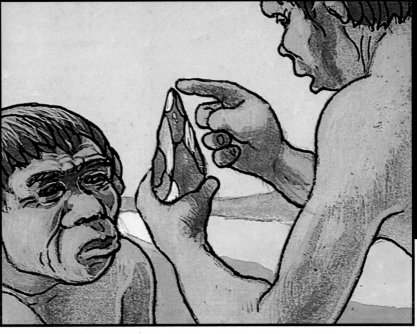

Homo habilis **invents the ancestor of the variable-speed power drill.**

THUMBS-UP TOOL TRICK GIVES HUMANS A HELPING HAND

2,000,000 BC

Watch out! There's a new idea about! That's the buzz around the African grassland as *Homo habilis*, the first recognizable human, saunters forth with his amazing new invention – the tool!

"Ever since we realized we didn't have to walk on our hands, we've been wondering what to do with our 'front feet'," a *Homo habilis* told us. "At last we've found the answer. After much experimentation we discovered that the twiddly parts at the end – now known as fingers – are not only great for picking berries and noses, but can also be used to make tools!

Tools? We asked top handyman Reggie Lugg to explain.

"Well, you see, a tool is something that does something better than hands – like scissors, dental floss and variable-speed drills with hammer-action for solid walls. Of course, we haven't invented these things yet, but we've made a respectable start by chipping stones to give them a sharp edge. On their own, sharp stones make very good knives. But tie a piece of wood onto them and you've got an axe, or even a spear!"

HACKING

Habilis means "skilled", and there's no doubt that *Homo habilis* is living up to his name. He's chipping and hacking like there's no tomorrow. In fact, he looks set to take over the whole world!

Ape-man *Australopithecus* is resigned to extinction. But they've got a few points to raise before they go.

"These new hominids may be clever, but they're a messy bunch," said one ape-person. "They leave their little shards of sharpened stone lying all over the place. What if our kids cut themselves on one of these things? We've still got another 800,000 years to go before we die out, so we think they ought to be more considerate. I'll bet people will still be picking up their mess millions of years from now."

Pleased to meat you!

Hunter-gatherers Come Out Top As Meat Mania Sweeps Globe

2,000,000 BC

It's Pick 'n' Mix time for us hominids as we face up to a brand new menu. Until now, we've had to content ourselves with picking berries, roots and the odd vegetable. Thanks to *Homo habilis*, however, a new item has been added to the menu – meat!

RUM

"Blearggh! Can't stand the stuff! Give me a nice rummage in the shrubs," said top *Australopithecus* ape-man and vegetarian, Ronnie Lurch.

But veggies like Lurch are up against stiff competition. Almost every kind of animal, from a gazelle to a quagga*, can find green stuff and eat it quicker than ape-men can. The only way to survive is to eat meat as well as veg.

GO FORTH

"It's all very well saying to go forth and gather," said leading *Homo habilis* Cornelius Gogg. "But in today's competitive environment you need to hunt too. That's why we're carving a niche for ourselves as hunter-gatherers."

The new breed of hunter-gatherers have set themselves a strict agenda. They've got a month in each area to strip all available vegetation, kill whatever they can, and then move on

This stuff is packed full of protein and is very tasty! It's more difficult to catch than a plant, but experts say it's definitely worth the extra effort.

to new ground.

Ape-men have responded with a detailed manifesto called 'Veg Is Best'. But their pledge that 'Brussel Sprouts Taste Nice' has been greeted with widespread derision.

*Modern-day hunter-gatherers please note: a quagga is a washed-out zebra which disappeared around AD 1900, so don't bother looking for it now.

THINK BIG

Here we go, here we go! A bunch of burly hominids flex those all important brain muscles.

SIZE MATTERS, SAY BRAIN GURUS

2,000,000 BC

A brain may not appear as immediately useful as a good set of teeth," head expert Professor Elmer Yarg said yesterday, "but it's indispensable if you want to get ahead in life. And research has shown that the bigger it is, the better you'll do."

LACK

Prof. Yarg and his colleagues claim that big brains make up for our lack of fangs, talons, tusks, claws, poison glands and other frightening things.

"If you have a big brain you can outwit creatures with smaller brains," said Prof. Yarg. **"It's that simple**. And as humans have got the biggest brains in the world we can outwit anything.

"Physically, we're weak and vulnerable. But we've got it up top and that's what counts. I wouldn't be surprised if we became the leading creatures on the planet."

AHEM

Opponents have slammed the big-brain theory on the grounds that human female's birth canals are not big enough to deliver children with big brains.

Prof. Yarg has the answer. "It's very straightforward. What happens is that we're born with small brains and then they increase in size as we grow older. Other species do this, but they don't do it as well as we do. A human baby's brain is 25% of what it will be in adulthood. A chimpanzee, by comparison, is born with 65% of its total brain power."

(Adult human brains are almost twice as big as chimpanzees and by the 20th century AD they'll be three times as big. Wow!)

"Granted, there are some drawbacks. While the baby's brain is growing, it's completely dependent on its parents. A baboon can look after itself after 12 months, whereas it takes a good six years for human kids to get the hang of things. So that means an awful lot more time and effort for the parents."

BRAIN OR BRAWN?

Decide for yourself which is best with our handy check list!

MAN	TIGER
Small	Big and hairy
Weedy little fingers	Fangs-and-all
Thinks	Roars
Sharpens Arrows	Sharpens Claws
Gets Friends	Gets Irritable
Makes Ambush	Makes Terrifying Faces
Home Before Dinner	Is dinner

HERE AT THE SENTINEL WE SAY THERE'S NO CONTEST!!! IT LOOKS LIKE THE BRAIN IS THE DEADLIEST WEAPON OF ALL.

PERSPIRATION? NO SWEAT!

MAN CHILLS OUT

2,000,000 BC

Do your smelly armpits embarrass you? Well don't you worry. According to the latest evidence, sweating buckets is a major bonus.

Dr. Oscar Snig explains all:

"Living as we do in Africa, it is vital to be able to keep cool. The basic way of doing this for most species is to lie in the shade, put out your tongue and pant. But this makes you look silly and is only effective in short bursts. If you do it on the run, you get dizzy and fall over – not to mention finding your mouth full of flies. That's why all the big predators tend not to do much round about midday."

LYING IN THE SUN

"Humans can't afford to lie around, especially at midday when the pickings'll be good, since the other carnivores are out of the way. So we've come up with two classy ways of keeping cool AND being able to hunt at the same time. First of all, we've lost most of our body hair. And secondly, we've learned how to sweat.

"Sweating is an incredibly efficient form of temperature control. The moment you get too hot, your body oozes water which cools you by evaporation. This means you can chase those pesky gazelles without having to stop every few minutes for a pant."

EXCESS

However, Snig warns, excess perspiration can be dangerous. Humans can only tolerate water loss amounting to 10% of their total body weight. Overly-enthusiastic sweaters run a risk of becoming dehydrated.

"It's very important to replace lost fluid. Some animals can store water very effectively – a camel, for example, can take aboard about 20 buckets of water in 10 minutes. Humans can only store a hundredth of that in the same time. Therefore I'd advise people to sweat only in areas where there are plenty of rivers and streams."

SENTINEL VERDICT:

Smell bad. It's the way forward. And you can forget about unsightly sweat stains because we don't wear clothes.

Dr. Snig's book *Why We're Not Camels* comes out in August. RRP 15.99 pebbles.

NEXT WEEK: ARE HICCUPS A HELP?

A hominid doing some sweating. Unfortunately for his chums it'll be two million years before someone invents the underarm deoderant.

"THEY WERE SMALL AND STUPID!"

NEW GENERATION TRASHES 'SKILLED' BREED

Homo habilis – Yesterday's man.

1,700,000 BC

The latest race of humans has arrived! They're big, they're brainy, they're the best – they're *Homo erectus!*

The new kids on the block take a dim view of their ancestors, *Homo habilis*, whom they brand as "stunted dimwits."

"They may have been clever for their time," said Al 'Upright' Ugg, "but compared to us they're nothing. We're a good 50cm (20in) taller, we're over 20kg (44lbs) heavier and as for our brains – well, let's just say you can think a whole lot better with an extra whole 15% of the gray crinkly stuff."

TOOLS

With their greater size and their advanced tool-making capabilities, *Homo erectus* are certainly making their mark on the evolutionary scene. But some of them are asking the question, 'How come we're so big?'

"Easy," said Al. "Big animals need less energy, relative to their body weight, than small animals. Marmosets, for example, eat proportionally three times as much as a human. So if food is scarce, it's actually more efficient to be big. Still confused? Never mind. You've got plenty of time to figure it out because we're going to be here for the next 1.5 million years!"

FIRE IN THE HOLE

Bright Sparks Cause Flame Sensation

450,000 BC

It's hot, it makes you sweat and it's not curry. Yes, it's FIRE!

Previously considered somewhat frightening, the amazing red stuff has become man's best friend. All over the world, humans are using it to cook, to keep warm and to frighten wild beasts.

STRIKES

"There's nothing new about fire," said Norris Nik, President of the Hearth Trust. "You can find it all over the place – bush fires, lightning strikes and volcanoes, for example. But the breakthrough has been introducing it to the home. What you do is make a little pile of stuff, then you find your nearest source of fire, stick a long piece of wood into it and hurry back to light your stuff. If the stuff doesn't burn – and if it's stone or earth it probably won't – try a pile of different stuff. It sounds complicated but it's very simple really."

LOTS

Fire has lots of things going for it, the main one being that it gives us humans more control of our surroundings.

"Before, we depended on the Sun for heat and light," enthused Norris. "Now we can keep warm and dry wherever we are. This not only spells an end to dank caves but it means we can survive in cold places like Europe. And if any Ice Age comes along we can just sit it out."

Fire. Once you've tamed it you can't live without it, and it has so many uses. These hungry hominids are using it to confuse and frighten their dinner.

GROOMING

Scientists aren't sure what fire is, but the current opinion is that it may be some kind of animal.

"In its natural state, fire can be extremely danger-ous. However, it is easily tamed and makes a perfect household pet. It's easy to look after, requiring no grooming or vet's visits, and survives happily on a diet of twigs and dry grass. But it does tend to die if given too much to drink.

"Its only drawback is that it leaves nasty stains on the ceiling – but if you have bats already you'll be used to that."

WHAT A DUMP!

Europe a "cultural wasteland"

478,000 BC

Paris in the springtime? Swinging London? Rome, the eternal city? Pah! Give us a break!

Are we disappointed or what? Having trudged all the way to Europe we've found it's got no croissants, no fancy pasta shapes, no cute little cities, no castles and no scandal-prone royal families. In fact, it has a noticeable lack of anything interesting at all.

SHIVER

"It's a cold, miserable place with a lot of mountains, forests and rivers," said shivering Debby Klunk, one of the first wave of settlers. "In the north it's nothing but snow and ice. If we stay here long enough I wouldn't be at all surprised if we ended up with pale skins, an embarrassing amount of body hair and a deplorable sense of rhythm. We should never have left Africa."

BAD

However, sources re-veal that Europe isn't as bad as it's made out to be. For starters it's a lot drier than Africa. Moreover, it's got an abundance of animals and is therefore a tip-top destination for hunters.

As numbers grow in the African grasslands and humans begin to feel the pinch we say: "Go North young man!"

LET'S STEPPE ON IT!

MAN GETS INTO THE ASIAN SWING

400,000 BC

"Europe? Why go there?" asks laid-back hominid Hussein Ogg, basking outside his Asian cave. "That's a place for stupid people."

Hussein has a point. Besides being cold and nasty, Europe is also very small. Asia, on the other hand, is mostly warm, is crammed with herds of wildlife, has millions of acres of grassland, and stretches from the Mediterranean to the Pacific.

TOP TRIP

According to a recent hunter-gatherer survey, Asia is our No. 1 destination. Visitors enjoy:
• Nice climate
• Open spaces
• Plenty of food
•The opportunity to become Chinese and invent practically everything before anybody else does.

ENDLESS

Particular attention has been focused on three main rivers – the

Life in a cave, somewhere in Asia. These people could even be heading for China!

Euphrates in Mesopotamia, the Yellow in China and the Indus in India.

"Asia has endless potential," said migration rep. Sally-Sue Grunk. "But it's the big river systems which seem to be the main draw. People say conditions are very comfortable there and given enough time they might even settle down and start farming."

THERE'S NO PLACE LIKE HOME!

By Sentinel correspondent KEN ZOG

Cave shortage prompts hut-building spree

380,000 BC

The world is echoing to the sound of wolf whistles as humans hitch up their furs, dust off their tasteless jokes and get into some serious construction work.

Building has become big business thanks to the pressures of growing populations and an increasing shortage of accommodation.

"Pah, who did your drains? It'll cost you to have them done properly," say builders.

JUST

"There just aren't enough caves to go round," said Len Mukk (building, decorating and allied trades). "People are coming up and saying, 'Len, knock me up a hut will you? Nothing fancy – just enough space for me and the wife, with somewhere to stick the rest of the family.' So I tell 'em it'll take two weeks and we go from there – strictly pebbles-in-hand, mind you. You can't give credit in today's economic climate."

FLIMSY

Len and his mates are particularly busy in Europe, where decent caves are rare outside of southern France.

"Now and then a customer complains that his home's too flimsy. So I say, 'Look son. You're a hunter-gatherer. You're on the move all the time. You don't want nothing permanent. I've built you a nice little one-room hut out of leafy branches. You've got a row of central posts and some stonework around the edges so's it doesn't blow away. There's a hearth in the middle and space for you all to huddle down in your furs at night. It'll last you the season. Then you'll be moving on. What more do you want? If you're after the Palace of Versailles you should have said so.' There's no reasoning with some, is there?"

HIPPOS IN THE THAMES?

PALM TREES IN GREENLAND?

What's going on?

An Investigative Special Report By Olsen Mug*

130,000 BC

Weather! Can't live with it, can't live without it. One millennium you're shivering in your furs, and the next you're squabbling over who gets the suntan lotion first. Hot, cold, hot, cold – it's enough to make you dizzy.

Our unpredictable climate has been a source of irritation for hundreds of thousands of years. But thanks to a special investigation by *Sentinel* super-sleuth, Olsen Mug*, we now know why it acts like it does.

LIES

"The secret lies in the way the Earth goes around the Sun," says Olsen Mug*. "Its orbit isn't always the same. Sometimes it takes us farther away from the Sun, and sometimes it takes us closer.

"This means that we have successive Ice Ages, with glaciers reaching as far south as London and New York, followed by

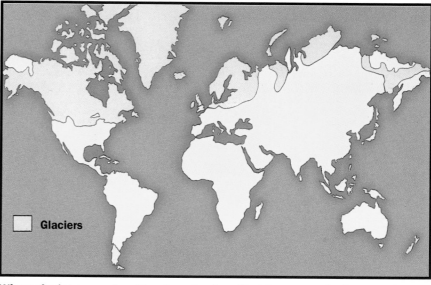

Where the ice goes when there's an Ice Age. (Just in case you're interested...)

Glaciers

ice-free periods when the earth is warm and fertile, lions wander through Europe, and Britons shelter beneath palm trees, and have to plaster on Factor 20 mud when they sunbathe."

TRAP

"This also explains the puzzling phenomenon of why, at times, land is sometimes above the sea and sometimes beneath it.

When it's cold, most of the world's water is trapped in glaciers and sea levels are low. But when it gets hot, the glaciers melt and we have lots of rain, therefore sea levels rise."

AWKWARD

"Of course, all this tooing and froing does have its awkward moments.

Imagine you're a hippo, wallowing in the Thames.

Then along comes an Ice Age and everybody starts pointing and acting like you don't belong. How embarrassing! And then you have other problems, like not being able to survive because it's too cold, and all the plants you usually eat don't grow where you live anymore. It does make life difficult."

SPELL

How long can we expect this to continue? "Almost indefinitely," says Olsen Mug*. "A prolonged warm spell is predicted from about 13,000 BC, but things will start cooling off around the 21st century AD.

"Maybe by then, however, they'll have discovered the secret of global warming."

IT'S A KNOCKOUT!

100,000 BC

Wise man wins human race

The name's Sap – Hom double sap." Yes, it's hands up to *Homo sapiens sapiens*, the hominid who's licensed to kill.

Despite stiff competition *Hom. sap. sap.* – "the wisest of the wise" – has won

through to become the top species on Earth.

"It's all to do with being extremely clever," one *Homo sapiens sapiens* admitted modestly. "With our advanced skills we are in *every* way superior to any other type of being."

TOOLS

It is all true. *Homo sapiens sapiens* has the most powerful brain of any hominid. And with this massive amount of grey stuff, they have been

able to create increasingly complex tools and, above all, develope a sophisticated language. (You can read more about this on pages 24-25, word fans.)

WEIGHT LOSS

It doesn't matter that *Hom. sap. sap.* is only two-thirds the weight of predecessor *Homo erectus*. Being able to speak properly means they can plan, exchange ideas and generally stir things up to their own benefit.

"We may be less bulky than previous species but we have evolved THE definitive brain size," says Dr. Heinrich Zag, an expert in his field. "There will be no comparable brain for the foreseeable future. People in 2000 AD may look back and say, 'Oh how uncivilized they were!' But the fact is, our brains and bodies are exactly the same as those hominids on the 7:30am train from Richmond."

OLSEN MUG
Special Reporter

G'DAY!

CAVEMATES DISCOVER AUSTRALIA!!

50,000 BC

First it was Europe, then it was Asia. Now humankind has taken over God's own garden, the land of the roo and the billabong – Australia!

UNDERSIDE

"Strewth, it's peculiar out here, mate," said Bob Awk, one of the first settlers. "The place is hot as a billycan's underside for starters. And the wildlife – well, either someone's playing a joke or they've been left to evolve on their own for too long. Take the kangaroo – big feller, bounds along on its hind legs and carries its kids in a little pouch. Believe me, you don't find that kind of creature anywhere else in the world. Same goes for the wallaby, the koala, the kookaburra and the duck-billed platypus. Queer as a three-dollar bill, the lot of 'em. And as for the XXXXXXX flies…"

"Still, the surfing's good and there's some impressive deserts we can go walkabout in. Could be worse."

GATHER

Australia may be special, but it's not half as special as the way it was colonized. From what our reporters can gather, a huge number of *Homo sapiens sapiens* in Indonesia simply got in their boats and said, "Let's go to Australia." And off they went!

That's pretty amazing, especially when our fortune-tellers predict that it'll be another 51,788 years before anybody else realizes Australia exists.

And, they say, guess what the new bunch of *Hom. sap. saps.* will call the old bunch of *Hom. sap. saps.* when they find them in the 18th century AD? Aborigines! That's from the Latin "*Ab Origine*" which means "From the beginning."

"Well," says Bob, "if we're from the beginning, does that mean they're the end? Future hominids should give that a bit of thought."

Bob Awk and cavemate go in search of Australia's weird and wonderful wildlife.

"DEAD END" SHOCK FOR ALTERNATIVES

NEANDERTHALS TOLD "YOU'RE NOBODIES"

40,000 BC

Neanderthals have been doing their best to become an alternative race of humans. But their hopes were quashed at a recent convention of hominids when it was revealed that they lacked all the major qualifications.

DEVASTATED

"I'm devastated!" said beetle-browed Grr Ngg. "We seriously thought we were going places. But as the convention wore on, we realized that we were way behind the competition!"

When the low-slung, chunky Neanderthals first appeared in about 230,000 BC their prospects were as good as anybody else's. True, they looked a bit brutish and ape-like, but they were pretty sophisticated. They cared for their old and sick, they developed a primitive religion and buried their dead with flowers and gifts – though some experts have dismissed this as "mere corpse disposal".

YAK

"It was *"Hom-oh-so-high-and-mighty"* sapiens sapiens who spelled our downfall," said Grr. "We couldn't match his tool-making skills and we simply couldn't understand what he was yakking on about. That was our big failing – speech. *Hom sap sap* can say things like 'Hello gorgeous, how about a date?' All we can do is grunt a bit and make vivid hand signals. We're washed up. By 30,000 BC we won't be here and everyone will say 'Where have those interesting alternative type humans gone?'"

LOST LORE OF THE NEANDERTHALS

No. 1 of our occasional series brings you the secrets of Neanderthal etiquette.

DO THE NEANDER MEANDER!

Your step-by-stumble guide to low-brow deportment.

THINGS TO GET RIGHT

1. Knees bent
2. Chin out
3. Fists curled
4. Brow furrowed

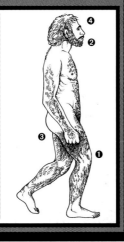

LET'S COME TOGETHER!

GOOD VIBES FOR TRIBES

Being in a big group of fellow hominids is much more fun that mooching around on your own, even if you do end up seeing far more of Uncle Zog than you'd care too.

30,000 BC

It's true – solitary scavenging can damage your health! According to reports you're likely to wither and die unless you're part of a tribe.

Communal living has been the rage for some time now. It started way back when early hominids stood upright and had to care for their children. This led to…

1. Small groups of hominids sticking together.

Then there came the business of hunting which, in order to be successful, required…

2. Cooperation with other groups.

After that came language, and as everyone knows if you speak, you need someone to speak to, so that led to…

3. Gossip, general chit-chat and telling Waffly Zog to shut up on the mammoth hunt.

Then came the pressures of migrating to different places, facing ferocious foreign beasts and checking the toilet for poisonous spiders. This encouraged us to…

4. Group together in the face of adversity in even greater numbers.

And so we formed tribes!

BAND

What's a tribe? Simple. We tend to hunt and gather in groups of 30 or so (12 adults and their kids). When 20 of these groups get together they form a band of around 600. This is a tribe. We meet for big hunts, the odd ceremony and all sorts of other things – like making up new words, exchanging ideas, and most important of all pairing up and having lots of little hominids.

So, at the end of the day, whether you're in Cairo or Cambridge, you're definitely safer with a tribe!

CAVE DWELLERS IN GRAFFITI UPROAR

"BUT IS IT ART?" SAY CRITICS

15,000 BC

French cave dwellers from Lascaux, in the Dordogne, are hopping mad. They've been branded as "destructive layabouts" – all on account of a little wall painting.

"They're vandals," said Lascaux local Mme. Bovary D'Ag. "Before these people moved in, the caves were in excellent condition. Now they're covered in graffiti which will cost a great deal to remove. They call it art. But I've seen them at it. They frolic around, daubing half-finished pictures of animals on the wall and then, late at night, some bright spark'll fill his mouth with paint and spray it out to make an outline of his hand. Frankly, they're a menace."

PLIGHT

"Oh, the plight of the struggling artist!" moaned Vincent van Ugh, a cave painter. "These paintings aren't graffiti. They're the first clear sign of man's artistic ability. They prove we can move beyond the day-to-day business of staying alive and can devote ourselves to more complex activity.

"What's more, art is a vital part of our kids' upbringing. Look. Here's a bull. And here's its hoof print. See? During the long winter months we put a lot of effort into these paintings so that our children can recognize animals and their tracks. It makes the hunting season so much easier. Imagine what would happen if we didn't do it. We'd have kids rushing at a cave lion shouting, "Gazelle! Easy meat!"

A CHILD OF FIVE COULD DO IT

Locals aren't convinced. "Some of the graffiti is quite unrecognizable as man or beast," says Mme. Bovary. "And look at the roof. It's covered in soot. They must have been lighting fires indoors. We don't need these kind of tenants. They're little better than squatters."

The unappreciated cave artists have agreed to move on. But they refuse to remove either the wall paintings or the layers of broken flints and small bones which cover the floor.

"The landlord wants to keep our deposits? Right. There they are, he can keep them!"

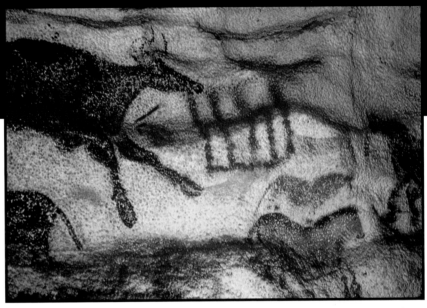

"Cows in French Art". Number one in a series of 100 great cow paintings. Collect the set!

HAND SIGNAL

News has come in that our Stone-Age artists are mostly right-handed. From a sample of 158 hand outlines discovered in the French cave of Gargas, 136 were painted by the right hand and only 22 by the left.

But our art expert warns: "These figures could be misleading. We need to include further data from findings in Germany, Portugal, Italy and Sicily to get a fuller picture of which hand is more commonly used in the European Community."

A report is expected within the next 32,000 years.

THE BUCK

DOESN'T STOP HERE!

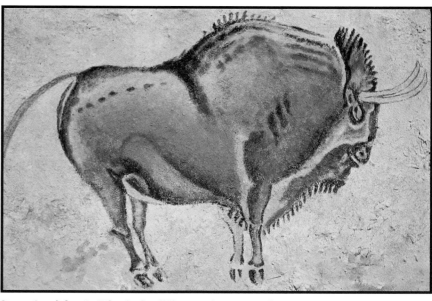

Stone Age joke: Q. What's the difference between a bat and a bison? A. If you don't know I certainly won't be asking you to go hunting! (Cue polite laughter.)

LAND OF OPPORTUNITY BECKONS

12,000 BC

It's a whole new continent! Intrepid trekkers in northern Siberia have discovered a land bridge leading from the Eurasian continent to America!

UNPLEASANT

Early reports say America is a cold and unpleasant place with little going for it.

"You'd have to be an Eskimo to survive there," said one disappointed colonist. "It's like living in Alaska."

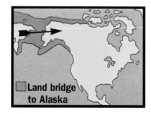

They went thataway!

However, geographical experts have pointed out that the place they've found is, in fact, Alaska, and that a sunnier climate awaits to the south.

Sentinel reporters have followed emigrants on their great trek, and can confirm that America gets hotter the farther down you go.

PASS

"First you pass through this cold area," says cub-reporter Jimmy Olsen-Clod, "Then you reach a country of big open spaces and endless opportunity. It's a fantastic place. There's endless prairies with million-strong herds of bison, and fields and fields of things like beans and corn."

"These foods are brand-new to us. But then so are a lot of other things here – turkeys, avocados, guinea-pigs, squashes and an irritating little dog called a Chihuahua."

Jimmy Olsen-Clod predicts that it'll take at least 2,000 years to reach the bottom of the continent.

"There's so much to see and explore. I reckon we won't be in Chile until 10,000 BC at the earliest."

WE'RE GOING TO POT

"Not a copy," say Japanese

"It's all our own work," insist Japanese potters.

12,000 BC

Japan has invented the most useful piece of pottery to date – the pot.

"It is a major breakthrough," said Professor Tanaka Stig. "We are now able to construct containers of any type we like simply by shaping lumps of clay and baking them in a covered pit."

"Unfortunately we are not able to use these pots as much as we would like. They are, alas, too heavy and too fragile to fit in with our hunting and gathering existence. Never-the-less, the art of pottery is here to stay and will undoubtedly be useful if people settle down to become farmers."

CLAIM

Opponents are already claiming the invention is a mere copy, and point to the existence of pottery skills in Czechoslovakia as far back as 25,000 BC.

LACKING

However, Professor Stig haughtily dismisses the earlier examples of pottery as "mere statuettes" which are "utterly lacking in usefulness."

"Pottery is a genuine first for Japan," he insists "and should fill us with justifiable national pride."

12

MAMMOTH SHORTAGE

CAUSES CONCERN

LIFESTYLE COLLAPSE PREDICTED FOR MANY

12,000 BC

Residents of eastern Europe and northern Asia are in big trouble. The mammoth, their main source of food, is disappearing FAST.

The mammoth has been a big item for centuries. Hunters have valued it for its legendary size (*Ed. actually, it's slightly smaller than an elephant*), its ivory tusks, its wonderful woolly hide and equally woolly brain.

Mammoths are so stupid and cumbersome that people have had no trouble laying an ambush and picking them off as they plod through the countryside. Sometimes they didn't even have to kill them. Quite often they found dead ones deep frozen and covered in ice and snow. All they had to do then was thaw them out at leisure using the miracle of fire.

SHREW

But all that's in the past. Nowadays, hunters lying in wait on the mammoth trail count themselves lucky if they bag a pygmy shrew.

What's happened? Mrs. Dunk, from the Russian village of Kostienki, tells all: "It's the men! They wouldn't stop killing mammoths. I told them they'd have problems if they carried on, but they took no notice. Now look what's happened. We've run out of the things. What can I do? Mr. Dunk won't touch his tea unless there's a big chunk of mammoth on the plate."

HALF

Experts say Mrs. Dunk is half right. The climate around Kostienki is also changing. It used to be freezing cold, and now it's getting warmer. And as the snow and ice retreats to the north, so the few remaining mammoths are following after it.

"Yes," bellowed a mammoth spokesperson, "we've all got these thick shaggy coats, so we like things nice and cold. This hot weather makes us all sweaty and bad tempered, so we're following our chums the reindeer to colder climes, where we can bask around in snow drifts."

This is very bad news for Kostienki, which has taken mammoth-mania to the limits. Not only do its inhabitants eat mammoths but they even build houses out of them. The doors are made of tusks and the walls are made of various other bones. The whole thing is pinned together with smaller bones, tied up with mammoth sinew and covered with hide.

Bone sweet bone – it's a mammoth house.

The framework alone of a typical mammoth-house, 5m (16ft) wide, weighs a staggering 21,000kg (46,000lb)! And some of their houses are much bigger than that!

THERE'S MORE

And what do you do in Kostienki when it's a bit cold? You throw a few mammoth bones on the fire! What do you do if you feel like creating a figurine of old Mrs. Zunk with her big nose? You get out your knife and a chunk of mammoth tusk!

MAD

Tools, toys, houses, food, clothes, furniture, knick-knacks – they're mammoth mad. In the whole village there's hardly a spoon or a needle that didn't start life as part of a mammoth.

So what are the Kostienkians going to do now?

"It's a clear choice," said Mr. Dunk. "We either make do with something else or go north in search of any remaining mammoths."

Bye-bye mammoth, we're missing you already!

Experts say overhunting, a changing environment and having a small brain has finished off the mammoth.

MAMMOTH UPDATE NEXT WEEK

FARMING FRENZY
HITS FERTILE CRESCENT

HUNTER GATHERERS WARN OF "MUTANT INVASION"

Some new-fangled farmers buckle down to some reaping what they sow, counting their chickens, and not letting one bad apple spoil the whole barrel.

7,500 BC

It's put-your-feet-up time in the Middle East, as folk discover the delights of farming.

Lifestyle experts from the Fertile Crescent ("It's a big lump of land running from Egypt to Iran, including the bottom bit of Turkey," says our Geography Correspondent) have found that folk live much more comfortably if they stop hunting and gathering, and take up farming instead.

SEED

What is farming? We asked a local agri-spokesman: "It's simple. You throw a few handfuls of seed around and wait for it to grow. Then you eat whatever it grows into. In between times you wander about waving a big stick, shouting, "Get off my land!" It's more exciting than picking berries and it's a whole lot easier than chasing

antelopes, I can tell you!"

But hunter-gatherers are lobbying for agriculture to be outlawed. "It's a menace to the natural order and it's putting us out of business," said a representative. "Farmers are selecting mutant plants which grow bigger than normal. And then they're planting them! It ought to be banned NOW!"

DESTROY

Farmers have laughed off suggestions that agriculture will destroy the countryside. "In the Fertile Crescent we're growing wheat, barley, peas, lentils – the works. It's the up-and-coming thing. India, China and South America will all be at it soon. And I'll tell you why. 15 square km (5.82 square miles) of fields can support 150 farmers. It takes 650 square km (250 square miles) to support 25 hunter-gatherers. Need I say more?"

STAINS

In a further break from tradition, farmers are building villages. These groups of dwellings are made from wood and stone, are usually found near a spring, and are designed to last for several years. Opponents say that villages are only the start and will lead to mega-

settlements with inner-city crime and graffiti-stained underpasses.

Hunter-gatherers are planning a "Hunt 'n Gather" protest march to draw attention to this unpleasant prospect. Their precise route is unknown but they are expected to wander in small, unhappy groups across Africa, Europe and Asia.

It's fertile and it's a crescent.

A STITCH IN TIME...

FUR FLIES AS FLAX SPARKS CLOTHING CRAZE

7,500 BC

It's official! Those Kill-things-and-wear-'em days are over. From now on it's pelts off and clothes on as the rag trade takes over!

Thanks to an

enterprising bunch of farmers, we no longer have to wear furs. Instead we can wear "cloth". This miracle fabric is guaranteed to be light, comfortable, quickly mended and easily replaced.

FLAX FAX

Sentinel reporters have identified the source of "cloth" as a plant called flax. According to informants, raw flax has to be soaked, pounded vigorously and then

Fashionable flax takes hours of dedicated work to process into the new miracle material "cloth".

rubbed on the thigh to make a weavable strand.

"It's hard work," agreed style guru Giovanni Lugg, "But it's worth the trouble. As for furs, they're completely out of

fashion – unless you live somewhere really cold. All that hair, and those rubbery fleshy tendrils. Ugh! Take it from me. Cloth's the people's choice."

TAME THAT BEAST
DOMESTICATION SENSATION!

Farming isn't just about crops. You'll need tame animals too. Here at the *Sentinel* we've drawn up a handy guide to a happy barnyard. Follow our chart to what stings and bites and what doesn't (or oughtn't to, at any rate) and you'll never go hunting or gathering again.

Aurochs

Stands 1.8m (6ft) at the shoulder. Muscly and bad-tempered. Has big, curved horns. Dislikes red rags. Provides a great deal of meat, leather and milk. Bellows and goes "Moo".

VERDICT – *An unlikely candidate, but since it provides so much, it's worth the trouble. Capture a few, breed from the placid ones and Hey Presto! you've got cows.*

Snake

Comes in all sizes. Slithery. Often poisonous. Impossible to milk. Unreliable egg-layer. Goes "Hiss".

VERDICT – *Don't bother. But keep a few on the refuse tip because they eat rats.*

Sheep and goat

About knee-height. Has horns. Provides warm, thick wool, milk and meat. Goes "Baa" and "Mehh".

VERDICT – *Ideal for the farm. They're herd animals, so once you've caught a few young 'uns they'll think you're herd leader and will do what you tell 'em (sort of).*

Wild boar

Smaller than sheep. Fat. Bristly. Has tusks and twirly tail. Provides bacon, chops and crackling. Goes "Oink".

VERDICT – *Yummy! Every home should have one. Is intelligent and eats anything, so is a natural for those rundown filth-strewn farms. Needs almost no taming. Comes home at night of its own accord. Often called Pig.*

Cat

Small. Plain, striped or tabby. Edible only on TV documentaries about funny foreigners. Goes "Miaouw" and "Browwp". Can scratch when irritated.

VERDICT – *Will accept domestication with a superior shrug. Eats mice, rats, small rabbits and birds and leaves their indigestible parts on your floor. Tends to trip you up but can be kicked very satisfactorily. Likes scratching furniture which is OK so long as your sitting log doesn't evolve into a sofa which you've upholstered at great expense. Comforting lap accessory.*

Believe it or not, over time this thing can be bred into a French poodle! (Would we lie to you?!?)

Tiger

Large, striped, frightening thing. Big teeth. Big appetite. Prone to scenes of explicit violence. Goes "Wraaaaaaagh."

VERDICT – *Only worth keeping if you have a particularly irksome milkman or if you belong to the "I-think-pit-bulls-and-Dobermans-are-soft" school of pet lovers. Otherwise forget it. Try its lesser cousin, the cat.*

Wolf

Small, rangy scavenger. Howls at night. Not worth eating but plays educational role in bedtime stories. Goes "Woof".

VERDICT – *A pack animal, so if you get a puppy it'll follow you around. Will help you out hunting, will fetch your slippers when you come home and will bark all day if you leave it inside.*

Fly

Has wings. Small and black. Plenty of eggs but too small to see. Creepy eyes. Spits on food. Tastes through feet. Goes "Buzz".

VERDICT – *Impossible to domesticate. Avoid like the plague.*

WARNING

Take care not to breed from animals that are too closely related, otherwise THIS could happen, or worse!

AGRICULTURE
OR AGRI-VATION?

Farmers say "Baa!" to animals

6,500 BC

Farming, which many thought would be a great leap forward for humankind, isn't such a good idea after all.

"We should never have given up hunting and gathering," says farmer Giles Gnug from Jericho, in the Fertile Crescent. "Agriculture is hard work, the diet's less varied, bandits keep stealing our food and we catch all these nasty new diseases."

GERMS

Diseases? Yes. If you live close to animals for too long, you catch viruses from them. The result is that human beings, who've never had a cold in their lives, are now prone to all sorts of deadly things like measles, smallpox and influenza.

"And that's not all," says farmer Giles. "If you live in a village, as most farmers do, surrounded by lots of people and all their filth, that means you're much likelier to catch whatever's going around than if you're hunting and gathering on the plains.

"Dysentery, typhoid, tuberculosis – you name it, we've got it. And some of these villages are in really unhealthy places. I've heard of this farming community at Çatal Hüyük in Turkey, for example, which is surrounded by mosquito-infested marshes and everyone catches malaria and dies at an early age. But then it was one of the first settlements, so maybe they didn't know any better."

In fact, most farmers can expect to die before they're 35 – or 30 if they're women.

So why do people do it? "Ah well," says Giles. "The trouble is there's so many of us. Once we started to get a regular supply of food we bred like rabbits, and now we're stuck with it. If we went back to hunting and gathering we'd all starve. It's too late to change now."

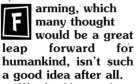

DID YOU KNOW...

- Nothing grows in the Sahara because all the goodness has been washed out of the soil by massive amounts of rainfall.

- The hefty old Aurochs – giant ancestor of the cow – won't be extinct until AD 1671.

- A typical Stone-Age head of corn is only the size of a thumb nail! (This is why we haven't bothered inventing pointy things to stick in the ends of corn-on-the-cob!)

Lost for smalltalk? Read The *Sentinel*!

Sheep. They may look cute and cuddly, but beneath the thin veneer of baaahsome amiability there lies a deadly, malevolent menace to mankind.

HOW IRRIGATING

Water load of old ditches!

3,500 BC

Wouldn't it be nice if we could grow more crops? Well now we can – thanks to irrigation, a cunning method of bringing water to places that are otherwise as dry as a desert.

Everyone knows that a bit of water helps crops grow, and that river mud is tip-top stuff for growing things in. But what do you do if you've got water in some places and not in others? Simple. You dig a ditch so that water flows from the watery places to the non-watery places. This way you'll turn a barren wasteland into a moist, silt-filled paradise where wheat waves golden in the breeze.

COMPLAINTS

Huge harvests have been recorded in countries such as Mesopotamia and Egypt where irrigation is commonplace.

But the people who dig the ditches are not happy with their lot.

"It's hard work," said one field hand. "We not only have to build these ditches but we have to maintain them. You've got to clear away the silt, you've got to make sure the water runs where you want it to, and then you've got to farm the fields. And then you've probably got to dig more ditches because some bright spark has decided to irrigate the entire Arabian desert."

MASSIVE

The widespread fear is that irrigation is too difficult for farmers to do on their own, and that it will give rise to a massive workforce paid by a single, all powerful government.

"This means we'll end up with kings and stuff. They'll demand taxes to pay the workers and this will lead to a lot of hard work for us peasants," said a peasant.

TRANSPORT SPECIAL

"YOU KNOW YOU'RE GOING PLACES WITH THE SENTINEL!"

WHEEL MEET AGAIN

The Shape Of The Future

3,000 BC

It's round, it's made of wood, and it's the greatest scientific break-through since the sharp stone. Yes, it's the WHEEL!

Humans are on the road at last, and the world is rumbling to the sound of traffic as we go wheel crazy.

A potter at a wheel. Would you believe this is the first step toward the Ferrari Testarossa?

POTS

According to our reporters, the wheel was first invented by potters, who needed a round, flat thing that they could spin a lump of muddy clay on to make pot-making easier. Then one smarty-pants said, "Hey! Why not turn a couple of these on their sides, attach them to a cart, and see what happens!"

Well, the rest is history.

CANS

Nowadays, anybody who's even vaguely with-it has a set of wheels. Teenager

Suzie Zagg says: "They're so cool! Because they go merrily round and round rather than drag unpleasantly along the ground, you can go places faster, and carry heavier weights than ever before!"

NUTS

Opponents are already dismissing the miracle invention as "merely an altered square." They say that although wheels allow people to move things more easily, they do have a big disadvantage: **they need a smoothish surface to travel over.**

Given that a lot of

our terrain is made up of rocks, ravines, steep hills and impenetrable wood-land, it'll be a while before the wheel reaches its full potential.

BREATH

"Wheels are OK, but I'm not holding my breath," says mule-driver Abdullah Zupp. "In the future, whenever there's a major civilization, somebody will build roads and things will be hunky-dory.

"But when those civilizations collapse, the first thing to go is the roads… well, no roads, no wheels. Believe me, this new technology's all very clever, but the smart money's staying with pack animals."

SETTLE DOWN, SETTLE DOWN

A city. Citizens will have to wait around 5,000 years before they can complain about how bad the buses are.

LIFE IS HOTTER IN SUMER!

3,000 BC

It's all change in Sumer, the Fertile Crescent's most up-and-coming region. The world's first city, Uruk, has become the biggest draw since cave painting.

"It's like a village, but much, much bigger," says reporter H. P. Sos. "The authorities saw how people were settling down and forming communities wherever there was enough land and water to support farming. So they decided to go one step farther. Result: the city."

Uruk really is something different. Not only is it bigger than a village but the way it's run is entirely new. It's ruled

Here's Uruk!

by a single king who organizes citizens to dig irrigation canals, collect farm produce, police the streets and, above all, pay him taxes.

There's a big temple in the middle of the city, which is dedicated to a god. Everybody is expected to supply the god with offerings of grain.

The king takes this grain and uses it to pay people to dig more canals, collect more farm produce, police more streets and collect more taxes so he can pay other people to defend the city, build walls around it, erect a bigger temple, and bully the previous people into digging more canals, producing more grain and paying more taxes. (Got that straight?)

HARD

But Uruk isn't only about hardship. It's also about TRADE! The city contains lots of non-farming citizens who make their living by supplying farmers with things they don't have time to make for themselves – chairs, tables, beds, pots, jewels, garden gnomes and so on.

LONG

What this means is that, so long as you've got the grain coming in, a city will support as many trades as there is demand for them. This, in turn, means that someone can survive without farming themselves.

"Cities are the hot-bed of invention," says H. P. Sos. "I predict Uruk's example will be followed across Asia, from India to China. Once you start building these things, there's no turning back."

WRITE ON!

Is it a squiggle, or is it a WORD?

Clay Tablets Get Full Marks

3,000 BC

Speaking is old hat, according to citizens in Mesopotamia. They've come up with a revolutionary method of communication which involves scratching symbols on clay tablets. Enthusiasts have already given it a name – WRITING!

"Writing's very easy," said Bart Jugg, a scribe. "All you have to do is draw a picture of the thing you want to describe. If you want to say you've got ten goats, you draw ten pictures of a goat. If you want to talk about the Sun, you draw something round with a few lines sticking out."

"After a little practice, you don't have to draw an actual goat. Instead you can do a shorthand squiggle and everybody will recognize it as 'goat'. You can also use symbols for less obvious things. Day and night, for example. What do they look like? Easy – a sun for day and a moon for night. Some symbols are less obvious – such as an arrow, which is our sign for life. But honestly, so long as everybody knows what each symbol means it doesn't matter what they look like. You could draw an elephant as the sign for a teaspoon and that would be fine."

Royal employees are the people most likely to benefit from writing. Temple scribes will particularly welcome the development as they have to record every bit of tax paid by every man or woman in the region.

NEW THREAT TO STONE

2,500 BC

Reports are coming in of a brand new alloy called bronze. (Science fans will know that an alloy is a mixture of metals.) Developed in South-east Asia, bronze is a mixture of copper and tin. Manufacturers are hailing it as the hardest metal yet made. They have already issued a limited number of bronze weapons and expect to produce tailor-made bronze body-protection shortly.

BRONZED OFF

Supporters say the alloy marks a new era – the Bronze Age. Opponents maintain stone is still best. "If you want to avoid an arrow you don't need metal. All you have to do is duck behind the nearest rock."
The debate continues.

Metalwork – it's a dirty job, but someone's got to do it.

THE EDITOR SPEAKS

The Get Ahead Sentinel – You Know It Makes Sense

Well, the Stone Age is over at last. ABOUT TIME TOO! Stone is SO unglamorous. If you want to get ahead in the world you're not going to do it by chipping away at lumps of flint. It's OK if you're starting out. But let's face it. It's not the kind of technology that's going to get us to the Moon, IS IT?

HUNTING AND GATHERING

It kept us fit, provided a varied diet and allowed us to exist in a natural state alongside the rest of the animal kingdom. But all good things come to an end. And when you think about it, it did keep population levels very low. If we'd stuck at it most of us wouldn't be here. Since the *SENTINEL* always puts its readers first, we say that's bad news. THE MORE OF YOU THE BETTER!!!

FIRE

Wasn't that a breakthrough? We think it'll provide the world's energy needs, in one form or another, for thousands and thousands of years. In fact, we vote it the NUMBER ONE discovery of the Stone Age!!!

MAMMOTHS

Farewell, big woolly friends. You were great while you lasted, and we shall miss your fearsome bellow. But as they say in Çatal Hüyük – this place ain't big enough for the both of us.

EVOLUTION

Whaddya reckon? WE don't think we need it any more. After all, you only evolve in order to adapt to new environments. But since we can pretty well control our environment we don't need to adapt any more. How about THAT?!!! But there's a long way to go yet. Who knows, if they ever invent computer keyboards we might have to evolve 26 fingers.
LET'S WAIT AND SEE!

CITIES

We love 'em. Lots of buzz, lots of new ideas, lots of jobs, lots of wealthy people = lots more people reading the *SENTINEL!* THAT'S PROGRESS FOR YOU!!!

INSTRUMENTS OF DEATH

"Sticks and stones may break my bones but words will never hurt me." Anyone told they have a face like a baboon's bottom may quibble, but who could deny that sticks and stones do break bones with alarming efficiency.

Experts say that weapons are here to stay. So whether you want to kill a chicken or an attacking nomad, the choice is clear. If you're not armed you're extinct. It's that simple.

In a special reader's service, our weapons correspondent Roy Zogg answers your killing queries.

Chomp

Dear Roy,

We're a fairly harmless bunch when you look at us. We've got dainty little fingers instead of sharp claws, and our teeth can just about chew an apple, rather than bite the head off our prey with a single chomp. We're obviously meant to be plant munching, cuddly little creatures who like cooing at butterflies and hugging trees. So how come we're waving weapons around like there's no tomorrow?

Larry Zugg, 42 Sabre-Tooth Avenue, Hutsville

Having dainty fingers means you can make things with them. You don't see lions lashing together bows and arrows with their big nasty paws do you? Your hand on its own can't do much as a weapon, but pick up a rock or a sharp stick and you're in business!

Two good reasons for making weapons:
One. Try defending yourself against a pan-ther without one.
Two. If you want to eat something more interesting than berries and seeds, chances are you'll have to catch it. True, you could hang around until you come across a half-eaten gazelle, but why wait, when you can KILL IT YOURSELF!

Ferocious

Dear Roy,

This hunting is a frightening business, even if you have got a sharp stick or a flint axe! My chum Joe Gorr says it's best to hunt the biggest animals like mammoths, but I think this is too dangerous, and we should stick to killing a few dormice every now and then.

Bob Stigg, 14a Cave Crescent, Tarrpitts

Aaaaah, the great big or small debate. Face facts, Mr. Stigg, kill a mammoth and you can keep your family fed for a month. Kill a dor-mouse, and you're squabbling over who gets what for breakfast, and you can forget about lunch and tea. I know mammoths can look pretty ferocious, but take it from me they're worth the extra effort.

Worms

Dear Roy,

I'm a pretty eager hunter, with plenty of raw courage, but I'm not having much luck. Whenever I try and kill a mammoth it runs away before I can get near it.

Jack Grok, "Dungatherin", Fossil

What you need, Mr. Grok, is TEAMWORK. Get together a bunch of pals armed with clubs and spears. No bows and arrows, or slingshots, you've got to get right up close to down a mammoth. (Tell them to get to your cave at sunrise too, – the early man catcheth the mammoth.)

All huddle together in a circle. Then you say, "OK guys, what are we gonna do?" and they all shout, "Kill a mammoth!" Then you all march off into the plain going "Whoop whoop", "Yeeeahhh", and stuff like that. All the noise will rouse a sleeping

LETTER OF THE WEEK

Muuuuurdah

Dear Roy,

We all know that weapons are very good for hunting, but guess what I heard yesterday – you can even kill people with them! Quite a shock that.

Harold Jodd, A hole in the ground, Clubland

Yes, Mr. Jodd, it's quite the latest thing. We've had weapons for ages, but until quite recently we've just used them to hunt. (Although, to be frank, there has been the odd argument over a mate or a gazelle that spilled over into a murder.)

Lately, what with fertile land getting a little scarcer now there's more of us humans around, and some of us settling down in farms and towns while others roam around, some bright sparks have realized you can kill your way to wealth and prosperity rather than work hard at it!

This is called warfare, and it basically involves all the skills we've learned from hunting – same weapons, same cooperating in groups – only the people that do it are called soldiers.

mammoth who will gal-lumph up to you to complain. This is where teamwork comes in.

While a couple of you distract its attention, the rest of you sneak around behind it. Before the mammoth can say "What's that smell" your hunting party will have it surrounded. Then you all attack at once with spears and clubs, and it's goodbye mammoth, and hello hearty mammoth steaks! These kind of tactics work perfectly well for lions and hyenas, so they can certainly work for you too.

Homo chickiens

Dear Roy,

Yes, it's me again, Bob Stigg. It's all very well saying hunt the big stuff. I reckon you have to be crazy to want to get close enough to stick a makeshift spear into something that's fighting mad, stomping around with feet the size of cartwheels, and about the size of a five-bedroom cave.

Bob Stigg, 14a Cave Crescent, Tarrpitts

Cluck, cluck, Stigg, laid any eggs recently? But still, it takes all kinds I always say. Maybe you're good at making pots?

BASHEM & RUNN

FOR ALL YOUR SLAUGHTERING NEEDS

Still going clubbing? You're obsolete! Catch up on all the latest hi-tech weaponry, including the phenomenal no-bodily-contact bow and arrow, at a settlement showroom near you NOW!

The classics

Flint hand axe

For those on a tight budget. Simply grab and stab. What could be easier! 1 pebble

Stick

Another budget special, and still as useful as ever. Sharpen with flint hand axe for added effectiveness. 1 pebble

The best of the beast

Antelope bone
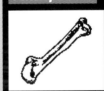
More wallop for your pebbles than any other thigh bone available! 3 pebbles

Antelope horn
The perfect dagger, for those right-up-close encounters. Still only 4 pebbles

Tooled-up

Bola

Swing around the head and throw. You don't see baboons doing this! Ideal for those small to middle-sized prey. 7 pebbles

Spear

Fire-hardened tip for penetration power where you really need it. Buy of the week. Only 5 pebbles!

Deluxe spear

With hand-lashed flint tip. Will pierce even the toughest hide. 8 pebbles

Deluxe axe
Try our new-improved deluxe axe, too. Stone top with added handle, gives you extra zing in your swing! 10 pebbles

The very latest

Spear thrower

More power to your shoulder! Improves spear range by up to 50%. Simply lob and collect. A hit every time! 7 pebbles

Sword
Think of it as a super dagger. It's longer, so you can stab from a safe distance. Available in copper and bronze. 10-15 pebbles

Bow and arrow

The ultimate in warfare safety. Lightweight and portable. Long range (Up to 50m (160ft)). Fast – your arrows fly swifter than a swooping hawk. Arrow projectile effective on all prey up to size of antelope and humans. 10 pebbles

BASHEM AND RUNN - SLAUGHTERING SINCE 240,000BC

The Stone Age Sentinel

MRS. OGG'S STONE AGE BEAUTY PAGE

Put the stunningly sensational back into the Stone Age, with the Fashion and Beauty column you can't afford to miss!

MRS. OGG — VOTED TOP STYLE COLUMNIST OF THE ERA BY READERS OF CAVEWEAR WEEKLY

SO WHAT'S HAPPENING IN YOUR CAVE?

BEAUTY AT ITS MOST BASIC

SWAGGER

• Readers out to trap a mate will be interested to know that body painting is IN. Red clay is plentiful enough, and washes off with a simple application of water.

Other adornments to put a swagger in your stagger include ambergris perfume (this comes from whale intestines, and smells far nicer than you'd think) and spruce tree leaf resin to sweeten the breath.

You can't go wrong with a few feathers too, draped in your hair or clothing.

BEADY

• Even though they're such hard work to make, beads will

A charming necklace adds allure to any outfit.

always be fashionable. I know it can take up to three hours to make a single polished bead from a sliver of mammoth tusk. But once it's done, it'll stay like that forever.

You can make beads from animal teeth, seashells, soapstone, and even pebbles. When you've got a good number, string them together to make a necklace, or sew them onto clothing, using a bone needle and some wool thread.

Then you'll have something of beauty that can be passed on through the generations, and treasured by your descendants for all eternity!

HAIR WEAR NEWS

• Try braiding. This means weaving three strands into one. Not only does it keep you out of mischief, it's the perfect antidote to boring, long straight hair.

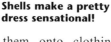

Shells make a pretty dress sensational!

FREE FACT SLAB
on clothes dyes available now!

FASHION TIPS

What's all the rage with the new style "clothes"?

FUR ENOUGH

Natural materials are this season's hottest body covering, and fur is still the number one choice for Stone Age trend-setters.

It's warm, it's easy on the eye, and it doesn't take too many brain cells to realize how to wear it. It's not perfect of course – it stinks like an old goat (especially if it *IS* an old goat) and it gets soggy when it rains. Still, if you want style and sophis-tication, you've got to pay the price!

LEATHER OR NOT

Catching up in popularity is the fabric of the future – leather. It's like fur but without the hair (you have to scrape this off.) Leather takes a while to prepare before you wear it. It has to be "tanned" (coated in a liquid called tannin to preserve it), then pulled tight across a frame to stretch it.

Leather can be cut into any shape, which means you can get it to fit as snugly as you like. You can also dye it pretty shades, or cut patterns in it.

It's extremely hard-wearing, and really keeps out the wind and the rain.

WOOL REALLY

Readers who like to peer at the very outer rim of the cutting edge of fashion technology will be curious about another new fabric. It's called wool, and it comes from those docile and bleating creatures, sheep. You can pluck it off the sheep as it sheds its coat, but don't wear it just as it is, it'll only blow off.

What you need to do is twist the wool around a wooden spindle to make a thin thread. Then you take the thread and weave it carefully together in a loom. Its very warm and versatile!

A loom. You can make socks with this!

NEXT WEEK: MAKE YOUR OWN BONE BROOCH

SENTINEL LIFESTYLE SPECIAL

HAVE AN ICE DAY

THERE'S NO BUSINESS LIKE SNOW BUSINESS SAYS TOP INUIT

8,000 BC

We humans have spread to almost every inhospitable corner of the world. From the howling wastes of Siberia to the baking plains of Arizona, we're there! But how do you make a living in a land where much of the sea is frozen solid and almost the only natural resources are seals and whales and ice and snow?

It's a piece of cake, says top Inuit Barry Yagg of the Arctic circle. You just have to make do with the little bit of everything that's actually available. Find out how he does it with the *Sentinel*'s roving reporter Don Stigg.

Don Stigg. So what do you eat out there? I bet you get sick of seafood!

Barry Yagg. During the summer we get to eat reindeer and deer. It's winter that's mainly seafood – seal, walrus, fish – but also the odd polar bear if we can catch one. Incidentally, if you ever do catch a polar bear, don't eat the liver. It's so poisonous it'll kill you.

DS. You'll need something a bit more substantial than a hook and line to catch a seal!

BY. Too true. Sometimes we use kayak canoes and hunt with harpoons. Our kayaks are made entirely from animals – bone frame and skin covering, treated with a waterproof glue made from boiling up various animal bits and pieces.

The other way we catch sea life is by digging holes in the ice. Seals pop up in them from time to time for a breath of air, and we nab them then. (We learned this trick from our arch enemy the polar bear.)

DS. So what does the fashionable Inuit wear for a day out?

BY. From the top of our one-piece tunic and hood, to the tip of our waterproof socks and boots, all our clothes are made from animals. They're mainly the leathery hides of seals and walruses, and fur from foxes and hares. These materials keep

Rudolph Reindeer's red nose would never again guide Santa through a foggy Christmas Eve.

their natural owners nice and snug, and do the trick for us too.

We like our clothes to be airtight but loose, so there's a layer of air to warm up next to our skin. We use bone needles and animal guts to sew the clothes together.

DS. Is it really true you live in ice houses?

BY. Sometimes... In the summer we're no different from everyone else. We make little huts from animal hides wrapped around a bone frame.

In the winter we also make shelters called igloos, from blocks of ice coated with snow. We have a little ice window at the top too. They make surprisingly warm little dens.

DS. There's so little wood around, what do you do for fuel?

BY. Any wood we find we use for weapons.

Fortunately, our animals come to the rescue once again. The sea mammals here, such as seals and whales, are covered in a layer of thick fat called blubber, which keeps out the cold. Blubber burns very well, so we heat food with it. We also brighten up our igloos with little blubber-burning lamps!

DS. It all sounds ingenious! But honestly, why would anyone want to live somewhere where it's so freezing cold?

BY. If your idea of heaven is a beach in Majorca, then it's obviously not for you. But we like it out here – it's not too crowded, we don't have tribes of passing nomads burning our villages and stealing our corn, and if it's always cold, you soon stop complaining about it because you've never known anything else!

NEXT WEEK: SOME LIKE IT HOT — MEET THE DESERT DWELLERS!

YOU WHAT???

Get with the new-style speech in the Sentinel column that TELLS IT LIKE IT IS!

"Errr, me think it a wolf!!!" The game of Charades swiftly follows the invention of speech.

THINGS YOU NEVER KNEW ABOUT TALKING

1 Experts think that we hominids have been able to talk since *Homo habilis* in 2,000,000 BC, who could say a few basic words like *"food"*, *"drink"* and *"do you come here often"*.

2 *Homo erectus* polished up his grammar and vocabulary a bit, and was able to string together the odd sentence. *"Not... woolly... mammoth... again. Me... want... smoked... salmon."*

3 Only *Homo Sapiens* has been able to talk properly, as our mouths and throats are the right shape for rapid, sophisticated conversation. *"If I see you wearing that filthy animal skin one more time, I'm going to throw it in the fire. D'you hear? And don't look at me like that when I'm talking to you."*

4 Humans are not the only creatures that talk to each other. Lots of animals grunt and squawk to communicate. Some insects even exchange smells to tell each other what they think. (Don't go getting any ideas...)

5 Some animals even have a small vocabulary. The Vervet monkey has about 10 different grunts and eeks, including one for eagle and one for cheetah.

6 Humans on the other hand have THOUSANDS OF WORDS for things, and can string these words together to explain complex new ideas, teach old dogs new tricks, and let other people know exactly how they feel. (Pretty bad! Top of the world! etc, etc.)

7 These words can also describe things other people have not seen, anticipate events in the future and recall events in the past. Try doing that with a few grunts and barks.

8 To make words your tongue goes to 50 different positions in your mouth.

9 Speech experts think it was the need to gather food together and cooperate to stay alive, that led us to develop our complex languages.

10 Although words for the same thing are different all over the world, what is similar about all human speech are the basic rules of grammar. (This means the way words are arranged.)

IT'S A... CAVE

There's a word for everything these days. Tree, river, mammoth – you name it, we've got it! But where <u>do</u> words come from? Language eggheads have thought about this, and come up with several theories. Here at the *SENTINEL* we cast a critical eye on what they're saying...

EXPERTS SAY	THE SENTINEL SAYS
Words began as imitations of natural sounds.	Works OK for Whooosh, Splash, Burp, Woof and Meow. But how do you explain Prehistoric, Cave painting, Knife and fork... the list is endless.
Words began as utterances along with emotional reactions.	Works OK for Aaaaaagh, Bleurrrrrgh and Waaaaagh, but try writing a poem with those!
Words were prompted by facial accompaniments to gestures we made to one another.	Call us crabby old cynics, but apart from a lip-smacking "Yum Yum", we can't think of anything else that fits this description.

COMMENT

THE SENTINEL SAYS

It looks like language is quite a mystery. But wherever words come from, one thing's for sure – everyone in your tribe has to use the same words to mean the same thing. After all, it's no good saying "Go and play hide and seek with a sabre-toothed tiger", if what you really mean is "Your High and Mightiness, I would be most delighted to marry your daughter."

A SENTINEL SPECIAL OFFER IN CONJUNCTION WITH THE WILLIAM GAKK SELF-HELP FOUNDATION

Are you a poor talker?

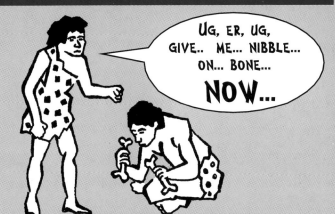

UG, ER, UG, GIVE.. ME... NIBBLE... ON... BONE... NOW...

Do you shrink from contact with your fellow humans because your sentence construction is laughably primitive? Do you suffer from loose vowels?

Banish the embarrassment of shoddy conversation with William Gakk's teach-yourself classic, "Between you and me..." The Bible for poor speakers everywhere.

LEARN

• The basic sounds that go to make up words. For example:

Ag, Eg, Ig, Og, Ug and many more...

• How to string together that all important sentence.

• How you say words affects the way people hear them.

A COMPLIMENT

YOU LOOK LOVELY!

SURPRISED
YOU... LOOK... LOVELY!!!

A COMMAND

YOU, LOOK LOVELY!

AN INSULT

YOU???, LOOK LOVELY??? HAHAHA

WRONG

TOOTH! OUT, SABRE- THERE'S A LOOK TIGER

RIGHT
LOOK OUT, THERE'S A SABRE-TOOTHED TIGER!

Popularity, respect, and a warm feeling of superiority over Neanderthals, apes and chimps can be yours for only 5 pebbles, with William Gakk's "Between you and me..."

Send no money now. Allow 28 days for delivery.

Indicate below if you do/do not wish to receive more similar self-help titles. Think carefully now, you'll be missing out on...

NEW TITLES
* Mammoth killing made easy
* 100 ways to survive an encounter with a sabre-toothed tiger
* Fresh ways with rancid meat
* Cave decorating for fun and profit

Being a wise and noble creature I wish to better myself. Please send more books and fleece me for every pebble I've got. ☐

I wish to remain in disgraceful prehistoric ignorance, no better than the lizards and slugs. Send no more books. ☐

THE WILLIAM GAKK SELF-HELP FOUNDATION, GAKK HOUSE, PALEOLITH HILL, RIFT VALLEY

GET STUFFED

WHAT'S COOKING?

with the Sentinel's cookery correspondent Pierre de Zoque

What's cooking, *mes amis*? Cooking is when you heat something up before you eat it!

Yes, you lazy bones, I know it takes more effort, but not only does cooked food taste, look and smell nicer, it's easier to digest and much better for you. (Nutritionists among you will be interested to know that this is because heating food makes it easier for humans to digest proteins and carbohydrates in it.)

We all know the story about the piece of mammoth meat that fell on the fire and tasted much nicer after it had sizzled a bit, but just throwing meat on a fire isn't exactly what you'd call *haute cuisine*. So what else can you do? Well, there's no end to human ingenuity...

CAKE

• If you must cook directly in a fire (and it is rather *passé* these days) try caking your meat in a juicy coating of good thick mud – it'll make it a lot more succulent, and reduces the drying up and shrinkage that direct heat often causes. Don't forget to break off the mud before you eat it!

HOLE

• Slow cooking is always better – try wrapping your meat in a big leaf and cooking on embers rather than a roaring fire.

If you're feeling really sophisticated you can make an oven by digging a hole in the ground, filling the bottom with red-hot embers and covering up the top with a thick covering of leaves, twigs and straw. Be warned though, it can take several days to cook your food, so forward planning is called for.

PLUCK

• Another way to cook is by boiling – this means heating water until it bubbles, and then popping your food in. (Be sure to extract it with a small knife or stick. Do not, under any circumstances, pluck it from the water with your bare hands, no matter how hungry you are.)

If you're reading this before your tribe has invented cooking pots you'll have to boil the water in a big turtle shell or reptile skin. Some enterprising chefs in Central America have even gone to the trouble of hollowing out a large stone.

SHOOT

Readers in Asia may like to clean out a thick bamboo shoot and fill that with meat, veg and a little water. Keep the bamboo far enough away from the heat to stop it catching fire, and you'll have a delicious meal. *Bon appetit*, as we like to say in this part of the world.

Hunters! Deer make a tasty dish, but people are <u>so</u> soppy about them. Tell your family they're eating warthog, or they may never speak to you again.

IN STYLE

FOOD FACT HOT POT

HANDY HINTS
FOR HUNGRY READERS

FISHY STORIES

Fish make a fabulous feast and they're cheap and wholesome!

They're not the brightest sparks in the world, and anyone wanting a pet to cuddle and adore would be ill-advised to keep one, but MAKE NO MISTAKE fish make a fabulous feast!

But how do you get hold of these silvery, slippery, succulent delicacies? FIND OUT with our infallible guide below.

BATTING

North American readers have seen Grizzly Bears do it by batting fish out of the water with their paws. Although we're quite a bit brighter than Grizzlies, for some reason we never got the hang of this.

Pierre says: *Buf! Worth a go if you're desperate.*

CLUBBING

You're no fool when you use a tool! Mind you, the splashing drives off any fish you haven't hit for miles around, and do watch out you don't club your own foot.

Pierre says: *Alors! It's a bit crude, but then this IS the Stone Age after all.*

TRAPPING

Gather up loads of sticks and laboriously lace them together to make a solid square barrier. Make several of these and then painstakingly arrange them in a V-shape reaching from the middle of the river to the bank, with a little gap at the pointy end of the V to let the fish in. Secure them to the river bed using boulders. When fish venture in, they're much easier to catch as they can't escape!

Pierre says: *Zut, mes amis! This sounds harder work than killing a mammoth.*

This man knows that fish bring style and sophistication to any table.

FISHING BOATS

If you're reading this before 8000BC, when we invent the oar, you'll have to wait a while, unless you're really foolhardy. With oars we'll have a more-than-likely chance of getting back alive when we venture out to sea in little reed rafts or dugout wooden canoes.

The best way to catch fish out at sea is with a big net. You can make one of

• Readers in the chillier parts of the world will be interested to know that meat keeps fresh much longer if you bury it in the ground. This is particularly useful if you've killed something really big, and you can't carry it all back to your cave.

• Those of you who are still hunter-gatherers may like to try digging into the ground, rather than just picking fruit and vegetables from the trees and the top soil. Readers in Europe will be interested to know that several nutritious and (fairly) digestible vegetables, such as the turnip, onion and radish can be dug up with very little effort.

American readers will be able to find potatoes and yams.

All these vegetables can be spotted by their tell-tale shoots, and they all taste much nicer after you've boiled them for 20 minutes.

• Insects make an ideal snack! Yes, it's true! Dried locusts are 75% protein and 20% fat. (That only leaves 5% grisly bits too horrible to contemplate.) So, *courage, mes enfants,* next time you're out on a forage and hunger strikes, munch on a moth!

these with twisted strands of hair or twine all roped together.

Pierre says: *Mon Dieu! Quite the most dangerous fishing technique available.*

Sharks, whirlpools, deadly currents and tides, blistering winds and huge, huge waves await. Still, it's quite pleasant when the sun's out, and you're in with a serious chance of catching a big load of fish.

FISH HOOK

Make a hook from a horn, using a flint tool. Attach a length of string made from wool or gut. Place worm on hook. Put in river with other end of string tied to big toe. Nod off to sleep. When toe feels a twitch, pull in line – you've scored!

Pierre says: *Formidable! This sounds too good to be true!*

NEXT WEEK: FAST FOOD AND HOW TO CATCH IT

Dazzy Dork's

WHAT'S HAPPENING COLUMN

SO WHO PUT THE BOMP IN THE BEAT?

Noted music profs reckon the first music happened when we discovered we could SING. Maybe we tried to imitate animal noises, maybe it was a nice hot day and we started to hum *Summertime and the living is easy* – who knows!

Then we started clapping our hands and banging sticks together, and discovered RHYTHM. Once we'd discovered that, the urge to shake our funky tail feathers and GET DOWN came upon us, and we started dancing.

Finally, we began to invent musical instruments. Maybe this started when a hunter noticed that his bow string went THWONGGGG when he fired an arrow, and he thought, "I could write a symphony with this!"

"You put your left leg in, and your left leg out..." If <u>that's</u> what it's all about, say dancers, we'll sit this one out.

DANCE FLOOR NEWS FLASH

Movers and shakers – we all like to stamp our feet when we're strutting our funky stuff, so why not beef up that beat with an anklet of shells from the beach?

If you live inland, save yourself a trip to the seaside by stringing together rows of bones or teeth to give your dance steps that added KER-CHINKKK!

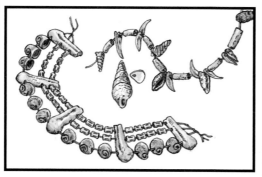

These sophisticated percussion instruments are operated by the ankle or wrist.

STONE-AGE TOP FIVE

1. Jailhouse Auroch **Elvis Zogley**

2. Where the tracks have no name **Ug2**

3. (I can't get no) huntin'-action **The Stones**

4. Eye of the (sabre-toothed) tiger **Bokk**

5. I'm a firestarter **Stigg and the Dumps**

INSTRUMENT NEWS

TOOT THAT FLUTE, ZOOT

So what's hot in the world of MUSICAL INSTRUMENTS?

BUDUM BUDUM

Drummers! If you're still banging a stick on a tree, you've missed the boat maaaan! Get on the scene by stretching an animal skin over a clay pot or coconut half. You can play this with your fingers, or a stick. Alternatively, a mammoth skull makes a wonderful drum and gives a deeply satisfying K-DONK when you hit it with a heavy stick. And unlike a tree, you can take these kind of drums anywhere!

PLINK PLINK

Tight strings make all sorts of interesting sounds, but they're so QUIET. Try placing the string over the mouth of a pot as you twang it, or holding the string next to your open mouth – you'll find it makes quite a difference to the volume (not to mention the state of your teeth.)

TOOT TOOT

Which smart alec with nothing better to do discovered you could make musical notes by blowing into a bone? Gosh, that must have been an extremely long, wet Sunday afternoon! Well you CAN, and here's how.

- Take one medium sized bird bone.
- Hollow it out.
- Add a little tube to blow into at one end.
- Make four holes along the length of the bone.

You can make different whistling noises by covering up different holes.

Be sure to tell your musician pals that this is called a flute. We'll be seeing a lot more of this kind of instrument in the future!

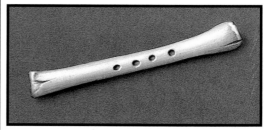

The flute with the tootiest toot this side of Toot House, Toot Street, Tootville!

DAZZY DORK'S NOTABLE NOTE OF THE DAY!

Hey kids! They say "music hath charms to soothe the savage beast". Personally, I'd rather face a tiger armed with a long spear than a bone flute, but, HEY, who can deny the STRANGE POWER of music!

GOOD HEALTH

with Robin Hukk, the Sentinel's medical correspondent

The column that keeps YOU up to the minute with the world of HEALTH and MEDICINE.

GOOD NEWS FOR SOME

Sentinel readers don't need me to tell you that it's a dangerous, unpleasant world out there. We get parched in the summer heat, and then we spend the winter shivering in our miserable tents and huts. We could get eaten by a pack of wolves one minute, or murdered by a gang of passing nomads the next.

THINGS

But don't despair, things are looking up. Thanks to recent improvements in diet, and more sophisticated weapons to protect us from predators, the average *Hom sap sap* man of 10,000 BC can now expect to live for a phenomenal 30 years!

DRAWS

There's not such good news for the ladies, however. Having drawn the biological short straw of child-bearing duties, most of you can still expect a visit from the grim reaper in your mid 20s. Still, chin up, at least you don't have to go mammoth hunting!

Healthy outdoor pursuits and a good diet all mean we're living longer.

ILL-UMINATING!

Readers often ask where illnesses come from. Most of us in the medical profession believe that minor ailments, such as runny noses, or constipation, are just part of the great ebb and flow of human existence.

However, really big ailments, like being too poorly to stand up, or being covered in lurid boils, are due to s u p e r n a t u r a l causes. Perhaps the gods are angry with you, or a malevolent demon has cast a spell on you.

Either way, if you're <u>that</u> ill, something awesome thinks you've really blotted your copy book.

TREATMENT CORNER

Two techniques to tell you about on the treatment front. The first is for minor ailments and the second is serious do-or-die stuff.

1. Upset stomach? Nagging headache? Festering cut? "Put on those gardening gloves," say tribes who have caught on to the fact that many plants contain healing substances. You can eat them directly, or boil them up in water, or make a paste to put on a wound, the variations are endless. The 64,000 pebble question is which plant for what ailment? Here at the *Sentinel* information is very sketchy, so we say "Have fun finding out!"

Take two of these, three times a day, with water.

2. Hold tight! Medical opinion has it that the gods make people ill by putting something bad into their body like a demon or a worm, or taking something out – like the patient's soul. Treatment for these ailments consists of either putting the soul back, or casting the intruder out. In such cases plant medicine can sometimes be effective, but more often than not, drastic methods are called for.

WHICH WITCH?

You may need to go to the expense of asking your local witchdoctor to perform a healing ceremony. (This will involve a lot of dancing and chanting, so be considerate and warn the people next door.)

WHOLE HOLE

Failing that, you could go for a trepanning. This involves having a hole drilled in your head. The advantages are that the demon or worm can then escape, or your soul can get back in. The disadvantages are extreme pain and likely death. Still, it's always worth a try if you're desperate!

THE BEGINNER'S GUIDE TO BITING THE DUST

ANOTHER READER'S SERVICE

OUR FUNERAL CORRESPONDENT DAN DED REPORTS ON THE ULTIMATE SEND-OFF

Being buried is becoming increasingly fashionable among modern day hominids. In fact it's a sure sign that life is looking up! When you find you have time to think about what happens after you bite the dust, it means life isn't quite as nasty, brutish and short as it used to be.

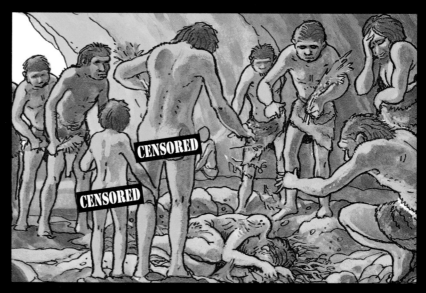

Funerals in Stone Age times are refreshingly informal, and stiff, black suits are definitely not required. It is essential, though, to bring flowers.

Testify!

Being the bright sparks we are, we've decided that we have a soul which lives on after death, and that dying is simply the moment when the soul leaves the body.

Whether you believe it goes to Heaven, the great Mammoth hunting ground in the sky, or simply lurks around your tomb or cave, depends on what idea your tribe has come up with.

Vultures

In the olden days, when we were *Homo habilis* and *Homo erectus*, experts think we were so busy finding food and avoiding being eaten we didn't make a fuss about dying at all.

If you dropped down dead, everybody else just left you there until you were eaten by a vulture. But these days we like to send our loved ones off in style, and here at the *Sentinel* we've been nosing around to see how it's done.

Neanderthal style

40,000 BC
Neanderthals were the first hominids to bury their dead, and they certainly went extinct

with a flourish!
• They dug a hole in the floor of a cave and laid the body on pine branches in a sleeping position, with its head resting on a stone pillow.
• Then they covered the body with flowers, and added some tools and a little food in case they'd be needed in the afterlife. Then they covered everything up with a nice snug layer of soil.*

Flowers will brighten up any funeral, and cost virtually nothing!

Homo Sapiens style

27,000 BC onwards
As you'd expect, *Hom Sap* does things with a bit more sophistication.
• If you're pretty important then you're buried in some really fancy clothing – furs, hats embroidered with seashells, tunics with fox-tooth decoration, you know the sort of stuff.
• In Russia they like to bury important people with THOUSANDS of elaborately carved little

mammoth-ivory beads arranged in rows around the body.
• In France and Czechoslovakia they cover the bodies with red clay. (We think this represents blood and life.) In parts of France they also wrap the dead tightly in cloth to prevent the spirit re-entering the body and making a nuisance of itself. (Spoilsports! Here at the *Sentinel*, we think this

Funerals can be fun, so be prepared to let your hair down!

might make for an exciting evening's entertainment. After all, it'll be a while yet before anyone gets around to inventing television.)

Stones

And if you're reading this after 4,500 BC you may be interested to know that in Europe they're burying their dead in really impressive megaliths.

These are artificial caves made up of massive, heavy stones. They make an ideal shelter for a dead body, or depending on their size, a whole bunch of dead bodies.

So there, being dead doesn't have to mean being lonely. Now there's a comforting thought!

Au naturel

Finally, over in North America, *Hom Sap* is doing things the simple way. They don't bother with anything elaborate, and rightly so. What could be easier than your so-called "Sky Burial"?

What you do is put your deceased in a high spot – up on a mountain, the top of a tree – and leave them to the weather and any passing animal who feels like a nibble.

When there's just a pile of bones left, you take these away and bury them. Ahhh, we do like to be different, don't we!?!

*Experts now disagree about the intention of Neanderthal burials. See page 10 for details.

Note to reader. Bottoms were a common sight in the Stone Ages, even at funerals. However, out of respect for the dead, we have removed them from view in our illustration.

SENTINEL SUPERNATURAL SPECIAL
STAGMAN!

WILL KURRR MEETS A MAN WITH ANTLERS ON HIS HEAD

A secret camera captures Rik Vog's witchdoctor rituals for the *SENTINEL*. Hey Rik, don't put a spell on us!

Let's face it. There's got to be more to existence than "Kill mammoths, then die". What's life all about? Do supernatural beings control our lives? Can we persuade the gods to look after US, rather than that tribe in the next valley who never invites us to their parties?

In this special feature, *Sentinel* religion correspondent Will Kurrr interviews a man who thinks he has the answers. It's Witchdoctor Rick Vog, of Les Trois Frères, France.

Will Kurrr: So Rik, what's with the antlers and everything?

Rick Vog: Hi, Will. This is my witchdoctor outfit. I wear it to frighten little children! Ha ha ha, just kidding. Actually, the antlers and stag mask are part of my priestly garments, along with a generous daubing of body paint.

I get dressed up like this at religious ceremonies, where all the men in our tribe gather together in a deep dark cave. I lead them through sacred rituals to ensure that the stags and deer that we hunt will continue to live in our part of the world, and we'll never go hungry.

WK: So what do you do exactly?

RV: BIG SECRET. If I told you in detail other tribes would copy us, and they'd lure our animals away. I can tell you we do a lot of dancing, and chanting, and we hand around magical objects carved out of antler and bone, and we sacrifice some animals too.

WK: So what's the point of that?

RV: It's MAGIC! You have to perform your rituals exactly right of course. Mix up your chants, or hand around the sacred object the wrong way, and it doesn't work! I've been doing this for five years, and our tribe has never gone hungry once.

WK: So how does it work?

RV: There are lots of spirits floating around out there. They live in the most beautiful parts of the land, like waterfalls or the forest.

There are spirits in the air, and water, and earth, and fire. Some are good, some are evil. The whole point of these rituals is to keep the friendly spirits sweet with sacrifices and worship, so they'll keep you in food and good weather. If you neglect them, they leave you to the mercy of bad spirits, and that means your tribe starves because there's nothing to hunt, and everyone suffers from diseases.

WK: It sounds like a pretty important job!

RV: Too right. You can't leave anything to chance these days. We need to put a huge amount of time and effort into these ceremonies to keep us fed and healthy.

Besides which, dressing up like this is much more fun than hunting mammoths, or picking berries, but don't tell anyone in my tribe I told you!

THE SENTINEL — IT'S SPOOKILY GOOD!

A SENTINEL QUIZ FOR THE WHOLE FAMILY TO ENJOY!!!

NAME THAT TOOL!

QUESTIONABLE QUESTIONS FOR THE MECHANICALLY MINDED

We all know that tools have enabled us to RULE THE WORLD, and anyone worth a stuffed field mouse knows what an axe or a spear looks like. But what about THESE odd looking things? Guess what they are, as we ask "What on Earth is THAT?"

❶
a) A bangle?
b) A tray?
c) An early attempt at wallpaper?

❷
a) er.. Is it a pastry shaper?
b) It's a saw.
c) Scrubbing brush?

❸
a) Hang on, I know this. It's for straightening spears, isn't it?
b) Is it some kind of stone pillow?
c) It's a chopstick rest.

❹
a) That's got to be a chisel.
b) No. It's a saxophone mouthpiece. I know. My brother plays one.
c) It's a fractional distillation chamber.

❺
a) Now that's a toothpick.
b) No, it's a spade.
c) You're both wrong. It's a drill.

❻
a) It's a microscope.
b) No, hang on, it's a needle!
c) You're both wrong again. It's a transmission gear connecting rod, and I know that for a FACT.

❼
a) Hmmmm. That looks like a harpoon to me.
b) Yes, I think you're right. Although it could be a back scratcher.
c) You haven't got a clue. It's OBVIOUS that it's a hat stand.

❽
a) It's a dugout canoe.
b) Naaaah, it's a toothbrush holder.
c) You're both complete cretins. Any fool can see that it's some sort of wheelbarrow.
a) I don't like your manner. Take that, punk! (CLUNK, THONK, BOP BOP BOP.)
c) Aaaaaaaaagh.

❾
a) Now that's got to be a lava hammerstone.
b) Come off it, it's just a piece of rock, anyone can see that.

ANSWERS

❶ b) It's a tray made out of tree bark. You can collect berries in this.

❷ b) It's a saw. It's just right for cutting meat and grass.

❸ a) It's for straightening spears. You place your slightly bent wooden pole in it, and bend it 'til it's straight. Piece of cake!

❹ a) It's a chisel all right. You can shape antler, bone and wood with the sharp end of that.

❺ c) They were both wrong, it is a drill! You can make little holes in hide, fur, ivory, wood, in fact anything you like, with this tool.

❻ c). No, I'm just kidding, it's really b). You can make one of these with a sliver of ivory and tools 4 and 5.

❼ a) Of course it's a harpoon.

❽ a) Although the *Sentinel* in no way approves or condones any acts of gratuitous violence, we have to agree with a) that this item is most definitely a dugout canoe.

❾ b) Ha ha. Fooled you. It IS just a piece of rock. Incidentally, a lava hammerstone is what you use when you want to hit and shape another piece of stone.

EGYPTIAN ECHO

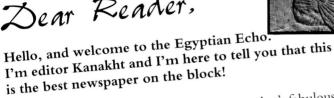

Dear Reader,

Hello, and welcome to the Egyptian Echo. I'm editor Kanakht and I'm here to tell you that this is the best newspaper on the block!

At the Echo we aim to bring you everything that's fabulous in NEWS and FEATURES. You can see from our contents list that the paper is split into two main sections. First we have news, which takes YOU THE READER through 2,000 years of history. The news comes in three parts, which are the same as the three main eras of Egyptian history – Old Kingdom, Middle Kingdom, and New Kingdom.

Then you've got 13 fascinating pages of features – fashion, pets, dreams, health and the like, all of which remained more or less the same throughout the entire Ancient Egyptian era. Included with that there's our fantastic sphinxational free give-away board game PHARO, that's fun for all the family. Only with the Echo – the paper with a pyramid in its pocket!!

Happy reading readers, and remember –
THE ECHO IS BEST FOR NEWS AND VIEWS!

Editor Kanakht
Egyptian Echo
Pyramid Row
Memphis

Kanakht

THE
EGYPTIAN ECHO

was written by
Paul Dowswell
and designed by
Karen Tomlins

With thanks to Charles Freeman, our Ancient Egyptian consultant.

Ian Jackson, Guy Smith, Peter Dennis, Richard Draper, Louise Nixon, Gerald Wood and Robert Walster provided the illustrations.

EGYPTIAN ECHO
ON OTHER PAGES

NEWS PAGES

Old Kingdom news
Smiting, pyramids and hieroglyphs. 34-37

Middle Kingdom news
Smiting, jewels and foreigners. 38-39

New Kingdom news
Smiting, god-swapping and mummies. 40-49

FREE GIFT

Your phenomenal Pharo board game 50

FEATURES

Fashion
*Dress to impress Tut style.
Bata's Beauty Spot.* 52-53
Dreams
What do they really mean? 54
Health
Dr. Ahhk is the Echo's doc on the spot. 55
Arts
Royal portrait controversy. 56-57

ENTERTAINMENT

Your sensational B - Z guide to throwing parties, snubbing your guests and being sick with style. 58-59

PROBLEM PAGE

Riveting reading for life's twists and turns. 60

PETS CORNER

Goose watch
Nine things you never knew about geese. 61

QUIZ CONTEST

Wholesome and educational entertainment for a rainy Sunday afternoon. 62

ADS

Small ads
*Looking for a job?
Don't start here!!* 63

SPORTS REVIEW

Hunting news
Cat chaos in the Delta. 64

NARMER NAILS NORTH TO SOUTH

"I'M IN CHARGE" SAYS SCOURGE OF SQUABBLING EGYPT

3100 BC

Tough tribal leaders trembled with terror as King Narmer declared himself ruler of both Upper and Lower Egypt. "I'm in charge now," the former king of Upper Egypt told royal reporters, "and anyone who says I'm not is in BIG TROUBLE."

Not since the Sun god Ra created the world and sent his fellow gods to rule over us has there been such upheaval. For the first time ever the marshlands of the lower Nile Delta and the thin farmlands of the upper Nile Valley are now one country.

Unpleasantness

Despite some general laying waste and other unpleasantness involving death and destruction, most Egyptians are relieved that Narmer has brought to an end centuries of squabbling between these two regions of Egypt.

Cagey

But who is this shadowy figure who has now declared himself "Lord of the Two Lands" and claims to be the gods' representative on Earth? Palace pals are cagey about his true identity. "His mother calls him Narmer," said one, "but he's also known as Menes, and some people even think he's called Aha."

When questioned about his

WHO, WHAT AND WHERE

Assorted tribal chiefs in Lower Egypt

MEMPHIS

King Narmer in Upper Egypt

Your at-a-glance guide to who's smiting who.

multiple names a royal spokesman replied, "Narmer, Menes, Aha – call him what you like - just so long as it's 'King of Upper and Lower Egypt'."

Where did you get that hat?

Meanwhile tongues were wagging as fashion watchers predicted a revolutionary new design for the royal crown. Palace insiders have in fact confirmed that Narmer will be combining the conical white crown of Upper Egypt with the red wedge crown of Lower Egypt.

Fashion chiefs were quick to praise the new design. " In a sense," said hat pundit Horem Khauf, " Narmer is quite literally combining his twin roles in one bold statement, and declaring that two hats are better than one, in a very real sense."

Royal wedding due

Narmer's first act as leader of a united Egypt is to set up a capital at Memphis – midway between the two territories. Meanwhile political analysts predict that Narmer will follow a policy of reconciliation with the Delta, marry a Delta princess and attempt to mix lower Egyptian gods and traditions into the culture of Upper Egypt.

You're history, punk! Narmer negotiates his way to a united Egypt. Horus the falcon god helps out.

Proclamation from His Majesty the Pharaoh

Applicants from loyal servants are invited for the following government posts:

Vizier of Upper Egypt
Sole charge of Upper Egypt. Based in Thebes. *(Ref. B/45.)*

Vizier of Lower Egypt
Sole charge of Lower Egypt. Based in Memphis. *(Ref. B/46)*

Chief Treasury Official
Must know how many beans make five. Ability to count without use of fingers and toes an advantage. *(Ref.B/47)*

Chief Granaries Official
Some experience separating wheat from chaff essential. *(Ref.B/48)*

Chief of Royal Works
Experience of construction projects employing 100,000 or more workers, and almost entire resources of nation would be useful. *(Ref. B/49)*

Chief Cattle Official
Would suit former farmer. No vegetarians. *(Ref. B/50)*

Chief Foreign Affairs Official
Multilingual and gestural skills an asset, plus ability to look fierce and uncompromising. *(Ref.B/51)*

Apply immediately to His most Esteemed and Glorious Majesty the King of Egypt – son of the great god Ra, Royal Palace, Memphis.

The Government of Egypt is not an equal opportunities employer.

IT'S PYRA-MANIA!!

World's greatest wonder unveiled at Giza

Sharp point

Giant beehive, to keep his majesty supplied with honey for the rest of eternity. (Also probable site of burial chamber.)

Exit route for bees. (Shown larger than actual size.)

Another corridor

Big corridor, with lots of pictures on the walls.

Another room

Underground canal system, with express barge link to Memphis.

The interior of the pyramid is a big secret. However, we have obtained a blueprint. No one's sure what's what, so our expert at the Echo has made a few guesses.

2550 BC

It's Pyramid Week in the Echo, and all of Egypt is going pyramid-crazy! After 20 years of toil and turmoil the Great Pyramid of Pharaoh Khufu is finally finished.

As a team of 100,000 sweating peasants polished up the limestone exterior and cleaned up the debris around the site at Giza, northwest of Memphis, Pharaoh Khufu and his royal entourage went on a regal tour of inspection.

His majesty lingered in the burial chamber at the heart of the pyramid to examine the imposing granite sarcophagus which will be his final resting place.

Ha ha ha!

Turning to royal reporters he declared: "So! My burial monument is ready at last. When I die I shall be safe in the knowledge that my body will be preserved forever in this magnificent structure, and my spirit will ascend to the heavens to take its place among the stars through this stairway to the sky. This is the greatest wonder of all the seven wonders of the world, and it's **mine, all mine**!!! Ha ha ha ha!!!"

Gleaming

Located next to the gleaming white pyramid is a magnificent temple to be used for Khufu's burial service, and within its shadow are lesser tombs awaiting Khufu's family and his many court officials. Competition for a burial spot here is intense, as it is well known that being buried next to the Pharaoh will enable royal insiders to continue to serve their King in his afterlife, and also guarantee them a place in the next world.

Massive

Meanwhile, unconfirmed reports suggest that Khufu's son Khephren is planning an equally massive monument for himself, to be started as soon as he becomes Pharaoh.

But some outsiders are questioning the wisdom of such huge burial monuments. "Just imagine what else the Egyptians could have done with all those resources and manpower," said one Sumerian trader, "like invest it in education. Still, I suppose it keeps them out of mischief!" But Pharaoh Khufu was unconcerned. "Who needs a degree in astronomy to heave a massive slab of granite to the top of my pyramid?" he asked the Echo. "Besides, give a peasant a few qualifications and he starts getting above himself."

Pyra-facts

Five fascinating pyra-facts about Khufu's pyramid

❶ It's breath-takingly block-tabulous. As many as 2,500,000 limestone and granite blocks have been used in its construction.

❷ Although the limestone comes from local quarries, the granite has been ferried along the Nile from Aswan – 800km (500 miles) away.

❸ It's tun-believably heavy – over 6,000,000 tonnes (tons) in fact.

❹ It's a gigantic compass. The four sides are almost exactly aligned to north, south, east and west.

❺ The outer limestone blocks fit so perfectly together it's impossible to insert a knife blade between them.

CRACKPOT CORNER

You'd think that everyone would know that the Pharaoh is a god and his pyramid is a ladder to help place him among the other gods in the sky. But Egypt's pyramids have provoked all sorts of crackpot theories about what they're here for. Here are just a few of them...

THEORY	THE ECHO SAYS
The pyramids are huge granaries for times of famine.	*Have a bigger breakfast, then you won't be so obsessed with food.*
The angles of internal walls and corridors hold hidden messages about the secrets of the universe.	*Stop reading that papyrus and go out and have some fun.*
Small table-top size paper pyramids have a mystical ability to keep fresh any fruit and milk placed within them. (So do great big pyramids...)	*Here – buy this magic amulet. It's only 12 gold rings, and it's <u>guaranteed</u> to make you irresistibly attractive, unbelievably rich, and immensely popular!*
The pyramids have been built by visitors from another planet.	*We think you've been picking the wrong kind of mushrooms.*

VOWEL PLAY

"Consonants only" script spells trouble for god of wisdom

Is Thoth a thilly thothage?

Everyone knows that Thoth the god of wisdom gave Egypt the great gift of writing (or "words of the gods" as we Egyptians like to call our beautiful hieroglyphs). Since our history began and scribes first put pen to papyrus, hieroglyphs have been part of Egyptian life.

Courting controversy, or just plain awkward? Some hieroglyphs, yesterday.

Here to stay

Without them we wouldn't be able to record the great deeds of our gods and Pharaohs on tombs and monuments. Left to right, right to left, even top to bottom – whichever way you write them, hieroglyphs are here to stay.

Mithtake

However, some student scribes are daring to whisper that **Thoth hath made a mithtake.** They say hieroglyphs could do with some vowels!
 Nebmare nakht, 11, explained.

"Written down, our word for beautiful "nefer" looks like this in hieroglyphs –

– that's "nfr". Why can't we use some symbols for the e sounds, or a, i and u for that matter?"

Dim

"And another thing" piped in Nan Akht, 10, "in the dim and distant future archeologists and explorers from other lands are going to find these things in tombs and monuments and be flummoxed."

They're going to say 'Is it Nufur, Nifir, Nafur or Nefir or what?? Lets call the whole thing off.'"

Ears cut off

But scribe school tutors were quick to dismiss their pupils' comments and have punished their impertinence severely. "These two boys have both been beaten to within an inch (26mm) of their lives, in fact they're lucky not to have had their ears cut off," said Scoros Sekhmet, head teacher at the King Khafre School for Scribes.

Don't know they're born

"Besides, I don't know what they're moaning about. There are only 700 characters to learn, and they've got 12 years to learn them in. Young people these days. They don't know they're born."

EGYPTIAN ECHO
PAGE 36 COMMENT

GT STFFD!!

Only a few nobles and smart alecs can read and write. And so what if funny foreigners will have trouble deciphering our language in the distant future. Who wants them poking their noses into our business anyway?

Why bother

OK, so maybe vowels *would* make hieroglyphs easier to read, but who said life was meant to be easy? The **ECHO** says **What you don't know you don't miss!**

Shrug means one million

Any dolt can understand numbers, says mathematician

Mathematicians picked up on the "no vowels" debate yesterday, and have scoffed at scribes and their incredibly complex system of writing. "Nothing can match the simple purity of our wonderful counting system," said top scholar Al Ghebra. "I means one, II means two, III is three, until you get to 10 then it's ∩. That's really easy. When you get to 100 it's a squiggle. 1,000 is a flowery looking thing, and 10,000 is a severed finger. ("Because it just IS," he told a puzzled *Echo* reporter.) 100,000 is some funny furry thing with a tail, and as for one million – it's some bloke going "Pah, I don't know. How do you expect me to count THAT MANY?"

Egyptian counting A beginners guide

I	I
∩	10
℮	100
⌇	1,000
⌐	10,000
𓆤	100,000
𓁨	1,000,000

Numbers are written from smallest to largest.

SCRIBES

THAT OUTDATED OLD CLAY SLAB WEIGHING YOU DOWN?

Say goodbye to handwriting misery with Egypt's greatest export – new formula PAPYRUS from *Papco* ©tm

Just compare new formula papyrus with your standard Sumerian clay writing tablet.

PAPYRUS		CLAY TABLET	
Durable		Shatters when dropped	
Light and portable		What a weight!	
Can be folded		You must be joking...	
Write daintily with pen and ink		Wield a clumsy hammer and chisel	
Can be easily scrubbed for reuse		Major scouring required for reuse	

Made with top quality *Cyperus papyrus* marsh reed, freshly plucked from the banks of the Nile. Peeled and sliced, and laid into interlocking strips, our papyrus is beaten 3,000 times with the finest mallets, set out to dry, and polished for 48 hours with stones and shells. Only when our experts have decreed it is the *smoothest of the smooth* is it passed on to YOU – the world's most discerning scribes.

TAKE UP THE *Papco* ©TM OFFER OF 10 FREE PAPYRUS SHEETS, AND YOU'LL NEVER BUY CLAY TABLETS AGAIN!

KINGDOM CRUMBLES
AS SET TAKES CONTROL

2100 BC

Special report from our calamity and pestilence correspondent Ohdir Whaat–kanthematabe

Despair, destruction, destitution and decay – that's just four things beginning with D they're saying about Egypt today. As I walk through the streets of famine-hit Thebes, this is truly a land where Set the god of disorder has turned the world upside down.

Swagger

Slave girls swagger by decked in gold and silver jewels, noble women weep into their frayed linen dresses, surly children, seeing no future in their life, rebuke their parents saying, "I didn't ask to be born", "I hate you", and "It's not fair."

In a country unused to civil war, starvation and anarchy, these are terrible times.

Feeble

Many I spoke to are quick to blame the situation on the collapse of the pharaoh's power following the especially long reign of Pepi II. After his death rival clans based in Thebes and Herakleopolis are battling for control of the kingdom, and hostile tribes are adding to the chaos by invading from both east and west.

Set – lawless and disordered.

CALAMITY AND PESTILENCE – NOT POPULAR IN EGYPT

Wailing, gnashing of teeth, and major complaining greet the collapse of order in Old Kingdom Egypt.

Man with five names reunites Egypt

2050 BC

Rejoice! Rejoice! That's the word on everyone's lips. Theban prince Mentuhotep II has triumphed over the Herakleopolitan princes, and is set to unite the country and bring to an end 100 years of disorder.

Sweat

Wiping the sweat and dust of battle from his eyes at a hastily convened press conference, Mentuhotep announced, "I intend to unite Egypt and bring to an end 100 years of disorder."

And another thing

"And another thing," he added, "I'm going to build several forts in the desert to make sure the borders are safe from invading tribes, and I'm going to go south to occupy Nubia. This is the beginning of a golden age in Egyptian history. You can't have a golden age without gold, and there's certainly plenty of it down there!"

Mentuhotep – the multi monikered monarch
THOSE OTHER FOUR NAMES IN FULL

S'ankhibtawy	"He who breathes life into the heart of the Two Lands"
Nebhepetre	"The Son of Ra"
Netjerihedjet	"Divine is the white crown"
Sematawy	"He who unifies the Two Lands"

"Mister Chuckle-trousers" is, strangely enough, not one of the many names of Mentuhotep.

FEUDING EGYPT
FALLS TO FILTHY FOREIGNERS

1660 BC

400 years of peace and prosperity have ended with an invasion. For the first time in its 1600 year history much of the mighty Egyptian nation is under the control of a foreign power.

Taking advantage of a period of decline and feuding with Egypt once again split into two rival dynasties, the Hyksos tribe have swept down from Palestine and overrun the lands of lower Egypt.

Hooligans

The filthy foreign barbarians have been behaving like football hooligans on a drunken weekend and have:

- Burned our cities.
- Razed our temples.
- Been horrible to the locals.
- Set up their own capital in Avaris.
- Made our kings in Thebes pay them taxes.

Not all bad

But some Egyptians insist that the Hyksos aren't all bad. "They do have a tendency to loot and pillage, particularly on a dull Sunday afternoon," said Khon Shotep, a merchant from Buto, "but they like Egypt so much they've adopted our language and culture."

Horse

"And they've brought some very useful things with them," he continued. "They had the novel idea of putting a harness on a horse so that it could pull a chariot. They brought newfangled upright looms, which are much easier to weave cloth on than our old floor looms, and they've introduced new instruments such as lyres and lutes into Egyptian music."

Fortune

But most Egyptians remain unconvinced, and fortune tellers predict some serious smiting awaits the foreign intruders.

Some Hyksos soldiers stealing corn, razing temples and burning cities. The locals don't like them.

HYKSOS HEXPELLED

AHMOSE ON THE LOOSE

A hippopotamus. A major player in the Egyptian campaign to drive away the Hyksos.

1550 BC

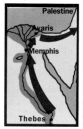

Ahmose's route to victory

120 years of foreign domination have come to an end. Theban King Ahmose I has cured Egypt of a nasty dose of the Hyksosis! The mighty monarch has swept north from his Theban power base to suppress the Hyksos tribe, who had overrun the delta region. The Echo is pleased to report that His Majesty has annihilated the alien intruders.

Uneasy

Upper Egypt has endured an uneasy peace with the foreign invaders, and relations have always been uncomfortable. Not only were the Theban kings **forced** to pay taxes to the Hyksos, but the interlopers **insisted** on venerating Set the god of disorder, AND **complained** about our hippopotami keeping them awake at night with their bellowing.

Domination

In his victory speech Ahmose told reporters, "We've given them a good hiding, and they **won't be back**! Once we've reconquered Nubia nothing will stand in the way of WORLD DOMINATION!!"

Sex change pharaoh claims dad was a god

Ma and Pa Hatshepsut, aka Mr. and Mrs. Tuthmosis I.

1470 BC

Pharaoh Hatshepsut, who has ruled Egypt brilliantly for nearly 20 years, is a WOMAN. And that's not all. She claims her dad is none other than Amun – king of the gods!! So says a secret source from inside the royal circle at Thebes.

Sauce!

The palace insider (whose identity cannot be disclosed for fear of his immediate execution) revealed to the Echo that Hatshepsut, who appears in statues as a man, and is

Hatshepsut yesterday, worrying her pretty little head about affairs of state.

addressed as "His Majesty", is undoubtedly a woman. "It was giving birth to two daughters that really gave the game away," he said.

Polish

The shadowy source, who works in the palace as a crown polisher, agreed to tell all to the Echo for a fee of three goats, four jars of wine, and a baboon.

He went on to reveal that Hatshepsut also maintains that her father is Amun. "Well the story is that the king of the gods was wandering around one day when he saw Mrs. Ahmose, that's Hatshepsut's mother. He was absolutely THUNDERSTRUCK by her beauty. Being a god, like, he didn't mess around, he just disguised himself as Ahmose's actual husband Tuthmosis I. Lucky fellow – that's not a bad trick if you ask my opinion!"

But this **double-shock-horror stunner of a scandal** is unlikely to tarnish Hatshepsut's regal reputation. The Pharaoh has **ruled** with great dignity. She has **restored** many buildings destroyed by the Hyksos, led the Egyptian army into battle in Nubia and the eastern empire, and even sent a **successful trading expedition** to the far off African land of Punt.

PAGE 40 COMMENT

Miss is a hit!

Everyone knows that having men as pharaohs is part of the god-given **natural order** of things. Like going to school or being a government official, it is **simply something** a lady should not worry her pretty little head about. However, under the circumstances the Echo has to say: **"Well done Ma'am – NOT BAD FOR A WOMAN!!"**

WE'RE IN THE MONEY

(WELL WE WOULD BE IF IT HAD BEEN INVENTED)

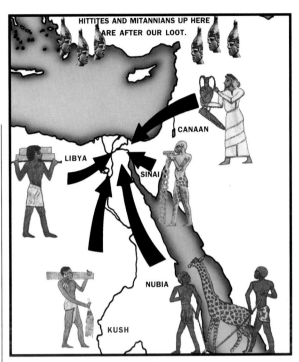

HITTITES AND MITANNIANS UP HERE ARE AFTER OUR LOOT.

LIBYA

CANAAN

SINAI

NUBIA

KUSH

LOOK WHAT WE'VE GOT!! Egypt's greatest ever empire.

1457 BC

Tuthmosis III, the mightiest of all warrior pharaohs, has added yet another feather to his cap with the defeat of the Mitannian army. The Egyptian Empire is now at its greatest extent EVER.

As trade flourishes, and tribute and taxes pour in from foreign lands, Egypt is set to become IMMENSELY WEALTHY!

Threat

But Tuthmosis's task has not been an easy one. The lands of Canaan (see map), acquired by Tuthmosis's grandfather Tuthmosis I, have been under constant threat from Egypt's two arch eastern rivals, the Hittites and the Mitannians.

Warpath

Tuthmosis III decided the Hits and the Mits needed STRAIGHTENING OUT, and has gone on the warpath 17 times against them.

He harassed the Hits who

TUTHMOSIS III. He had a snake in his hat, rather than a feather.

threw in the towel before it came to an out-and-out punch-up, but he had to mash the Mits at the battle of Megiddo before they declared "enough is enough".

Couldn't be done

"They said it couldn't be done," he boasted to royal reporters after the battle, "but they were not great men of vision, genius and immense personal charisma – like me." Tuthmosis went on to explain how, against the advice of all his top generals, he had led his army over a steep mountain path, surprised the Mitannian forces from behind, and crushed them utterly.

Coining it in

The successful campaign now leaves Egypt free to enjoy the benefits of its substantial empire. With silver and tin coming in from Canaan, salt and wine from Libya, copper and turquoise from Sinai, gold and slaves from Nubia, and ebony and ivory from Kush, the Echo says Good times are here, and they can only get better!

AKHTOY'S ABODES

44 Sneferu St, Memphis

All sorts of property at prices YOU* can afford!!

Elegant country mansion

Most charming executive 16 room residence, within easy reach of Thebes, so ideal for professional man • Panoramic views of surrounding desert • Traditional unbaked brick construction with stone/wood frames and pillars • Beautifully decorated, with bright floral/geometric designs on plaster • Imposing ramp to substantial "temple style" entrance. Windows placed high in house to minimize penetrating sunlight. (All frames painted in "glare guard" brown paint.) • Bathroom with limestone tub and splash slabs. Toilet with fine stone "keyhole" seat • Magnificent reception room, with matching pillars. Triangular vents on roof to catch refreshing north wind • Own grounds with pool containing water birds • Kitchen on roof. Cool cellar incorporating plentiful water storage facilities (four large jars).

Superb town house

BACK ON MARKET

Individual and most impressive Eighteenth Dynasty town house occupying unique location in heart of Memphis • Would suit royal official • Expansive grounds, with own well. Imposing doorway carved with inscriptions venerating owner • Three floors with 30 rooms in total • Ground floor comprised of baking and cloth-making area open to courtyard • Principal floor comprised of impressive main reception room with brilliant blue ceiling, and living quarters for family • Master bedroom with adjoining bathroom and brick/wood "seat style" toilet with pot and sand container • Top floor comprised of office/living quarters. Each room complete with beautifully painted columns • Flat roof suitable for cooking area, and sleeping space for servants.

Worker's cottage

Delightful terraced dwelling built within safety of walled village • Mud construction. Near to fields. Plain "peasant fashion" mud walls, incorporating multiple niches for placement of statues to household gods • Thatch roof (with openings for light and ventilation) • Feature raised brick bed, in main bedroom. Cellar offering walk-in storage facility, set beneath earth style floor.

Character two-room hovel

Ideal first-time purchase on outskirts of Memphis • Two rooms with own internal wall (disintegrating) • Close proximity to Nile (prone to flooding). Part covered "open access" roof, giving generous light and ventilation • Near small stream for bathing, and close-by handy field with several bushes (non-prickly) for "other purposes". Healthy "good for you" style trek to nearest well.

Traditional town house

BARGAIN OF THE WEEK

Most sought-after premier residential location, enjoying benefits of bustling downtown Sais • Strong, unbaked brick construction will allow building of additional level on roof • Bedroom with semi-private partition – ideal for portable toilet • Opportunity for expansion, as several adjacent properties are derelict.

Akhtoy's descriptions of appliances/services or indeed entire residences should not be taken as a guarantee that these items are in working order, or even exist. We recommend that purchasers arrange for a qualified scribe to check these dwellings thoroughly.

*Depending on who you are.

SUN SETS ON "SON OF SUN"

Light goes out on Akhenaten

Akhenaten. He liked the sun and art, but lost control of Syria.

1336 BC

Akhenaten, the maverick pharaoh who venerated the sun and declared war on all the other gods of Egypt, is dead.

But even as the royal corpse grows cold, and the nation prepares to bury the most unconventional monarch in its history, political pundits are arguing over the merits of his rule.

"Akhenaten cast several very large boulders into the placid lotus pond of Egyptian society, and the waves they made have created unheard of upheaval in a hitherto changeless land," said the Echo's royal correspondent shortly before the editor said, "You're fired".

Amen to Aten

Akhenaten came to the throne as Amenhoptep IV in 1352. But the sun-crazy sovereign took a new name – meaning *pious servant of Aten*– six years into his reign. Although he ruled over a land of many gods, Akhenaten became convinced that there was only one god – and that god was the SUN ITSELF– known as THE ATEN.

Sunstroke

Egyptians wondered if their pharaoh was suffering from sunstroke, as Akhenaten declared:

• The sun was his FATHER.
• ONLY AKHENATEN and his family could worship The Aten – everyone else had to worship Akhenaten.
• Worship of all other gods was FORBIDDEN.
• The great temples of Amun, king of the gods, were to be SHUT DOWN.
• Statues of all other gods were to be SMASHED, and their names REMOVED from all statues and monuments.
• Homage was to be paid to The Aten in large courtyards OPEN TO THE SKY, and filled with altars where devotees could place fruits and flowers and other bountiful products of the sun.

Rival

But sunstroke may not have been the sole reason for these changes. Political observers are suggesting that Akhenaten promoted the worship of the sun because he feared that temples to the god Amun were becoming so rich and powerful that they competed with the pharaoh himself for control of the land.

So what

Yet despite the revolutionary nature of these changes the average Egyptian in the street was more than likely untouched by Akhenaten's new religion. Compared to the usual gods of Egypt the sun was faceless and characterless.

Most Egyptians have little shrines to their gods at home, and continued to worship at them, no matter what Akhenaten said.

THE REVOLUTIONARY RULER'S REGAL RECORD

Four *other* things Akhenaten did, apart from insisting everyone worship The Aten.

① Built a luxurious new capital called Akhetaten, midway between Memphis and Thebes.

② Lost control of the colony Egypt had established in Syria, which was taken over by the Hittites.

③ Married Nefertiti, said to be one of the most beautiful women in the world. (However, some gossips say that a shadow fell over their relationship, and she squabbled with Akhenaten before she died.)

Nefertiti

④ Encouraged artists to paint sweeping, graceful images full of life and movement, rather than stiff and stilted depictions of the items they portrayed.

Unforgettable – that's what you aren't

A palace scribe erasing all mention of Akhenaten from royal records.

HOREMHEB SET TO TURN AKHENATEN INTO INVISIBLE MAN

1320 BC

Pharaoh Horemheb has turned the tables on the most table-turning, topsy-turvy, back-to-front, upside-down pharaoh in history.

The former general turned monarch has told reporters he intends to wipe the name of Pharaoh Akhenaten from the very pages of history!! "Akhenaten tried to stamp out our gods, so now we're going to STAMP HIM OUT. Henceforth it will be forbidden to speak his name out loud, and he shall only be known as *that criminal*. All his statues and every inscription of his name shall be U T T E R L Y ERADICATED. All temples to his god, The Aten, are to be closed AT ONCE and then torn down."

Tut tut

He went on " Much of the harm caused by *that criminal* has been undone during the reign of my predecessor King Tut. Worship of the old gods has been restored, and the capital moved from Akhetaten back to Memphis. But I intend to erase his name from all records, and it's going to be like he never existed."

Godless? You need...

GODZ 4 UZ

UNIT 26, TEMPLE ROAD, ALEXANDRIA

THE FINEST COLLECTION OF STATUES, SHRINES AND AMULETS THIS SIDE OF THE RIVER OF DEATH.

CULTS, MINOR DEITIES, GODDESSES, IDOLS AND BIG LEAGUE GODS, WE'VE GOT THE LOT.

JUST LOOK AT THESE STATUES!!!

AMUN

He's everybody's darling. He's king of the gods.

TOP QUALITY

NUT

Look out below! Its **Nut** the sky goddess, all set to welcome you into the next world!*

IDEAL GIFT

TAWERET

Your tiny tot's cuddly bedtime pal. Protect your children with the hottest hippo in god-dom.

MIN

The god of fertility. Hello Big Boy!!! Available in three shades of lime green.*

BES

Burglary a problem? **Bes** get one of these!! **Bes** is guaranteed to guard your home and children, and keep out unwanted intruders.

2000 GODS

THOTH

Take a letter **Thoth...** The brainy beak-faced bookworm is god of wisdom and scribe to the other gods.

SOBEK

He's wetter than a wet week in Avaris. He's the god of water.

INTEREST FREE CREDIT OFFER

MA'AT

It's a fair cop!! **Ma'at** the goddess of justice and truth.

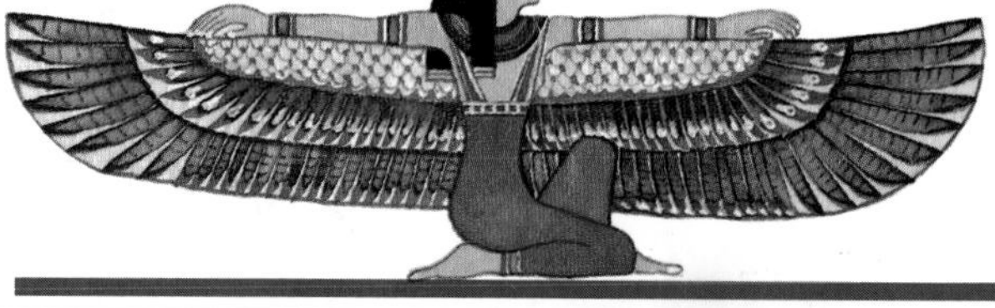

OSIRIS

King of the dead – he looks after you in the after-life.

BUY NOW PAY LATER

GOD WISE – WE'RE SIMPLY THE BEST!!

All clay statues come with authentic "marble-effect" finish.

FREE DELIVERY

*The publishers consider full reproduction of these particular deities unsuitable for a family newspaper.

SUPERPOWER STALEMATE ends in treaty

Ram and Hat say let's be pals

1268 BC

Egypt's arch rivals the Hittites woke up this morning to discover they are now our BEST FRIENDS. Pharaoh Ramesses II has signed the first state-to-state peace treaty in history with former foe and top Hittite Hattusilis III.

Silver

The treaty, which is engraved on a silver tablet, sets out several ground-breaking agreements between the Egyptians and Hittites. Among them are reassurances that:

• *We promise not to **pinch** their territory if they promise not to pinch ours.*
• *There'll be no more **jabbing, slugging and smiting** between us (no hostilities at all in fact, although hitting with pillows, tickling, and making mildly impudent remarks about each other are still allowed).*
• *We'll **support** each other if anyone else attacks us, no matter how big they are.*
• *Political rivals of Ramesses and Hattusilis will not be offered **refuge** in each other's country.*
• *Ramesses is to **marry** one of Hattusilis's daughters.*

Decades

The treaty ends decades of rivalry between the two great Middle East superpowers. Political observers attribute their willingness to compromise on the need to defend themselves from other nations in the region.

"There are too many other blood lusting, power hungry, land chomping, gold grubbing nations like the Syrians, Babylonians and Libyans out there for them to cope with," said Scholar Mengebet, of the Memphis Institute for Strategic Studies, Tactical Teaching and Military Methodology. (M.I.S.S.T.T.M.M. for short).

More temples

But whatever the reason, Ramesses II will now have more time and energy to spend on his great passion – BUILDING TEMPLES.

Reckless archers from the Ptah division shoot arrows into the air to celebrate the fact that we're now pals with the Hittites.

Pharaoh's bundle of joy

1240 BC

In between fighting off the Syrians, and building some of Egypt's fanciest temples and fortifications, Ramesses II is still finding time to entertain his 100 wives and concubines. Palace officials announced last night that the sprightly 76 year old pharaoh is a dad AGAIN! The latest pharaohette is thought to be his 200th child.

Son of Amun

Ramesses, who claims to be the son of Amun, king of the gods, has ruled Egypt for over 60 years, and has already outlived 10 of his sons. "There's plenty more where they came from," he quipped to waiting reporters on his way to inspect Abu Simbel, the memorial he is building in Nubia for recently deceased Chief Queen Nefertari.

Feverish

The new baby news sparked feverish speculation about the identity of the child's mother. Yesterday, bookmakers Luxbrux were offering odds of 7/1 on Asmunnikal, sultry daughter of top Hittite Hattusilis III. Other contenders include current chief queen Isi-nofret (10/1), and Nut, the sky goddess (10,000/1).

Superdad slams the Syries! His Majesty Ramesses II, taking time off from fatherhood to smite some Syrians.

SEA PEOPLE SCUTTLED

RAMESSES III DIVES IN WITH BOTH FISTS FLYING

1174 BC

Ramesses III's reputation as the guardian angel of Egypt has been sealed. Front line dispatches from the Nile Delta have confirmed that he has won a decisive naval battle against the latest in a long line of invading barbarians – the so-called Sea People.

Motley

For many years this motley alliance of miscellaneous Mediterraneans has been creeping toward our shores, intent on conquest, not to mention plundering and looting. Rampant Ramesses reacted with righteous wrath when their invasion fleet reached the Nile Delta. He wreaked havoc on the Mediterranean marauders, assisted by an army battle-hardened by his recent campaigns against invading Libyans. **The Sea People have been decisively splashed, ducked, held under water, and buried up to their necks in sand.**

Serious

The Sea People threat has been serious enough for every single Egyptian male of military age to be called into service. Ramesses told reporters, "These Sea People,

they're the Hyksos of the 1170s – settling wherever they like, and pillaging as they go. They've been on the warpath since Amenhotep III was a lad★, and they're not coming here, I can tell you."

★ *Note for scholars – c.1400BC*

Loyal

His loyal subjects were quick to praise their fiery king's briny show of belligerent brilliance, but seemed to be weary of the constant struggle to keep Egypt free from raiders and invaders. "Wars, we're ★★★★★★★ sick of them," said Meket aten, a chariot driver from Thebes. "If it's not the ★★★★★★★ Libyans invading us, it's these ★★★★★★★ Sea People. I'd hang them up by their ankles and throw crocodiles at them, if you ask me."

Ramesses in outright termination mode. His "no-nonsense" approach won the day.

Ramesses on the rampage.

ALL OUT STRIKE!

Wageless workers in wildcat walk-out

Workers' spokesman Ptah-emdjehuty claims he's starving.

1150 BC

The nation is reeling from the news that workers building the tomb of mighty warrior Ramesses III have GONE ON STRIKE.

In a shock move unprecedented in the Egyptian construction industry, the royal tomb craftsmen downed tools when their wages failed to arrive for the **second month running**.

Grain drain

"We get paid in goods and food," said workers' spokesman Ptah-emdjehuty, "and we're not doing any more work 'til we get some."

As he spoke an angry loin-cloth clothed mob gathered outside the half-completed tomb and began to chant: **"What do we want? – Grain, oil and linen, and a little bit of silver on special occasions!" "When do we want it? – NOW, or as soon as Ramesses sees fit – but he'd better hurry up because we're starving!"**

Fabric

Palace spokesman Vizier Ta was quick to condemn the striking workers, and blamed their lack of wages on a nationwide shortage of grain. "These people are politically motivated shirkers," he told the Echo. "The very fabric of the nation is decaying. The conscience of the population is withering"

Plot

The strike is indeed further evidence of the decline of Egyptian civilization. Despite brilliant military victories, the reign of Ramesses III has seen escalating price rises, disrupted trade, dishonest incompetent government, and even a plot to assassinate the King himself.

COFFINS FOR ALL OCCASIONS

Our coffins are made of the finest handcrafted wood, and are decorated to the highest standard with hand-painted magic designs.

They are **guaranteed** to offer you protection and a safe passage to the afterlife.

a) The Royal – solid gold coffin within stone sarcophagus

b) The Aristocrat – gilded wood

c) The Regular – wood

The Regular model

IT'S YOUR FUNERAL

The procession

Come as you are, with just the family. Alternatively, Dead World can supplement your funeral procession with a selection of professional mourners, priests, animals for sacrifice and porters to carry your belongings.

The "opening of the mouth" ceremony

We all know how important it is to get this right. The tomb door ritual to restore the life force to your dead body is too important to be left to lesser funeral services.

TOMB IT MAY CONCERN

This is where the size of your wallet really matters, but remember, you're dead for a long time, so penny-pinching here may seem like a false economy in the years to come!

There's no reason why you shouldn't continue to enjoy yourself in your tomb. Pack it out with your most desirable possessions. **The bigger the tomb, the more you can take with you.**

Magical pictures, and texts incorporating YOUR NAME, should adorn the walls of your tomb. This will ensure your spirit will continue to exist in the afterlife.

For an additional fee we can ENSURE that your spirit form is regularly supplied with essential food and drink.

(We also have a rock bottom "hole in the ground" service for those on an extremely tight budget.)

COURT REPORT

Brought to you by
Ma'at, the goddess of
JUSTICE & TRUTH

Headhunting boss nose best

Top estate official Nakht Sobk has had his nose cut off after a court at Abydos found him guilty of kidnapping a herdsman belonging to a rival estate. Sobk seized the man (who has not been named) because he was impressed by his sheepherding abilities. "You can't get good staff these days," he told the court. "So I told him he was being headhunted."

But neither the herdsman nor Judge Neferhotep was impressed by this line of argument. "The law is quite clear on this point," the judge told Sobk. "*If any man shall seize a herdsman and cause him to say 'ruin has befallen my cattle', then he shall be beaten with 200 blows and have his nose cut off.* Your exemplary record as a good citizen has saved you from the beating, but your lack of nose will serve as a permanent reminder that high officials cannot do just what they wish."

The Echo court artist's dramatic depiction of Sobk's trial. The estate official (waving arms) pleads for his nose.

Tool thief DEATH DRAMA

A Theban woman has been sentenced to death after a workers' court found her guilty of stealing tools from a fellow worker. The woman, known only as Herya, swore an oath in court protesting her innocence before the god Amun, and the Pharaoh himself. She did look silly, when shortly thereafter, a court official dispatched to her house dug up the very tools in question.

Worker-magistrate Henut Kagab was unequivocal in his sentence. "Exceedingly guilty is the citizeness Herya, and worthy of death." However, the workers' court does not have the power to carry out a death sentence, and Herya's case is to be heard by Vizier Kentika.

WORKERS IN CURSE OUTRAGE

Foreman Nemty Nakht is alleging that four of his workers spoke blasphemously against the Pharaoh. "I clearly heard one of these men say 'Pharaoh has a nose like a jackal and the character of a cantankerous baboon'," Nakht told the Theban workers' court.

He went on "Another said '... and he stinks like a jackal after a four week trek through the baking desert.' Then they all snickered like naughty student scribes."

The four workers deny the allegations, which, if proven, could result in their execution. They say they had recently discovered that Nakht had been illegally bartering granite building blocks for shipments of wine and ostrich feathers, and that he is trying to frame them.

The case continues.

RED FACES FOR TOE TORTURE TOMB ROBBERS

A Theban court heard yesterday how two peasants on a tomb robbing rampage had red faces when they went to sleep " on the job", and were caught red-handed.

Imhotep Intef and Itruri Kagab broke into the tomb of Bakenptah Amenhotep in Abydos. After a hard afternoon ransacking, plundering, looting and despoiling, they fell upon the food and wine Amenhotep's devoted wife Akh-menu had left to nourish his spirit, and gobbled down the lot.

Feeling tired, they decided to lie down for a while before they moved on. Tomb guards, alerted by what they described as "low rumbling noises" coming from within the tomb, moved in and made a swift arrest.

Feet

Judge Nebre was merciless with the men. "Tomb robbery is one of the great curses of the modern world," he told them. "Your guilt is established beyond all doubt. I sentence you to have your feet beaten with a big stick."

Intef and Kagab await their turn before Judge Nebre with other miscreants at the Theban court.

Hide-and-seek

Three thieves who stole 20 cattle hides from a tannery have been arrested and punished with a beating of 100 blows and five large cuts.

Judge Kanakht told the men, "God knows the wrong-doer, and punishes his sin with blood. Be thankful I have not ordered your ears to be cut off."

"District Five" face Vizier Kentika

Five district governors are being tried by Pharaoh's deputy, Vizier Kentika, in the highest court in the land. They face charges of withholding taxes, taking bribes, and failing to assess local estates. If found guilty the five face a life-threatening beating of 200 blows, and social and professional disgrace.

"Donkeys ate my taxes" pleads peasant

Ammun Enshi, a peasant from Selima, has been given a swift beating with a stick for late payment of taxes. Judge Anubis heard that Enshi had been unable to pay his taxes after a herd of donkeys ate half his corn crop. "Your misfortune has saved you from further punishment," the judge told Enshi. "But if you are unable to pay your taxes again, you will be conscripted into the Karnak temple building project."

Enshi is given a short, sharp shock. "It's disgraceful," says his mother.

Don't spill that salt or break that mirror, and definitely don't go walking under any ladders – it's

PESHED'S PROSPECTS

Greetings, O readers. I, Peshed, the Echo's oracular prophet of good days, bad days, and auspicious and inauspicious portents bring you news of the FUTURE.

The season of Akhet* is upon us, and here is my forecast for the next 120 days.

The 26th – a good day for ducks.

The first month of Akhet

The **26th day of the month** is a **hostile** day. It is the day when Horus the great protector, and Set the god of disorder, declared war upon each other and brought chaos and woe to the world.

Do not go out of doors between dusk and dawn, as great misfortune will befall you. Between dawn and dusk you may go about your business providing you do not partake in any of the following activities: bathing, boating, making a journey, eating fish or any other water-living creature, killing a goat, ox or duck, lighting a fire in the house, and listening to cheerful songs.

You are also forewarned that uttering the name of Set, the god of disorder, will ensure that your house **will never be free of squabbling and ill temper.**

The 6th – don't drink barley beer.

The second month of Akhet

I have much news for those who were born in this month.

Those born on the **fourth day of the month**. You are likely to die of fever. Always take a cloak when you go out, in case it rains and you catch a chill.

Those born on the **fifth day of the month.** You are likely to die of a broken heart. Perhaps you could become a hermit, and go and live on your own at the top of a mountain?

Those born on the **sixth day of the month.** You are likely to die of drink. Stay away from

that barley beer if you can possibly help it. Those born on the **ninth day of the month.** Congratulations, you are likely to die of old age. Make sure you have plenty of children, so at least some of the ingrates will be around to look after you when you are an old codger. Those born on the **23rd day of the month.** Snap, crunch, chomp. Watch out for crocodiles!!

Those born on the **27th day of the month.** Hssssssssss. Watch out for snakes!!

Those born on the **29th day of the month.** Your life will be much blessed and when you die you will be a highly respected gentleman, your worship, sir.

A local temple, yesterday.

The third month of Akhet

Peshed regrets to announce that he has no predictions for this month. Please consult your local temple oracle for details.

The 28th - 30th. Get planting!

The fourth month of Akhet

The **28th, 29th and 30th days of the month** are **good days.** On these days Horus and Set called an end to their struggle, and peace fell upon the world. These are good days to wage war against the enemies of Egypt, and on a more mundane level, to sow crops or begin to cultivate a piece of land.

*****Note to foreigners. The Egyptian year is divided into three seasons – Akhet, when the Nile floods its banks (July to October), Peret, when the waters recede (November to February) and Shemu, the time of harvest (March to June). There are four thirty-day months in each season.**

ECHOCOMMENT
SOCKS CRISIS
1030 BC

• 2,000 years of mainly uninterrupted peace and prosperity.

• The most extraordinary buildings in the world, EVER.

• Fantastic craftsmen and architects that make other nations green with envy.

• A system of government which usually stays in power by looking after its people – rather than hitting them regularly with a big stick.

We've had it all. <u>But are we going to be able to keep it?</u>

BURST

The Egyptian nation has had several great advantages over its rivals. Since the dawn of time the Nile River has burst its banks every July and poured fertilizing silt over the fields. When the waters recede we get to plant and harvest record-breaking crops. Since King Narmer united the region way back in 3100BC, we've made the most of this regular supply of food and built a **prosperous, ordered world** where government ruled, and craftsmen flourished. Being surrounded by sea and desert meant invasion by greedy outsiders was all but **impossible**.

ALL CHANGE

BUT THIS HAS ALL CHANGED. The Sahara Desert is getting **dryer**. In the west, wandering tribes from Libya are desperate to settle in our fertile land, **and they don't mind waving their swords around to do so**. Mediterranean and Asian armies are pouring in from the east, all itching to get their hands on **our** wealth.

ROTTEN RULERS

We've been telling them to get lost for twenty centuries – <u>so why worry now?</u> Because 50 years of **weak rulers** have led to a **crumbling** respect for the Pharaoh and the power he represents. **Corrupt** government officials are squandering Egypt's wealth. Squabbling Mediterranean powers have **disrupted** our great trading empire. The goldmines of Nubia are all **exhausted**. In the midst of all this the **threat** to our country from outsiders has never been **greater** – yet we've never been **less able** to resist it.

The Echo says the barbarians are at the gates. LET'S PULL OUR SOCKS UP – <u>BEFORE IT'S TOO LATE</u>.

PHARO

The sphinxational new game that's free with the ECHO

PHARO TAKES YOU ON A ROLLER COASTER RIDE THROUGH 20 CENTURIES OF EGYPTIAN HISTORY. JUST CHOOSE A MUMMY, THROW A DICE, AND OFF YOU GO...

2560BC
You, King Khufu, employ 100,000 men to make a pyramid of 2,500,000 limestone blocks. It remains tallest building in world until Eiffel Tower is erected in 1888. Pat yourself on the back, and go forward 2 spaces.

2660BC
You are architect Imhotep, and you build Egypt's first massive pyramid for King Djoser – the most impressive monument the world has yet seen. Go forward 1 space.

2550BC
Build sphinx and give travel writers the world over the opportunity to use the word "enigma"

2500BC
Begin to mummify dead, with intention of preserving bodies forever.

2345-2181BC
Power begins to slip from the hands of the pharaoh and into the provinces where strong nobles rule. Go back a space.

1390-1352BC
Feel extremely pleased with yourself. You are Amenhotep III and you're lucky enough to be in charge when Egypt is at the height of its power and majesty. Move forward 3 spaces.

1458-1425BC
Look out Palestine and Nubia – smitings ahoy! Tuthmosis III, the greatest of all warrior pharaohs, enlarges Egypt's Empire.

1506-1494BC
Take a leaf out of the Hyksos's book and expand Egyptian territory northeast into Asia, and south into Nubia.

1550BC (-1069BC)
NEW KINGDOM ERA. You are Ahmose I. You expel the Hyksos and a new golden age begins. Build a few temples and go forward 3 spaces.

1352BC
You are Akhenaten, and you announce that the sun god Aten is the one true god.

1330BC
You are King Tut and you say no he isn't and set about obliterating any evidence of Akhenaten's existence.

1295 (-1186)BC
Beginning of 19th Dynasty. It's mainly downhill after this, so enjoy yourself, it's later than you think!

1279-1213BC
You are Ramesses II and you combine a prolific career in warriorhood and building with an impressive 200 children. How DID you find the time? Smite the Hittites at the battle of Qadesh, make a peace treaty with them and go forward 3 spaces.

1186- 1069BC
Beginning of the 20th Dynasty. Egypt is beset by uppity tribes on all sides. They're getting restless and greedy. Watch out for those Sea People – they're really trying it on!!

RULES OF THE GAME
1. No fighting, sulking or cheating, even when you're losing.
2. Some spaces have instructions on them. **Obey them**, or face the wrath of **Set**, the god of disorder!!!

WAY BACK WHEN (Pre 5000BC)

Wander around the Nile region gathering berries, making mud pots, doing some fishing and being eaten by crocodiles. Not much of a life, but it's a living.

A LITTLE LATER (5000-4000BC)

Fertile soil around the Nile proves ideal for growing crops. You have enough food to stop worrying about where the next meal is coming from and start building towns, decorating pots and squabbling with local tribes. Move forward 1 space.

A LITTLE AFTER THAT (around 3500BC)

Two distinct kingdoms emerge from the mists of time – Hello there Upper and Lower Egypt!

3300BC

Start building rectangular looking houses with real bricks, instead of mud and sticks. Continue to squabble with local tribes.

3200BC

Devise writing in the form of hieroglyphs – one of the most beautiful scripts ever invented. Go forward 3 spaces.

3100BC

You are King Narmer. After some serious smiting you unite Upper and Lower Egypt. Success goes to your head and you declare yourself Egypt's first god king. Make Memphis the capital of Egypt and go forward 3 spaces.

2686BC (to 2150BC)

OLD KINGDOM ERA begins. Everything gets controlled from the capital. If you are an ordinary Egyptian you have to pay taxes and get conscripted to building projects, but on the other hand life is a lot more safe and settled. Go forward 2 spaces.

2700BC

Get really good at building. Go forward 2 spaces.

2725BC

Start burying kings with lots of possessions for the next world, so being dead doesn't affect their lifestyle too adversely.

2750BC

Craftsmen produce beautiful copper and gold artifacts. Hieratic script developed.

2800BC

Produce accurate calendar based on movement of stars.

2250BC

You are Pepi II and all your nobles and administrators think you're such a weed they no longer take any notice of you. Watch over the decline of the Old Kingdom, and see your country splinter into conflicting fragments.

2181BC

Disaster. Central government collapses. Famine sweeps the land. Golden age of tomb robbing, civil war and bloodshed. Your house is ransacked and no one can find a decent plumber. Go back 4 spaces.

2055BC (-1640BC)

Hurrah. Get back on course with the MIDDLE KINGDOM ERA.

2055BC

You are Mentuhotep II and you re-establish control of whole of Egypt and things settle down nicely. Go forward 3 spaces.

1985(-1975)BC

200 years of stability, trade, great literature and craftsmanship. Egypt is such a splendid place to live you can stay here for at least two turns (or longer if you feel like it!).

1990BC

Begin to smelt bronze. If you know what this means, go forward 2 spaces.

1650BC

Hyksos peoples sweep down from the north to take advantage of all this dithering and take over top part of Egypt. They do however bring some very useful tools with them – such as horse-drawn chariots, lyres, loots and sophisticated bows and arrows.

1783 (-1640) BC

Era of 13th Dynasty. Unlucky for some, including this lot. 50 pharaohs come and go in 150 years. Egypt splits into two. The bunch who run the land at the top have 76 kings in 100 years. It's all a colossal mess really.

1786BC

Oh no. Things are beginning to collapse again and everything falls into disrepair. The garden needs weeding, and just look at the carpet! Go back 3 spaces.

1980BC

You are Ammenemes I. You and several other pharaohs called Ammenemes reclaim vast tracts of !and from marshes, and build irrigation schemes, with the intention of increasing farmland and preventing famine. Go forward 2 spaces.

1184-1153BC

You are Ramesses III and you win a series of brilliant victories against the Sea People. Stay here for three turns, because things really go downhill from here onward.

1060BC

Oh dear, here we go again. Libyans, Ethiopians, in fact all sorts of barbarians, are invading your country. Withdraw all your troops to Egypt's original boundaries.

1000BC

The Golden age of Ancient Egypt is over. Tomb robbery reaches epidemic proportions. You even have to remove the bodies of recent pharaohs to a secret hiding place so they won't get ransacked.

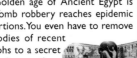

999 - 30BC

Not much to look forward to over the next millennium. Just lots of foreigners taking over. Some of them even have a try at being pharaohs. Egypt stays like this for 1,000 years until the Romans take it over in 30BC, and make it a province of Rome. Things don't improve much. You're just a Roman rather than an Egyptian.

Bata's beauty spot
Hot tips from the hottest lips in Memphis!

Hello girls! Bata here with another dispatch from the front line of the Echo's campaign to KEEP EGYPT BEAUTIFUL! So wiggle those hips, flutter those eyelids and LET'S GET GORGEOUS!!

Hair today... shorn tomorrow

Judging by your letters many of you are concerned about greying and thinning hair. A woman's lustrous black mane is her crowning glory and it's important to keep it looking attractive AT ALL TIMES.

For greying hair *a dark and mysterious mixture of black cow blood, black snake fat and raven's eggs will return your tresses to their former glory.*

Thinning hair *is more of a problem, but a preparation* *of mashed up fenugreek seeds rubbed well into the scalp has been known to slow the process down.*

The mane attraction. The first step to all-round beauty.

KOHLS FROM NUBIA

We've been wearing mesdemet (also known as kohl) as eye shadow since it was first brought back from our lands in Nubia. But did you know that not only does this magnificent black mineral make our eyes look dazzling, it also protects them? Lead sulphide, the main ingredient, acts as a disinfectant, keeps away the flies, and shields our eyes from the sun.

I spy with my little eye, something beginning with ⬜.

AS SWEET AS YOU ARE

Keep sweet in the baking heat with a deodorant preparation of myrrh, desert date seeds or frankincense, mixed together with the fatty oil of your choice. Incidentally, I'm often asked by noble ladies why peasants stink so much. The sad truth is that many Egyptians have never seen the inside of a bathroom, and can't afford the expense of keeping clean. Still, let's be thankful some of us can.

TOP FASHION
Dress to impress – King Tut style

Fortune tellers predict that in the distant future people will say "Clothes maketh the man," and for sure, none of us on the Echo would disagree with THAT!

Tut's top tips

A cloth around the loins might be all right for your run-of-the-mill farm hand, but connoisseurs of true style know that power and respect go hand in hand with a good tailor and jewel maker.

So here, with the help of our own teenage King Tut and his Queen, is the Echo's own guide for the top Egyptian after top marks in the style stakes.

FOR HIM

Clothes that say "I'm in charge"

Sandals – immaculate, gold plated, extremely uncomfortable. These shoes shout "I go everywhere by chariot."

Add instant authority with an elaborate **crown**. This hat does a lot more than keep the sun off your head!

The ever popular his 'n' hers wide gold **collar**, with precious jewels. The accessory that screams "I'VE GOT CASH COMING OUT OF MY EARS!!" Wear it plain, or with serpent, vulture or hawk head attachment, in fact any creature that inspires fear and respect will do. (Fashion hint: cow and sheep attachment not recommended.)

Refreshing **body oils** to keep you cool.

Jewels by Nofret's Nik-naks, Memphis.
Clothes by Faras Dwat, Giza. Throne – model's own.

FOR HER

Clothes that declare "I'm the daintiest doll in Upper Egypt"

White linen **dress** – timeless, elegant simplicity.

Braided **wig** on shaven head. Say goodbye to headlice misery. Gold tube braiding optional.

Jewel charms to ward off jealous spells and curses that are sure to be winging their way toward anyone as gorgeous as YOU!

Seductive peacock-feather **headdress**.

Stay feminine, fresh and flagrantly fragrant with sweet **lily oil**, even in the scorching sun.

Broad gold **bracelet**. A must – especially if it's a gift from someone even more important than you.

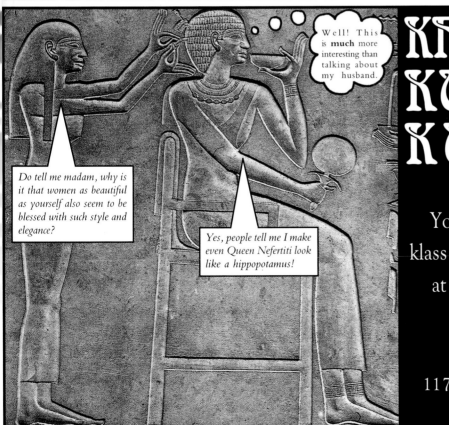

*Well! This is **much** more interesting than talking about my husband.*

Do tell me madam, why is it that women as beautiful as yourself also seem to be blessed with such style and elegance?

Yes, people tell me I make even Queen Nefertiti look like a hippopotamus!

BUY OF THE WEEK!

Wrinkle–stiltskin

They say beauty is a joy forever, but even the most enchanting vision of loveliness wakes up one morning to find those crows have left their feet in the corner of her eyes. Help is at hand with this new papyrus *The book of how to make the old young.* It shows how simple everyday products (such as fenugreek leaf) can be used to make ointment and lotions to wipe out wrinkles and blitz blotches!

DREAMS
What do they really mean?

What you eat, or indeed, what might eat you, are some of the many causes of unusual dreams.

"I had a funny dream last night." Was there ever a conversational gambit more likely to make your eyes glaze over? Let's face it, other people's dreams are really boring, but your own, well, they're really fascinating!

Dreams. We all have them, but what do they really mean? Many people believe that they are one way the gods use to talk to us on Earth. People also believe our dreams show us what lies in the future.

Dream team

Here's a quiz compiled by Echo dream correspondent Tash Khakty and top dream consultant Saq Neferti. See if you can guess the correct interpretation of these dreams, then check your answers to see what your dream interpretation says about YOU!

Dream one

I was standing under a waterfall which was pouring into a crystal clear river, and the water felt really clean and cold.

Meaning:

a) My roof is leaking and the water is pouring over me as I sleep.
b) The gods are smiling on me, and purifying me from all evil.
c) I haven't had a bath for ages, and I feel guilty about it.

Dream two

I was out in the fields and this absolutely massive cat appeared and stared at me for ages.

Meaning:

a) My cat has come into my bedroom and curled up on my head.
b) The gods are smiling on me and there is going to be a really big harvest.
c) A tom cat's been in here and sprayed on my pillow.

Dream three

I was with this really gorgeous man/woman (delete where not applicable), and we were kissing and canoodling and all that.

Meaning:

a) Heavens. It's Mr./Mrs. Hekhbet! Hmm, he/she always was rather cute!
b) The gods are angry with me and I will soon lose a close relative.
c) I was with this really gorgeous man/woman, and we were kissing and canoodling and all that.

Dream four

I was standing in the street, and this huge ostrich ran up to me and we tried to stare each other out.

Meaning:

a) My pillow is stuffed with ostrich feathers.
b) The gods are angry with me and misfortune will soon befall me.
c) Lanky cousin Mekmer is coming to stay. We can't stand each other!

Dream five

I was on this farm and feeding a herd of cattle and they were all mooing and everything.

Meaning:

a) I knew we shouldn't have bought a house too near to Farmer Senini's cow shed.
b) The gods are angry with me and my future is to wander the Earth aimlessly with no direction.
c) All my friends are completely bovine. I'm the only one with any spark about me.

Dream six

A purple baboon playing a lute started to sing a song about peeling onions, then it turned out to be the pharaoh, and I had to tell it what a wonderful singer it was.

Meaning:

a) I had too many figs to eat for supper.
b) I had too much cheese to eat for supper.
c) My uncle Merey is coming to stay. I can't stand him, but he's promised my family he'll pay for the repair of our roof and I've got to be nice to him.

ANSWERS

All the b's are the correct interpretations of the dreams, and are based on explanations found in the sacred Egyptian text *The Book of Dreams.*

Score 2 points for all answer b's. Score 1 point for all answer a's, and 0 points for all answer c's.

If you score between 9 and 12 – give yourself a big cheer and a pat on the back!

If you score between 6 and 8 – give yourself an indifferent shrug and say, "Phhh!"

If you score less than 6 – Give yourself a kick, and hiss like a snake!

What your answers say about you

Mostly a's. You are a highly practical person with little time for the spiritual world. Perhaps you should spend more time contemplating the afterlife.

Mostly b's. You are a very religious person in touch with the gods, and at one with the spiritual nature of the world.

Mostly c's. You are a hardened old cynic. Mend your ways or you'll be fed to a monster in the afterlife.

Ask Dr. Ahhk!

HE'S THE ECHO'S DOC ON THE SPOT

We all know a trip to the doctor's can be ruinously expensive. An ugly wound may be about to turn green, but if you haven't got those copper ingots, jars of figs, and three spare slaves to pay the doctor, then you'll just have to grin and bear it.

Until now. In another exclusive Echo readers' service, esteemed graduate of the famous medical academy of Per Bastet, Dr. Ahhkerkau (doctor of the Queen's toes and shepherd of the King's bottom) is AT YOUR SERVICE.

SMITTEN

Dear Dr. Ahhk,

Yesterday I was out smiting some Hittites. Some so-and-so slashed me with his sword and now I've got a nasty wound all down my arm. My dad splashed water over it, but it's still turned a lurid green. I can't afford some copper ingots, jars of figs and three spare slaves to pay my local doctor, and I'm afraid it might drop off, or worse. What can I do?

P. Tjebu, Tarkhan

Well P., that does sound nasty. Here is what you need to do. First of all cover the wound with a piece of fresh meat (stewing steak will do, you don't need to use best rump) and leave it there for one day. Then for the next few days you'll need to apply a daily fresh dressing of linen soaked in honey (and make sure it *is* changed every day). You may also like to pray fervently to the god Isis for a speedy recovery. Give it a week or so, get plenty of rest, and soon you will be as right as rain.

FOOLISH YOUTH

Dear Dr. Ahhk,

When I was a foolish youth and mixed with bad company, I shaved my head and had the words *KARNAK KOSH BOYS KICK TO KILL* tattooed across the top of my skull.

I am now 35 and have a prestigious job as a government tax inspector. Alas, I am also going bald. Every morning brings fresh horror. Please help, I am desperate.

J. Hatibi, Karnak.

Many patients come to me with worries about baldness, and I am pleased to tell you there is a quick and easy solution. Take one freshly dead crow (a chariot kill would do), remove one of its vertebra and crush to a fine powder. Sprinkle a smidgen of burned asses hoof over it, mix together with a dollop of black snake lard, and bake at 200°C (420°F) for twenty minutes. Rub gently into the affected area while the potion is still warm, but for Amun's sake DON'T EAT IT. Alternatively, you may wish to purchase a wig.

CROCODILE TEARS

Dear Dr. Ahhk,

Me and my friends want to take a river trip from el-Amarna to Aswan. I'd love to go but I'm petrified of being eaten by a crocodile, not to mention being stung by a scorpion, or bitten by a snake. My friends say an accident like this is highly unlikely, but I'm not so sure, and keep dreaming about huge gaping jaws and grinding teeth. What can I do?

W. Qedes, el-Amarna

Well W., you are a sissy. I have known lots of people who have been eaten by crocodiles, and it doesn't hurt that much. However, there is a sure-fire cure to your problems. You need to buy a stone amulet with the image of Horus the god wrestling with a crocodile, snake or scorpion engraved upon it. (These are available from *Godz 4 Uz*, *Nofret's Niknaks*, and all good amulet stores. Ask for the *Horus bite-guard©®* brands.) Pour water over the amulet, drink the drops that flow from it, and voilà – your safety is guaranteed.

Be sure to obtain a separate amulet depicting Horus wrestling with each of the animals you wish to gain protection from. Have a nice trip!

WHAT'S BEEN GOING ON HERE?

Dear Dr. Ahhk,

I woke up recently with severe back pains, and I've been having recurring headaches that last for days. My tongue has taken on an unpleasant yellowy coating and I also have several other symptoms unsuitable for a family newspaper such as this. What do you reckon?

R. Paheri, Panopolis.

Bad luck Mrs. P., you have what we doctors call a *fenet worm* gnawing away at your tooth. You probably contracted the worm by eating some bad food.

I shall tell you what I reckon, Mr. R. Peheri of 23 Naga el-Deir Road, Panopolis, I reckon you have been up to NO GOOD, and the god Osiris has sent a demon to torment you. Perhaps you have been "seeing" your friend's wife, or pilfering grain from the village stores? Whatever it is, I would suggest you STOP DOING IT IMMEDIATELY.

THIS WEEK'S STAR LETTER

WORM TROUBLE

Dear Dr. Ahhk,

I have a terrible toothache that's been keeping me awake all night. I've tried to treat it with cloves and olive oil, a hot poultice, and prayers and offerings to the great god Ma'at. Alas, nothing seems to work. What do you suggest?

P. Pepyankh (Mrs.), Naqada.

Bad luck Mrs. P., you have what we doctors call a *fenet worm* gnawing away at your tooth. You probably contracted the worm by eating some bad food.

These worms are the cause of many common ailments. They need to be driven out of the body as quickly as possible by the ingestion of foul potions. What you need to do is mix up an utterly repellent mixture of rotten vegetables, horse manure, jackal blood and mud from the banks of the Nile and then eat it three times a day. Wash it down with a glass of water, and avoid alcohol for the duration of the treatment. It's not a very nice remedy, but believe me, "Doctor knows best!" Keep at it for a week and it should do the trick!

You can write to Dr. Ahhkerkau at
The EGYPTIAN ECHO, Pyramid Row, Memphis

YOUR **ECHO** GUARANTEE OF GOOD HEALTH

Would YOU like to

- **portray the power of a proud and noble ruler?**
- **depict the poise of a gracious lady?**
- **evoke the startled stare of a man roused from sleep?**

Let ME show YOU how!

Khun Anup, painter at the palace library of sacred books, offers you the chance to join his famous painting and drawing course. This could enable you to get a job in the royal workshop, or as a tomb artist where you can guarantee your patron's immortality by painting an accurate likeness of him on the walls of his tomb.

New Courses available in

Relief carving
Sunken relief (cutting into stone to make a picture)

Raised relief (cutting stone away from around an image)

Some of the skills you'll learn on Khun's course

FORM AND CONVENTION

Who's the most important person in this picture? That's right, it's him in the middle. You can tell, as he's the biggest, followed by his wife, and his children. Servants are shown smallest of all.

Get this wrong, and you're in BIG TROUBLE!

EGYPTIAN PERSPECTIVE

Look at this table...

Wrong

You can't see what's on it from just one angle.

Right

That's better – now everything on the table can be seen.

It's especially important to master this technique for paintings on tomb walls, as the spirit of the deceased will be able to make use of all the items you depict.

THE MEANING OF THE PAINTS AT YOUR DISPOSAL –

White – for luxury and joy
Bright yellow – for gods' bodies
Pale yellow – for women's faces
Brown-red – for men's faces
Red – for evil and violence
Green – for water and youth
Blue – for the hair of gods
Black – for the earth

HOW TO MIX YOUR PAINTS

How to take simple materials such as earth, chalk, charcoal and soot, and mix them with other minerals and water, acacia tree gum and egg white to make almost any shade you like.

THE STRICT RULES YOU MUST ADHERE TO IN FIGURE ILLUSTRATION

Proportion

Figures can be drawn on a grid of 20 or so squares. There are strict rules about what goes where. For example the length of a forearm must **always** be three squares.

Perspective

The idea here is to show as much of the body as possible, without completely distorting the picture. The face is always in profile, but with the eye in full view. The torso is always seen from the front, but the lower body and legs from the side, with both legs showing.

ART FOR ATEN'S SAKE

Art-shock controversy for god-swap Akhe

The world of Egyptian art has been shaken to its very foundations by Pharaoh Akhenaten. Not content with telling everyone they can't worship the traditional deities of Egypt, the god-swap pharaoh has also turned the world of art upside down. **OUT** go stiff and formal portraits of the royal family, and depictions of the pharaoh as strong and handsome. **IN** come cheerful family scenes and warts-and-all depictions of the royal countenance.

Spark

The spark that set the bushfires of artistic controversy blazing is a new portrait of the royal family, unveiled yesterday.

In a raised stone relief the Pharaoh is shown with his wife Nefertiti and three of his young daughters. Baby Ankhesenpaaten **plays** with Queen Nefertiti's crown. Meketaten **perches** on her mother's knee. King Akhenaten **kisses** daughter Meritaten.

Flagrant

This scene of flagrantly carefree family life has sent shockwaves reverberating through the dignified world of Egyptian art, which is quite unused to such outrageous informality. Royal observers are especially startled by the fact that Nefertiti is even **sitting on Akhenaten's throne!**

The portrait that shocked a nation. Many feel kissing babies is rather undignified.

FAYOUM FEVER HITS ASWAN

Egypt's top music sensation, the Fayoum Four (featuring Fazzy Flute), are wowing the nation with their latest creation *Spend the day merrily (put ointment and fine oil to your nostrils)*. Guests who flocked to see them at a wedding in Aswan were treated to a two hour show by the near-naked quartet.

Currently on a tour of public festivals, parties and funeral ceremonies, the four are stunning audiences with their daring mixture of traditional Egyptian pipes and harps, and the latest flutes, lyres and lutes from Asia.

Smirk

Fazzy, 23, (real name Tefnakhte Mengebet) whose first public performance was playing to sweaty Nile Delta farm hands, has been romantically linked with Egypt's top juggler, Koptos. "We're just good friends," she smirked when questioned by reporters gathered at the show.

Noise

But village elders were unimpressed with the quartet. "You can't hear the words," said one. "And the music – it's just a noise."

A young fan (middle) rushes the stage as the flute, lute, harp and lyre quartet wow Aswan revellers.

DO THE HIPPO HIPPO SHAKE

A new dance is sweeping the country. Named after Egypt's sacred and much loved hippopotamus, the "hippo hippo shake" is a hip grinding, leg swirling, arm whirling sensation!

Cut it out

Just follow our cut-out-and-keep guide and you can't go wrong!

For you older "hippos" this dance can be a superb exercise routine to tone up those flabby muscles and burn off those extra calories. (Be sure to consult your doctor before embarking on any strenuous exercise, says the Echo's legal consultant!)

DO THE HIPPO HIPPO SHAKE

DANCE GUIDE

1. You shake your hips to the left...

2. ...put your leg up in the air.

3. You shake your hips to the right...

4. ...wave your arms like you don't care.

(Lyric reproduced by kind permission of Tefnakhte Mengebet/Memphis Music)

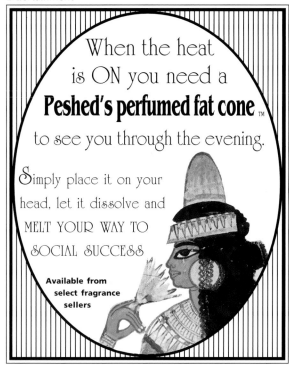
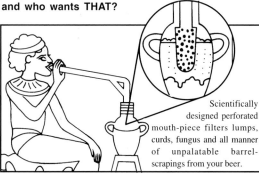
HEY, LET'S

Throw the party of your life with the Echo's B to Z guide to faultless entertaining

The long, light evenings are upon us and 'tis the season to be MERRY. Parties can be great fun, but they're also a handy way of impressing your boss, making your rivals look like cheapskates, and letting your relatives and friends know you're a successful, pretty powerful kind of guy.

Here's the Echo's **B** to **Z** guide to how to have the most FANTASTIC PARTY OF YOUR LIFE.

is for **B**EER. You'll need plenty of this, and wine, to make your party go with a swing. But remember "wine and beer make you feel queer" – so don't mix the two!

It also stands for **B**OREDOM. Be on the lookout for drooping eyes, and for that deadly moment when stifled yawns replace lively conversation. You'll need to act fast to pep things up, and bring on the musicians or the acrobats immediately.

 is for **D**ANCING. Not for your guests of course – no one would expect guests to dance at a party, but you'll need to hire some dancers to entertain your guests with a few pirouettes, when they've had enough food and gossip.

is for **F**LATTERY. Be sure to have a good range of outrageous compliments at the ready, so guests can admire your eloquence. <u>Do say</u> things like "Thou art secure and thine enemies are brought low!", and "Thou enterest into the presence of the Divine Judges, and thou cometh forth in triumph!" <u>Don't say</u> things like "Thou art not nearly as bad as people say thou art!" or "For a man of fifty, thou could be a lot fatter than thou art!"

It also stands for **F**LOWERS. Make sure every guest has a lotus flower to admire or sniff discreetly if the occasion demands it (see **I**.)

 is for **G**OLD and silver cups and plates. There's no point trying to impress your guests with wonderful food and drink if you're going to serve it on palm leaves and clay cups. Remember IF YOU'VE GOT IT, FLAUNT IT.

is for **H**ARPS. We all like music, and what better accompaniment to the merry tinkle of conversation than the merry tinkle of a tasteful harp.

is for **I**NCAPACITATED. Don't worry about your guests being sick – it just means they're HAVING A GOOD TIME. Be sure your servants have plenty of fresh water and towels to cope with those "little accidents".

is for "**J**UST ENOUGH IS NEVER ENOUGH". The whole point of a party is to get so thoroughly stuffed you put on three chins, and don't want to eat again for a MONTH! The more roast ox, goose, catfish and mullet you provide the better, along with enough drinks to drown a boatload of baboons.

PAAAARTY!!

Can you spot which of these lovely ladies is about to see her dinner again? Bring water immediately!!

is for **K**ARNAK, **K**HNEMHOTEP II, **K**IDNEY BEANS, **K**ALEIDOSCOPE, **K**ARAOKE, **K**ILLER BEES, and absolutely <u>NO WORDS AT ALL</u> to do with parties and entertaining in Ancient Egypt!

is for **M**USICIANS. As well as playing discreetly in the background, you'll also need music to accompany your dancers. The more musicians the merrier – a quartet at least.

It's become fashionable for musicians to sing about what a great time everybody is having, or to point out that their glasses are empty and they ought to drink more wine.

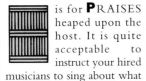 is for **N**IBBLES. Quaint little delicacies are just what you need when you've stuffed your face with ox and duck. Be sure to have a good supply of figs, dates and tasty little honeyed pastries.

is for **P**RAISES heaped upon the host. It is quite acceptable to instruct your hired musicians to sing about what a splendid fellow you are.

Who knows? Maybe the message will seep in!

is for **Q**UEEN OF PUDDINGS – a wonderful mixture of bread, custard, jam and meringue, unfortunately unknown to us Ancient Egyptians.

is for **R**ECEIVING GUESTS. If someone really important is coming, you must make a great show of being at the door to greet them as they arrive. Not only is this good manners, but it also allows the slobs next door, and your surly employees or farmhands to see you hobnobbing with royalty or similar posh people. You can greet lesser mortals in your reception room. Be sure to look down your nose at them, but don't snigger or sneer unless you really can't help it.

is for **S**EATING. Make sure you have the most important seat in the dining room – it's your party after all. If you have someone TITANICALLY important as a guest it's best to offer them a seat of similar elaborateness (people have been ruined for less). Guests of similar status should be seated around you.

If your party is very formal then men and women should sit separately. If it is informal, then husbands and wives may sit together if they so wish.

is for **S**HAMBLES – which is what your house will look like after the party.

is for **T**RANSPARENT CLOTHING. Your servants, dancers and musicians should all wear revealing clothing, or even better, NOTHING AT ALL. In the future people will get really indignant about this sort of thing, so MAKE THE MOST OF IT NOW!

is for "**TSH**!! Just look at old Harkhuf over there, eyeing up Miss Nebankh. Chubby middle-aged men aren't really her type."

is for **W**ATER. Almost the most essential ingredient of the evening. Cool vast amounts in great jars in your cellar, and make sure the servants have a plentiful supply.

is for **Z**ITHER. (SEE **H**). Quite the latest sensation from Asia.

Uncle Amen pouring oil on troubled waters.

Upset? A problem aired is a problem shared. The Echo's agony columnist "Uncle" Amenemope is at your service, with kind words and comforting advice to help restore your inner harmony. Just write away to

Dear Uncle Amen

Drunken baboon

Dear Uncle Amen,

I am so completely in love with this girl in our street that it's making me dizzier than a drunken baboon. Her hair is blacker than the night, her lips are redder than ripe dates, her voice is softer than a tinkling harp (*Yes, yes, get on with it – Uncle Amen*). Unfortunately, her family is much richer than mine and she won't even LOOK at me, never mind let me marry her.

Every night I lie awake dreaming of the day we can meet and rub noses, and I can tell the whole world she's mine forever. What can I do?

K.A., Memphis

Pull yourself together K. – everyone in Egypt has black hair, and most people have red lips, unless they're suffering from a particularly unpleasant ailment. Granted, not every girl has a voice like a tinkling harp, but <u>really</u>, she doesn't sound THAT special. Anyway, here is my advice;

Do not make a ferry on the river, and then strain to seek its fare.
Take the fare from him who is wealthy, and let pass him who is poor.
The gods prefer him who reveres the poor to him who worships the wealthy.

Now, isn't that a comfort?

Son is a scamp

Dear Uncle Amen,

We were so proud when our son went off to medical school at Per Bastet, but now his tutors write to us with terrible news. They say he neglects his pen and papyrus to abandon himself to dancing, drinking and consorting with all sorts of scamps and scallywags. Instead of studying the workings of the human heart and its attendant valves and channels, he frightens people in the street, lurching from one beer hall to another.

What can we do?

K.P., Luxor

Your son has strayed further into the abyss than a cat into a herd of basking crocodiles. His heart must be denser than a great obelisk. Try not to fret, and in the meantime you may like to reflect on this advice:

Do not say 'Today is like tomorrow' How will this end? Comes tomorrow, today has vanished. The deep has become the water's edge.

There, isn't that better?

Inde-*scribe*-able

Dear Uncle Amen,

My younger brother is training to be a scribe, and he's turned into the snootiest, cockiest little twerp this side of the fertile crescent. He keeps turning his nose up at me and says "I'm going to have the best job in the world, unlike you, a mere sailor, who might go to sea and be devoured by a storm, and unlike brother Rensi, who spends his days bending over in the boiling sun, toiling in the fields, and comes home stinking and exhausted."

What can I do to bring him down to earth?

B.N., Thebes

Grill or bake?

Dear Uncle Amen,

Please can you settle an argument that is bringing much discord to our household. I insist that the best way to cook mullet is to grill it with a knob of butter. My mother-in-law however, insists that baking it wrapped in palm leaves with garlic and onions, is by far the best way. The old bat beats me with a stick when I do it my way, and my husband just looks the other way and pretends nothing is happening.

What do you think?

P.K., Abydos

Between you and me I always say why go to the bother of stoking up an oven when you can grill over an open fire. Most fish taste the same whatever you do with them, so I'm with you on the fish question. However, reading between the lines, I detect a far more serious issue here than how to cook fish. Respect for elders is one of the fundamental cornerstones of our society, and you do seem to be rather lacking in it. Perhaps you would like to think about this:

Do not revile one older than you for she shall see the gods before you.
Let her not report you to them saying "My daughter -in-law hath reviled me"
Remember – A dog's food is from its master, it barks to him who gives it.

Do I detect a hint of jealousy here B.? Alas, your pestilent brother is right, and your sourness will make you disagreeable in the eyes of your family. I say to you:

Guard your tongue from harmful speech, then you will be loved by others.

You could console yourself by thinking he may end up spending his days counting jars of grain in a warehouse, while you yourself are enjoying the blessings of bracing breezes and plenty of sunshine. In the meantime, try and be nice to him – as a scribe he'll almost certainly end up as an influential, wealthy individual.

Goose in a whirlpool

Dear Uncle Amen,

I am so completely in love with this boy in our street that it's making me dizzier than a goose in a whirlpool. His hair is blacker than sloes. His lips are redder than beads of red jasper, and his voice is stronger than the roar of a ferocious crocodile.

Unfortunately he is already married, and he won't even LOOK at me, never mind anything else. Every night I wander in the garden, whispering my love to the flowers and the birds, and I dream of a day when we can walk together along the banks of the Nile, arm in arm.

A.R., Thebes

Well A, you are tottering on the brink of a deep ravine. If this fellow begins to think your hair is blacker than a very black blackcurrant, and your lips are redder than a very red redcurrant (let's assume he's not much of a poet) and wants to start seeing you too, then you'll be in bigger trouble than a camel in a snow storm. In fact, being a camel in a snow storm would be considerably better than being stoned to death, and then having your remains fed to wild dogs, which is what would happen if people found out about the two of you.

I offer you these words of advice…

Man is clay and straw, the god is his builder.
He tears down, he builds up daily.
Look at the bowl that is before you and let it serve your needs.

*What you really need is a distraction. I'm sending you the address of K.A. in Memphis (see **Drunken Baboon**, above) He sounds like a nice boy, and he also seems to be at a loose end. Perhaps you could get in touch?*

 * Note to scholars. These translations of *Amenemope's Instructions* are taken from Miriam Lichtheim's *Ancient Egyptian Literature* Three volumes ©1973-1980 Regents of the University of California.

Pet Geese?
YOU MUST BE HONKERS!

If Old Macdonald lived in Egypt, he would have kept geese in the house as well as on that farm.

Geese. We all like to eat them, but would YOU keep one as a PET? This idea isn't as fowl as it seems. Its plucky character and funny little ways have enabled the Nile goose to waddle into the hearts of householders throughout Egypt. It is allowed to paddle around the garden and even roam around inside the house.

Dog doesn't mind

Does the family dog seem to mind? Not a bit of it, and although geese don't get along so well with other popular household pets such as cats and monkeys, this mutual antagonism rarely stretches to more than the odd nip or squawk.

But best of all, say owners, a goose will keep burglars out of your house just as well as any guard dog, and it's far less fussy about its food.

Nine things you probably never knew about geese

❶ Rather disappointingly, a goose does not lay its eggs under a gooseberry bush.

❷ Despite its name the goose cannot do the goose step.

❸ In a fight between a cat and a goose, the cat will usually come off worse, unless it is especially fat and vicious.

❹ Geese cannot be trained to hunt crocodiles.

❺ A "dressed goose" is not one all done up for a night on the town – it's more likely to be one all done up for a few hours in the oven.

❻ Like us, geese have their own language. Because it has only two words – *honk* and *hssss* – it is especially easy to learn.

❼ Scholars think honk means "Hey, you there!!"

❽ They are less sure about hssss, but think it probably means "Get out of my way".

❾ Perhaps because of their limited vocabulary, there have been no great geese poets.

Animal laughs

Embalmer: "Would you like your cats turned into mummies, Madame?"
Lady:"On no, Mister. They're both Toms – I'll just have them stuffed."

Hyena: "OK, act friendly, and let him stroke you. Then wait 'til his back's turned, and we'll steal the chickens!!"

CATS – JUST HOW SACRED ARE THEY?

We may have tried and failed to make a pet out of the hyena, but we certainly succeeded with the cat. In fact, historians tell us that Egypt was the first place on Earth where cats became household pets.

When the humble African wild cat moved out of the marshes and into our houses, it quickly became Egypt's most adored animal.

Owns the place

It may act like it owns the place, and walks off in a haughty sulk when you boot it out of your chair, but many people believe that cats (or *miu* as they're known in Egypt) are actually sacred! Here's why ...

★ Bastet, the goddess of happiness, likes cats so much she even looks like a cat.

★ If you make certain prayers and spells over a cat, the spirit of Bastet will enter it. Bastet can indicate her feelings toward you through the cat's actions. For example if it licks your hand then Bastet is pleased with you. If it takes a lump out of your arm with its claws then you're in serious trouble.

★ When a cat dies the household where it lives goes into mourning, and everyone shaves their eyebrows. You wouldn't do that for any old animal would you?

Miu loves yah? We do!

61

WIN THIS BOAT!

A chariot may be quite Hyksosian, a horse on its own will save your feet, but everyone agrees (from godly kings to buzzing bees), that a boat upon the Nile is quite a treat!

So wrote Egypt's top songwriter Fazzy Flute in her hymn of praise to our greatest asset – the wonderful Nile river. To celebrate the beginning of the season of Akhet, when the Nile floods its banks and irrigates our fields, we're GIVING AWAY this magnificent deluxe sailing vessel.

All you have to do is answer the following 20 questions, and send them to us by the first day of the third week of the first month of Akhet, 1334BC. The first correct entry to be pulled from our bag will WIN THIS BOAT.

No cheating now!

The ECHO's fabulous Akhet season contest offers you the chance to GO BOATING IN STYLE!!

Just look at these features:

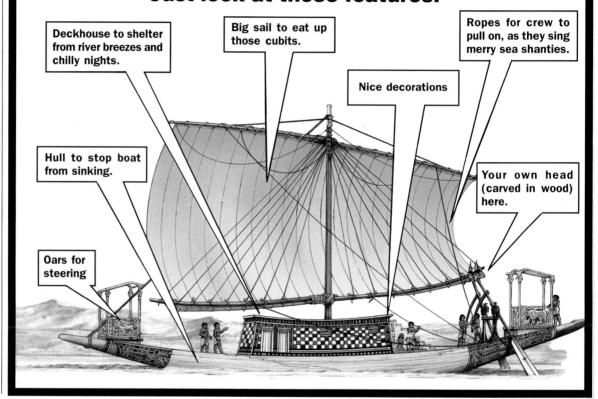

Deckhouse to shelter from river breezes and chilly nights.

Big sail to eat up those cubits.

Ropes for crew to pull on, as they sing merry sea shanties.

Nice decorations

Hull to stop boat from sinking.

Your own head (carved in wood) here.

Oars for steering

TWENTY QUIZZICAL QUESTIONS

1) What did Ramesses III do to the Sea People?
a) bought them all ice cream; b) smote them good and proper; c) sold them chariot insurance.

2) Which sacred pet likes to have mice for lunch?

3) Thilly thothage or divine intellectual thenthation?

4) What do you see in your dreams?
a) the future; b) the past; c) the present.

5) Hrglyphcs dnt hv ths...

6) Egyptian civilization (not to mention our floods, boats and crocodiles) would never have happened without which river?

7) Ancient Egyptians add up to 10,000 with one of these:
a) severed finger;
b) flowery squiggle;
c) sun-powered pocket calculator.

8) This royal he was really a she!

9) Big pointy-topped things where pharaohs were buried, which were made with millions of limestone blocks, and built by 100,000 workers.

10) Fashionable headwear for sweet-smelling parties:
a) hollowed-out crocodile head; b) perfumed fat cone; c) miner's hat with built-in torch.

11) Sun god who was eclipsed during the reign of King Tut.

12) This Egyptian capital was named after a city in Tennessee, USA – or was it the other way around?

13) Which flying ingredient is part of a cure for baldness? Is it:
a) the pilot's seat from a Boeing 747 (boiled and diced); b) the vertebra of a crow (crushed); c) the iron head on the tip of an arrow (melted).

14) Urns for your organs.

15) They kept the Hyksos awake with their bellowing.

16) You might have this cut off for stealing a shepherd.

17) It waddles, lays eggs, says honk and hiss, and you can eat it.

18) A marsh reed which is essential for writing.

19) They were Egypt's first invaders.

20) Workers on Ramesses III's tomb went on strike because:
a) they wanted to watch a football match; b) they wanted to bring down the government; c) they hadn't been paid their wages.

SPOT THE DIFFERENCE

Our artist has drawn two **almost identical** pictures of King Tut. One was drawn before noon, the other after a large lunch consisting of three jars of wine, two pitchers of barley beer, three olives and a couple of peanuts. There are nine crucial differences. Can you see what they are?

Spot the difference

Vulture and snake on hat replaced by dog (1) and cat (2). Nose ring (4). Right eyebrow missing (3). Flower earrings (5). Staff and crib replaced by flyswatter (6) and axe (7). "I love pyramids" badge on chest (8). Watch on left wrist (9).

KING TUT 1

KING TUT 2

THE ECHO'S WORLD OF WORK

Please reply to the appropriate Echo box number.

FULL TIME GENERAL

POTTER

Must have own potter's wheel, and not mind getting hands dirty. **BOX 24**

OVERSEER

Overseer required for craft workshop, to supervise stone carvers, vase throwers, joiners and jewel makers. Must have sharp eye for all known dodges, vivid vocabulary and big stick. Would suit former policeman. **BOX 33**

WOODWORK

Local armament manufacturer has several vacancies for:

Bow benders
Arrow testers (ability to perceive straight line essential)
Javelin sharpeners
No Hittites.
BOX 75

MINERS

Honest, hardworking men required for gold mine in Nubia. Must be strong, have constitution of ox, and not mind being attacked by roving desert tribesmen. **BOX 89**

CHARIOT MAKER

Usual skills. Ability to make round wheel essential. **BOX 43**

SILVERSMITH

Required for general jewel making, vase inlays, dishes, idols, cloud linings. Must be honest, get along with overseers, and not mind extremely close supervision. **BOX 123**

STATUE MAKER

Statue maker requires the following: Sculptors (own mallet and chisel an advantage), engravers (knowledge of hieroglyphs essential – badd spelers sevearly punnished), painters (blue and green only). **BOX 138**

MENIAL

BARBER

Good conversationalist wanted. Flexible hours. **BOX 147**

BRICKMAKER

Must be skilled in mixing mud, straw, water and sand. Also need water carrier. Training provided. Must get along with brickmakers. **BOX 152**

TEMPORARY GENERAL

QUARRYMEN

Quarrymen skilled in extraction of limestone, sandstone, alabaster etc. needed for expedition to eastern desert to locate and return suitable material for monument for Ramesses IV. Must be good at digging and hewing. Top rates (beer, bread _and_ water).
Also have vacancies for soldiers, waterbearers, horsemen and foremen. **BOX 184**

OBELISK ERECTORS

Must be good at pulling heavy loads and know a little about ropes and ramps. **BOX 196**

WOMEN'S WORK

TUTOR

It's a Lark singing school seeks tutor for classes. **BOX 199**

SHOP ASSISTANT

Hair Today wigmakers seek shop assistant for their retail outlet in Memphis. Knowledge of lice would be useful. **BOX 203**

CHATTY LADIES

Spinning workshop has three vacancies for cheerful, chatty ladies. **BOX 275**

ANSWERS TO "WIN A BOAT" QUIZ

For readers who missed the final date of our quiz contest we have kindly decided to provide the answers to the questions.

1) b – smote them good and proper (page 46)
2) cat (page 61)
3) b – the vertebra of a crow (page 55)
4) a – the future (page 54)
5) vowels (page 36)
6) the Nile (page 49)
7) a – severed finger (page 37)
8) Hatshepsut (page 40)
9) pyramids (page 35)
10) b –perfumed fat cone (page 58)
11) The Aten (page 43)
12) The other way around
13) b – the vertebra of a crow (page 55)
14) canopic jars (page 46)
15) hippopotami (page 40)
16) your nose (page 48)
17) a goose (page 61)
18) papyrus (page 37)
19) the Hyksos (page 39 and 40)
20) c – they hadn't been paid (page 47)

Bad luck if you got them wrong. Better luck next time!

EGYPTIAN ECHO Sport

HUNTING SPECIAL

QUACKING CAT-ASTROPHY
as Brhrwp goes ballistic

Nebamun 10 Crocodiles 1

Top Theban physician Nebamun and a hand-picked hunting expedition pitted their wits against a strong crocodile side in a nail-biting match on the Nile Delta marshes this Sunday. But following an outstanding performance by Brhrwp the family cat, they came away with an easy victory.

Despite blustery north winds and the ever present threat of a sandstorm, the patrician physician's expedition made a strong showing, catching four geese, a crane, two ducks and four pigeons.

Boggy

Nebamun's team, consisting of his wife, daughter, four servants, three decoy herons and the aforementioned family cat, quickly established their mastery of the marshes.

Gliding silently through the boggy Nile banks in a small wooden boat, Nebamun scored an easy early success when he pounced on a flock of geese

out having a quiet Sunday morning paddle.

The carnage continued. In what was to be the most outstanding event of the day, Brhrwp performed a magnificent four claw and jaw pounce on two pigeons and a goose.

After a break for lunch Nabamun's throwing stick accounted for a crane and two ducks, and there followed a quiet period of a couple of hours when everything saw them coming and flew away.

Splash

The one setback of the afternoon occurred when a papyrus boat containing three of Nabamun's servants capsized while stalking a small shoal of catfish. Unfortunately their splashes and shouts came to the attention of a horde of basking crocodiles, busy dozing by the river bank digesting a small deer they had devoured for dinner. Clearly it was time for desert, and as the three men swam rapidly for the safety of the river bank, two crocodiles wriggled into the river after them.

Two pigeons and a goose bite the dust as Brhrwp swoops to conquer.

The chase was short but not sweet. The two strongest swimming servants reached the bank just in time to see the third vanish in a blur of green skin and flashing white teeth.

But Nabamun was not discouraged. " Pah," he said sadly, grieving over the loss of a loyal and devoted servant, " there's plenty more where he came from!"

ECHO SPORTS COMMENT

TUT IN OSTRICH OUTRAGE

Ostrich lovers have accused King Tut of bad sportsmanship. Armed with a bow and arrow, four dogs and a two-horse chariot, the boy king recently killed 24 in a single morning.

As Tut is a god on Earth they have little chance of having their pleas heard. The Echo says **You might as well bury your heads in the sand!**

GREEK GAZETTE
ON OTHER PAGES

NEWS PAGES

Bronze Age 2900-1100 BC	66-7
"Cock and bull" says Cretan king	66
Dark Ages 1100-800 BC	68
Oh no, the Dorians are here...	68
Archaic Period 800-500 BC	68-71
Sparta talks tough	71
The Classical Age 500-323 BC	72-79
Marathon man in drop-dead dash	72
Why we don't like the Persians	74
King Phil's Macedonian mash-up	77
Gordians in knot fiasco	78
The Hellenistic Period 323-30 BC	80-81
Quadruple royal murder sensation	80
Corinth crushed in Roman rampage	81

FEATURES

The oracle speaks	83
Hot news, live from Delphi	
Thinking	84-85
Philosophy watch	
Arts	86-87
What's new in pots and buildings	
Entertainment	88-89
Top tips for holiday reading	
Health	90
Meet Hippocrates, the Doc from Kos	
Style	91
Chins, tunics, cloaks and girdles	
Democracy	92-93
What your vote means in today's Ancient Greece	
Small ads	94
Sport	95-96
Greece in games dispute	

GREEK GAZETTE

Dear Reader,

We're <u>bright</u>, we're <u>sharp</u>, and we're <u>stylish</u>! Over the next 32 pages you'll find out what we've achieved in only 1,500 years. We've • survived a monster volcano blast • gone in one side of the Dark Ages and come out the other side • beaten the Persians • built a stunning civilization • beaten the Persians again • conquered half the known world

Look! We've invented democracy. It'll be AGES before anyone improves on our system of government,
AND we've invented the idea of thinking,
AND we've invented the world's most beautiful architecture,
AND we've invented drama.

Regular readers will already know how world-beating we are. But if you're new to the classical age we hope this bumper special issue will blow your sandals off.

Happy reading folks!

Paidagogos

Paidagogos
Proprietor
The Greek Gazette

THE GREEK GAZETTE

was written by
FERGUS FLEMING

and designed by
KAREN TOMLINS

Edited by
PAUL DOWSWELL

Historical consultant
CHARLES FREEMAN

Illustrated by Guy Smith and Ian Jackson

Additional illustrations by Luis Rey, Richard Draper, Robert Walster, Gerald Wood, Peter Dennis, Nigel Wright and Gillian Hurry.

"COCK AND BULL!"
SAYS CRETAN KING

1600 BC

Crete King in Knossos Kontroversy

Theseus, the King of Athens, has fallen out with the King of Knossos following a dramatic visit to Crete – the island headquarters of Minoan civilization.

"I'd heard they were sacrificing Greek boys and girls to a monster, so I went there to kill it," said the hunky hero. "When I reached the capital, Knossos, I realized they needed some radical pest control. There was this big maze called a Labyrinth which contained a dreadful monster called a Minotaur. It was like a man but with a bull's head. And to keep it happy the Minoans fed it little Greek children.

"'Well,' I thought. 'This won't do.' So I went in and killed it and brought out its head as proof."

Thongs off to Theseus!

OUTRAGE

But the King of Knossos tells a different story.

"It's all a legend!" cried the outraged monarch. "This Greek peasant came in smelling of goats and got completely lost in our palace with all its rooms and corridors. He only thinks it's a labyrinth because he hasn't seen anything larger than an outdoor toilet. And as for the so-called Minotaur. Well! Everybody knows that's nonsense. What happens is that I wear a bull's mask during certain rituals because the bull is our national symbol.

"The fact of the matter is that the Greeks are jealous of what we've achieved here on Crete." The King is right. The Minoans have:

- *big palaces*
- *excellent water supply and drainage systems*
- *whole storerooms of large earthenware jars crammed with food, oil and wine*
- *an indecipherable form of writing called Linear A*
- *and a frightening national sport called bull-leaping in which you grab a charging bull by the horns and flip yourself over its back.*

"The Greeks don't have anything like this," said the King. "Pah! They'll never be a classical civilization."

A *Gazette* artist recreates Theseus's account of his showdown with the Minotaur. Guess who won!

THERA IT WAS – GONE!

1600 BC

The little island of Thera gave the Minoans a nasty shock yesterday. It blew up – and completely destroyed their civilization!

In an astonishing display of vitality, Thera transformed itself from a nice round island with a mountain in the middle into a large bay surrounded by a crescent-shaped piece of land and the odd rock sticking out above water.

"At first we thought it was a domestic accident," said one member of the emergency services. "But it proved to be the biggest volcanic eruption this millenium. Apparently the island was a dormant volcano. We don't know what set it off.

"However, preliminary investigations have ruled out arson."

HAVOC

The explosion caused havoc on Crete, which is only 110km (70 miles) away from Thera. Wearing only his night-shirt the King of Knossos gave his version of events.

"Last night the royal slumber was disturbed by the noise of earth tremors, massive tidal waves and widespread flooding. When I opened the window to complain I saw that the crops had been destroyed, the city had fallen down and our entire civilization had been wiped out."

His Majesty admits that Crete is no longer a major player in the Mediterranean.

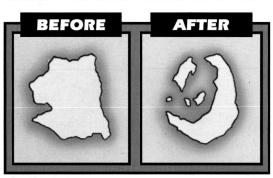

BEFORE   **AFTER**

Experts think a faulty gas oven is probably not to blame.

MYCE-'N-EASY DOES IT!

GREEKS COME ACROP-OLIS!!

 **1450 BC**

Who's who in Greece? The Mycenaeans, that's who. Nobody's quite sure where they came from, but they're the top dogs now. From their headquarters at Mycenae, they've set up settlements all over the country and have even conquered the Minoans.

"We may be just a ragtaggle of tribes," said a Mycenaean spokesman, "but we're skilled marauders and our culture has spread throughout Greece and beyond. We've founded strongholds like Athens and Thebes, and introduced our language and gods to the locals. We've even captured Knossos."

"The greatest thing we've done, though, is to introduce a new form of writing. On Crete they used Linear A which no one could understand apart from them. We've gone one better. We're calling ours Linear B. In the future people will look at Linear A and say, 'What a lot of meaningless squiggles!' Then they'll come to Linear B and say, 'Thank goodness! At last some writing that makes sense.'

"What's more, we've invented a whole new way of fortifying our towns. What we do is find a piece of high ground, surround it with a massive wall, and call it an acropolis. When people try to invade, we just hit them with swords and tell them to go away. And they do. Amazing!"

The *Gazette* says, "This is where Greek civilization really gets into its swing."

Now that we're more civilized we've got time to engage in idle pursuits, such as painting an octopus on the side of a pot.

TROJANS SLIP IN HORSE BUSINESS

1250 BC

Greeks make hay as Trojans whine

When Paris, Prince of Troy, ran off with beautiful Princess Helen of Greece he couldn't have made a worse mistake. King "Angry" Agamemnon sent his entire fleet to get her back.

"We besieged Troy for ten years and lost a lot of good men," said Angry at a press conference yesterday. "We were at our wits' end. But then we came up with a winning tactic. We pretended to run away and leave them a large wooden horse by way of saying sorry."

"Just what we always wanted!" thought the Trojans. They saw the Greeks had gone, and dragged the horse into town. But what they didn't realize was that the Greeks had only run away behind the nearest hill and that the horse was hollow and filled with elite troops.

When night fell the soldiers crept out of the horse, seized the town and opened the gates to let the Greek army in. They massacred half the population and turned the rest into slaves. No-one got away apart from a warrior named Aeneas, who escaped after having had most of his consonants removed.

Horse sense. The Trojans obviously didn't have any.

TOP POETS IN FACT FLAP

In a shock announcement, the Troy and Associated Ports Press Council (TRAPPCO) has slammed the accuracy of Greek reporting.

"Yes, the Trojan War did take place. No, it wasn't anything like Greek papers say it was," claimed a TRAPPCO spokesman. "What happened was that some minor Mycenaean lords destroyed the major trading city of Troy. But they didn't take ten years over it. And there was no Helen, no Paris and most certainly no wooden horse.

"The entire story has been invented by the Greek bards in order to glorify their country's achievements. Like Homer, for instance. In the past this man has published a number of misleading articles. Everyone knows his so-called epic *The Odyssey* – about some fellow who slays a one-eyed monster, oh, and something about a wicked witch who turns people into animals... What a fable that turned out to be!"

The Greek press angrily rejected the slur but TRAPPCO wasn't backing down.

"History will prove us right. You'll see."

HELLO
DARK AGES!

The Dorians Are Here!

"We're washed up!" In an exclusive interview Mycenaean peasant Totali Yatolos tells the *Gazette* how Greek civilization fell.

"Things were bad, I've got to admit. It started off with a string of poor harvests. Then it got to food shortages. And the next thing we knew it was famine.

"Those who could get out did. Apparently they've been roaming the Mediterranean, looting and raiding. As for the rest of us, we stayed put and fought between ourselves. That's when we noticed we'd been taken over by the Dorians."

So exactly who <u>are</u> the Dorians? "Nobody knows where we come from," a prominent Dorian told us helpfully. "In fact some people even think we're Greeks. As far as we're concerned civilization is finished. There's going to be no more Bronze Age, no more cities, no more trade.

OUTRAGE

"From now on it's all hard times and not much to eat. **We're nomads and we think everyone else should be.** We're going to be grazing their fields like there's no tomorrow. Oh yes. And because the art of writing has been lost we can do **what we like when we like** and there will be no records. Brilliant!"

Mr. Yatalos disagrees, but he's in no position to say so.

JUST LOOK WHAT THEY'VE DONE TO OUR POTS!!!

Before the Dorians

Clever, lively figures. Bright, varied glazes.

What we've got now

Muddy, brown stickmen. Call THAT art!?!

AAA! EEE! III! OOO! UUU!

WE'VE REALLY VOWELLED UP

It's official! Greek is the world's first written language to have vowels.

"We've really grabbed the ancient world by its ears," said Professor of Alphabets, Demi Mouros. "Like all great inventions it looks simple. But it's been quite a complicated process."

It all started when Prof. Mouros's team of Athenian experts studied a consonants-only alphabet used by Phoenician traders. They soon realized there was room for improvement.

"We noticed that the Phoenicians left it up to the reader to fill in the vowels. But this obviously wasn't good enough. Looking at some of their bills we noticed it was impossible to tell if they were invoicing for a cargo of sacks or a cargo of socks. Well, that's not quite true because we don't wear socks and we don't use sacks. But you get my drift. So we looked at ways of making things clearer. That's when we hit on the idea of vwls."

In a session of brainstorming the linguists came up with a range of noises to suit any occasion.

"We started off with five vowels –a, e, i, o and u. But then we thought we'd add a few more, in case of emergencies. As a result, Greek now boasts seven vowels which we call alpha, epsilon, eta, iota, omicron, upsilon and omega. That's α, ε, η, ι, o, υ and ω."

"Using them's easy. All you do is insert them between the consonants. For example, take the word crpls. Looks bizarre doesn't

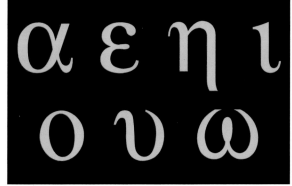

Vowels unveiled yesterday by Professor Mouros. Oracles predict a bright future for a,e,i,o and u, but not ω and η.

it? But just add a few vowels and Bingo! You've got acropolis."

"Of course, there have been one or two teething problems. Troublemakers have started inventing words which are almost all consonants with hardly any vowels at all – apophthegm, for example, which means a general truth." What a mouthful! We're advising anyone who comes across such a word to use a combination of simpler ones which everyone can understand."

Greeks are going crazy over the new alphabet. Many people can read and write it. And they're using it for all kinds of wacky purposes, like scrawling their names on pots. Some people have even started to write poems.

Major rulers, however, are furious. In their trade journal, *Ff Wth Thr Hds*, they have made it clear that they disapprove of the new development.

"It's disgraceful," said the King of Corinth. "**Before long people will be saying exactly what they like. Outrageous**!"

POLIS-ED TO MEET YOU!

"GOATS ARE OFF!" SAY CITIZENS

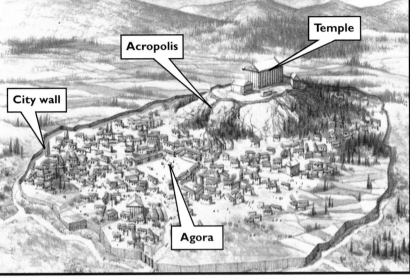

FRIEZE – IT'S THE POLIS! Not a frieze at all in fact, but an illustration by a *Gazette* artist.

700 BC

It's goodbye Dark Ages and hello civilization as Greece goes city-state crazy! Throughout the land people are forming states with their own aristocratic rulers, their own farmland and above all their own cities. They're so pleased with their new way of life they've given it a name – the polis.

"We got the idea from the east – places like Phoenicia and Turkey," said one satisfied aristo. "There they were with big, fortified cities, prosperous agriculture and sophisticated trade networks. And there we

were thinking, 'Ho-hum. Centuries of squalor lie ahead. If only we were like those guys in Asia Minor.' Then we realized: 'Hey! What have they got that we haven't? Nothing!' So we decided to copy them."

OUTRAGE

City-state mania is sweeping Greece. Places like Sparta, Corinth and Thebes are already classed as major-league polises. And hundreds of other newcomers are emerging.

As for the Dorians?

"Now and then you find some raggedy nomad trying to graze a herd of goats on polis land. **We just tell him to get lost.**"

POLIS FILE

Can you tell a polis from a hole in the ground? The *Gazette* gives you ten facts on the most wanted life in Ancient Greece.

• Size – unimportant. It's what you do with it that counts. Can range from Athens's 2,500 square km (1,000

square miles) to the island of Chios which supports four polises on an area one-third of the size.
• City – vital. Every polis must have one.
• Fields – very important. Otherwise everyone would starve.
• Agora – marketplace. Hub of the city.
• Acropolis – fortified citadel. Hide here when someone attacks.
• Temple – dedicated to

patron deity.
• Citizens – a must. Status usually hereditary.
• Slaves – essential. Otherwise citizens would have no free time.
• Metics – foreigners. Bring in valuable trade. Not allowed to be citizens.
• Army – well, farmers with swords actually. Useful for fighting other polises on dull days.

ARISTOS TOLD TO "HOP-LITE" OFF

They were jabbin' and a stabbin' at the Hop (lite).

650 BC

Polis life is being given a shake-up as Greek rulers are told: Toe the line or get out.

"We're sick and tired of them," said an outraged citizen. "They go around with their noses in the air, tax us heavily and take all the food when there's a famine. We haven't been able to do anything about

it in the past because they've got horses and chariots and can just ride us down. **But now we've got a secret weapon they can't beat – the hoplite!**"

Hoplites are the hottest new items in warfare. Heavily-armed infantrymen with shields and long spears, they form themselves into a long formation called a phalanx which the cavalry can't dent.

"It's terrible," complained

one ex-king. "We invented the hoplites to fight wars for us. But now if we don't do what they want they throw us out and put some ghastly man called a tyrant in charge. If you ask me, Greek civilization is going downhill."

Being a tyrant has become the most popular job in Greece. Everyone with any clout wants the position and if they can't find an aristo to depose

they chuck out another tyrant.

"Beats farming, which is what we'd be doing otherwise," said a hoplite. "And it's great fun. When you've got two armies facing up to each other it's **Godzilla-meets-King-Kong stuff**. Some people say they want proper laws and that. **But between you and me, we all need a little mayhem really.**"

ESTATE-FOR-CAKE SWAP SHOCK

Where the colonists are going, and where we hope most of them will stay.

Desperate Dan Delion, a colonist from Corinth, has made the worst deal of the century. He and some pals rowed a boat to Sicily intending to grab some land and parcel it out between them. But on the way his food ran out and he was so hungry that he swapped his share for a honey cake.

"I had no choice," he moaned. "My innards were emptier than a Dorian schoolroom. What else could I do?"

WORMS

Dan's tale has opened a can of colonial worms. Over the past few centuries thousands of Greeks have left the mainland for futures in countries all around the Mediterranean and Black Sea (see map for details).

The official line is that they're cultural ambassadors who are bringing Greek civilization and trade to places as far apart as Marseilles and Sebastopol.

BIG SNAG

But there are two big snags. **Not all the colonists want to go,** and when they get where they're going, **not everybody wants to see them there**.

"It's a real case of Don't Look Now," said an anxious Italian. "One minute you're lord and master of all you behold, the next there's a bunch of Greeks building towns and temples everywhere. We find it very upsetting that a load of total strangers should settle here without so much as a by-your-leave.

"They're mostly in the south, in places like Sicily. But if they could move even farther south we'd be very grateful. Better still, why don't they go home?"

However, the fact is that **many colonists would like to do exactly that.**

TOUGH

"I only left Corinth because there was no food," said Dan Delion. "I'd love to go back. But most of my shipmates can't. They're exiles, criminals and unemployed citizens. And anyway it's so far to row."

Back in Greece, the city-states are taking a tough line. "Come back? What nonsense!" said a Corinth spokesman. "These people are thieves and revolutionaries. All they do is eat our food which is in short enough supply as it is!

"And as for Mr. Delion's poverty. That's rich! We've had reports that in the Italian colony of Sybaris they sleep on rose petals and have banned roosters in case they wake them in the morning. Pah! **How soft can you get?**"

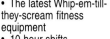
DRACO TAKES IT TO THE LIMIT

CRIMS IN A SPIN AT NEW LAWS

621 BC

There's no messing with tough-man Draco. The hard-hitting lawmaker from Athens has made it clear that he supports the maximum penalty for criminal activities – death.

"It's very worrying," said one Athenian thief. "We voted the man in because we'd had enough of tyrants and thought we needed a few laws. But we didn't count on this. **It's positively draconian.**"

BAG

Under the new regime you can be executed for the smallest transgression. Steal a bag of olives and you're for the high jump. Extreme? Not a bit. When we spoke to Draco himself he explained the situation.

"Crime's a problem in Athens like any other big city," he said. "It may seem unfair that thieves and murderers are treated alike. But a crime's a crime isn't it? Death is the obvious answer. I'm only sorry that we haven't come up with something nastier for the really bad offenders. Still. There's time yet."

A Greek worrying about what "Wacko" Draco will do next.

SPARTA TALKS TOUGH

PRIVATES ON PARADE

613 BC

The Spartans are seething. After 17 years of defeats and internal rebellions they've decided to get their act together.

"It's a simple matter," said one Spartan colonel. "Ever since the Dark Ages we've been the top dogs in this part of the country. But recently we've let things slide. From now on, every Spartan man is going to have to learn to be a soldier."

So, it's goodbye to sleeping late on Sunday. Instead, it's cold baths at dawn and marches at midnight for the brave boys in the barracks. And everybody has to go naked.

"We're rather astonished," said a Theban citizen. "Being good at fighting's one thing, but this is totally unreasonable. **The Spartans spend their whole time preparing for war**. Even the women have to stay fit so that they can have healthy warrior babies.

"While the men are in barracks their wives spend their time doing athletics. And they wear very short tunics or sometimes nothing at all! You can imagine how distracting that is.

"But then Sparta's always been a little odd. It doesn't allow foreigners into the country. It's got two kings. And as for its political system – well, let's just say nobody can make head nor tail of it."

Sparta has run up against one or two problems in its army-mania. The main one is that with all the men in barracks, there's nobody to look after the farms.

They got around this by making the local peasants do the farming. But the peasants dislike it so much that the Spartans have to spend their whole time putting down rebel-lions, leaving them with no time to fight their enemies.

"I've come up with a fantastic answer to this problem," one Spartan general told the *Gazette*. "We need to persuade other states to form the **Peloponnesian League**. We'll demand that everyone in southern Greece gives Sparta military assistance when it's needed."

A Spartan soldier. No doing the dusting, cooking the supper and looking after the children for this fellow!

THE PRICE IS RIGHT!

500 BC

What on earth is this???

Money. That's what I want.

That's the question being asked by shopkeepers throughout Greece. Well, the *Gazette*'s got the answer. It's a **coin**. Or, as our finance editor calls it, "A small, round piece of metal you can buy things with."

The great advantage of coins is that they're so handy. Before, everyone used to barter. This meant that if you wanted to sell a cow you'd have to exchange it for, say, a table, some pots, a load of firewood and maybe a stool or two. And if you wanted to buy some meat or eggs you'd have to go into town with a fish and a bag of carrots. Imagine dragging all that around with you! Now you can just saunter along with some money.

Coins were invented in the Turkish state of Lydia, and they've quickly caught on over here. They're made of gold, silver or electrum (a mixture of both) and have pictures on both sides so you can tell if someone's tried to chip pieces off.

They're so popular that every state is minting its own except Sparta.

"We're not having any of this namby-pamby stuff," said the Spartan Banker-General. "We use iron bars for currency. If anyone tries to overcharge, you simply open your wallet, take out a bar and whack him on the head. You couldn't do that with a coin could you?"

No you couldn't!

MEN ONLY

HOW TO DO IT

THE SPARTAN WAY

Your step by step guide to how to become a tough nut

❶ Be born healthy. Sickly kids are thrown into a ravine.

❷ Go to school. Learn everything about life in barracks – fighting, athletics, more fighting, patriotic war songs, fighting, combat training, fighting and male bonding.

❸ Age 18. Join the army. Live and eat in barracks. Enjoy harsh conditions.

❹ Age 30. Get married. Wife will wear man's clothes on wedding night. Return quickly to barracks.

❺ Enjoy further barracks life, visiting wife at rare intervals.

❻ Your estate is run by slaves, leaving you free to remain in barracks.

❼ Become old and leave army. Ramble on about the joys of barracks life.

STOP PRESS! EXCLUSIVE!

MARATHON MAN IN DROP-DEAD DASH

490 BC

Only a few hours ago top long-distance runner Phidippides staggered into Athens.

"I've just come from Marathon," he panted. "We've one…"

Then he dropped dead before he could finish his sentence. Citizens are scratching their heads. What was he trying to say? Luckily our sports correspondent, Vizzy Goth, can explain the mystery.

"It's quite simple. Phid was a dead serious athlete, always on the lookout for new races to win. He spotted the distance between Marathon and Athens and thought, "Hmmm! 42.195 km (25 miles 385 yards). Could be a great distance event here." So he gave it a try.

What he was trying to say before he died was, "We've one more race to compete in!"

HIGHLY UNLIKELY

"Yes, Viz," says our medical expert, "Doc" Epidaurus, "You're quite right. But you've left out an important detail. Before this epic event Phid had tried something even more ambitious. He'd run non-stop from Marathon to Sparta to warn them that the Persians were invading.

At several hundred miles this was clearly too far for competition purposes. And I think his death was a direct result of trying the Marathon-Athens dash when he hadn't warmed down enough. I think we should be warning kids not to try this at home."

"Too true Doc," says Vizzy Goth! "But even if they can't do it at home I'd like kids to know that the Marathon is now a competable distance!"
Remember! You read it first in the GAZETTE!!!

CORRECTION
489 BC
It has been drawn to the Gazette's attention that the story concerning Phidippides contains an error. His last words were in fact, "We've won!" referring to the epic battle at Marathon in which Athenian hoplites thrashed a Persian army twice their size, killing 6,400 of the enemy while sustaining only 192 casualties themselves, thereby boosting morale to such an extent that the battle would be remembered as an example of Athenian pluck and tenacity and as a reason why Athens should be the leading state in Greece. The Gazette apologizes for this inaccuracy.

"I like to sing as I go," Phidippides told the *Gazette* during his run. *"I get around, You better run, Run-run-runaway, that sort of thing."*

PERSIAN KING WHACKS HELLESPONT

The *Gazette* war artist depicts the bridge across the Hellespont. Watch out, there's a storm coming!!

480 BC

XERXES – A FEW VOWELS SHORT OF A FULL WORD

Greeks are laughing fit to burst as news comes in of the latest Persian fiasco. Having gathered the biggest invasion force in world history, King "Silly" Xerxes decided to invade Greece. But "Silly" went off the rails when he tried to cross the Hellespont, the strip of water dividing Greece from Turkey. He built a bridge by lashing together 300 boats and was all set to march across when a storm blew up and sent his bridge to the bottom.

"Silly" was so annoyed that he had the Hellespont punished.

• He gave it 300 lashes.
• Then he branded it with hot irons.
• Then he chained it by throwing a lot of shackles into the water.
• And then, just to show it how lightly it had got off, he beheaded all the bridge-builders.

What a laugh!
The *Gazette* says, **"Play it again Xerx!"**

HEY!
Guess what?

The *Gazette* has discovered the funniest thing yet. Xerxes isn't pronounced Exer-exes. He calls himself Serkzees! Even more reason to call him Silly! What a hoot!

OH DEAR, WHAT CAN "THERM" MATTER BE?

Our war artist depicts the battle of Thermopylae. "What I really like to draw is kittens," he complained.

PERSIANS CRUSH GREEKS IN MULTIPLE VICTORY SHOCK

480 BC

Greece was recovering yesterday from a bad dose of the Persian Blues. At the battle of Thermopylae King Xerxes's cool cats annihilated a Spartan army led by King Leonidas.

"It was a close-run thing," claimed Leonidas's next-of-kin. "There were only 7,000 of our men against the entire Persian army. We beat back three separate attacks until a traitor showed Xerxes how to get behind our positions. Our Leo ordered everyone to retreat, then stayed behind with 300 men and fought to the death."

It turns out King Xerxes isn't such a sad sack after all. After his first failure he built a second bridge over the Hellespont and trampled Greece into the ground. **Not only has he beaten the Spartans at Thermopylae but he's gone on to sack Athens.**

"Ha! Tremble puny Greeklings!" said the Persian monarch in a *Gazette* exclusive interview. "From now on you'll have to call me King 'Conqueror' Xerxes."

The secret behind the Persian success is a 10,000-strong band of elite soldiers called The Immortals. They do exactly what the king tells them and they're called immortal because as soon as one is killed another steps forward to take his place.

"This isn't the Greek way," said one Athenian officer. "Sparta's an exception of course. But generally we like to do things in a more democratic fashion. Like we did at Marathon, where we had a rota of ten generals alternating on a daily basis, with everyone voting what to do on each day. Come to think of it, it's a miracle we won.

"I'm not sure what the current consensus is. But if we can't beat the Persians on land I'm sure our navy can at sea."

STOP PRESS

479 BC

THREE-TIME WINNERS DITCH PERSIANS

At the battles of **Salamis** and **Mykale** a joint city-states navy has sent the Persians packing! Despite being outnumbered, our gallant boys rammed the Persian boats repeatedly with their trireme warships until every last one was at the bottom of the sea. At the same time a big bunch of hoplites annihilated The Immortals at **Plataea. HA HA HA!!!**

HANDS UP!
THERE'S A BALLOT IN THE CHAMBER!

CITIZENS GIVE TRIPLE-WHAMMY

461 BC

Athenian aristocrats are reeling as citizens give them the triple-whammy.

The **first blow** came in 594 BC when Solon introduced reforms to improve the lives of poorer people.

The **second smash** came in 508 when Cleisthenes announced that all citizens were equal.

The **knock-out clincher** came this year when Athenians rose up and seized all power for themselves. Pundits have already given the new system of government a name – **democracy**.

MOOD

Pericles, one of Athens's elected leaders, was in an expansive mood when he spoke to a *Gazette* reporter.

"What happened was that the earlier reforms weren't working as they should. Sure, we had an assembly and limited voting powers. But the city was still being run by a council of aristocrats called the Areopagus. Imagine our shame – being governed by something that sounds like an internal organ! There was only one solution: an armed uprising.

"We waited until our ruler had gone off with 4,000 hoplites to help Sparta put down a rebellion. Then we struck. It was all over in a matter of hours.

"Aristocratic rule is dead. From now on everything will be decided by a show of hands."

DOWN

Democracy has gone down well. Every citizen has an equal say, and all over Athens people are busy thinking up new things to vote on.

"I've just come back from a meeting," panted Aristotle Megaphon, a baker. "We came to all sorts of decisions – to break off relations with Sparta, to get ready for war, to appoint some generals and to build up the navy. **Isn't democracy fantastic**?"

> **FOR FULL DETAILS SEE OUR DEMOCRACY SPECIAL ON PAGES 92-93.**

Pericles. Crazy hat, but not so crazy political idea!

PERSIANS ON THE CARPET
GAZETTE PAGE 74 COMMENT

A Persian. This man might look funny, but that doesn't mean he won't burn your house and steal your chariot.

448 BC

12 GOOD REASONS why we don't like Persians

Let's face it. Everybody loathes them. And here's why. They're a load of bullies who've taken over the Middle East, overrun the Egyptians, invaded us twice and given us no end of grief with their funny beards and so-called Immortals. Just look at what they've done.

✗ Started from nothing in a particularly barren part of Iran.

✗ Took over next-door Media 550 BC.

✗ Seized Turkey 547 BC.

✗ Grabbed Palestine and Babylonia 539 BC.

✗ Occupied Egypt 525 BC.

✗ Moved into India 521 BC.

✗ But then...they invaded *us* in 490 BC and were totally TRASHED at Marathon.

✗ However...they invaded us again in 480 BC and *we* were wiped out at Thermopylae.

✗ Then they went on to sack Athens the same year.

✗ But *we* sent them packing at Salamis, Mykale and Plataea in 480 and 479 BC.

✗ Made a peace treaty with us in 449 BC.

✗ But they're still skulking about trying to have another go at us. Typically OUTRAGEOUS!

The Gazette says "Go home you feared and disliked people whom our oracles predict will eventually be conquered by the Greeks, peace treaty or no peace treaty."

That's telling them!

🏛 AN OFFICIAL ANNOUNCEMENT PLACED BY THE CITY-STATE OF ATHENS 🏛

YOU THERE!

Yes you, you weak little Aegean states who've hardly got two warships to rub together

★ Frightened of another Persian invasion?
★ Do you know what Persians do when they're really angry?
★ Did you know that after their recent defeat the Persians are **really, really** angry?
★ Are you shaking in your sandals?

Good. Now pay attention.
Because we're inviting you to join the Delian League.

What is the Delian League? It's a defensive alliance in which we pool our cash to support a rapid-response strike force to see off Persian invasions.

What does it mean for you? Very little. All you have to do is put your gold in a central fund on the island of Delos and do what we tell you.

What does it mean for us? We keep our fleet of 200 warships on constant alert ready to defend you against the vile Persians.

What could be better? Apply in writing while you still can.

Under the terms of the Delian League in the year 478 BC the state of Athens recognizes that there will be no Persian invasion and reserves the future right to spend all League gold to its own benefit – i.e on sprucing up the city, developing the economy, importing fancy goods, building the Parthenon, etc. – and the right thereby to call the 440s and thereafter the Athenian Golden Age, and the right to conquer any member states that may or may not put up a fuss and ultimately the right thereby to create an empire that stretches across the Aegean.

TRI-MENDOUS!!

The Gazette guide to the super ship they're calling the Trireme

Now hear this! They say bad things come in threes, and if you're a Persian or a Phoenician they don't come badder than Greece's new navy blockbuster **THE TRIREME.**

- three times the speed
- three times the control
- three times the ramming power

All thanks to new three level oar technology!

OARSMEN

Each seat comes complete with lacy cushion, waitress service and personal video screen. (Just kidding!)

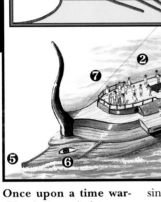

Once upon a time warships just carried troops who landed on shore to fight their battles. Then some bright spark found out you could actually fight at sea – ship to ship.

RAM

More recently naval tacticians have discovered that the most cost-effective, tough-on-them-and-soft-on-us technique is to ram the enemy to sink his ship. It's much less messy than hand-to-hand fighting. And much more fun too!

But ramming needs speed and control, and there's no better way to achieve that than **more oars**. So navy designers have hit on the idea of stacking the oarsmen three levels high along each side of the ship. The result – **the most powerful weapon this side of Zeus's thunderbolts!!**

CARP

However, the super ship does have its critics. There's no space to cook or sleep so the trireme can only operate within reach of a friendly port or beach. 24-hour blockades are also out of the question as the ship has to return to shore every night. But let's not quibble. The *Gazette* says "With boats like these Greece can RULE THE WAVES!!!!"

SLAM BAM THANK YOU RAM

TRIED AND TESTED TRIREME TACTICS

HEAD-ON

Give 'em all you've got with a head-on sideways assault!

BEHIND

A nasty shock from behind will break their oars. Then they're mincemeat!

CHECK OUT THESE FEATURES....

❶ Three banks of oarsmen whisk you along at speeds of up to 16kmph. (10mph).

❷ Crew of 200 salty sea dogs, including archers and hoplites to repel enemy boarders.

❸ Mast made from finest Macedonian spruce. Can be lowered for battle.

❹ Sail of toughest linen. Stow this away for ultimate control! (Stripes optional.)

❺ Bronze ram for those close encounters of the Aegean kind.

❻ Reinforced prow with big painted eye to frighten the opposition. Oooo!

❼ Upper-deck archers' nest. Aieee!

❽ Oars. Each a massive 4m (14ft). Wow!

❾ Leather rowlock covers. No water gets in when these are in place!

❿ Experienced captain from a top-locker aristocratic family. Aye aye, Sir!

NEXT WEEK: LONG SPEARS – ARE THEY WORTH THE EFFORT?

IT'S A PELOPO-KNEES-UP!

404 BC

Sparta's hard guys are whooping it up tonight. Why? Beeause the Peloponnesian War is over. After a hard 30 years struggle between Athens and Sparta, Sparta has finally WON!

"It took almost three decades but we got there in the end," explained Spartan general Lysander to our war correspondent. "Despite a number of setbacks we hammered them fair and square.

"The reason it took so long was because we had the best army in Greece but Athens had the best navy. Whenever we tried to besiege them they just brought in food by sea. Stalemate!

"Then we had this fantastic brainwave. We built a navy too! We followed the Athenians to a place called Aegospotami and waited until they'd all gone ashore for a picnic. After that it was easy. We captured 170 of their ships and executed 4,000 prisoners.

"The next year they surrendered. We pulled down their walls, got rid of their stupid democracy and installed not one but THIRTY tyrants to run the place.

"What a hoot! Have some more bread and water."

"What are *you* looking at?" A Spartan behaving badly.

MEN!

FIGHTING WELL BUT LOOKING DOWDY ? THEN ACT THE PART IN OUR HANDY UP-TO-THE MINUTE, ALL-WEATHER COMBAT GEAR.

SPARTAN SPECIALS

has a seasonal super-offer you can't resist:

STYLISH HELMET

Beaten from a single piece of bronze, this imposing headpiece features small eyeholes, a narrow slit for the nose and a metal crest to make you look taller. (Perfect for aggressive nodding and a must for those in-battle debates.)

CUIRASS

Made of layered linen, and decorated in the most martial style, this torso guard is ideal for the fighting soldier. Combines comfort with protection.

Ready made in three sizes: small, medium & massive

HEAVY SHIELD

Once you've deflected your foe's arrows, swords and daggers, you can give him a good whack on the nose with the reinforced bronze rim.

STURDY GREAVES

With our patented bronze shin guards you can wade through sword swipes, spear stabs and hostile coffee tables with impunity.

SWORD

A chop-chop here and a slash-slash there, never will be a bore, that is how we spend our days in the merry old time of war!

Guaranteed no rust

BIG CLOAK

Top-to-toe cover in case of cold weather. Also good for when you've lost a battle and need to be a nobody. (But don't forget to remove that distinctive helmet!)

LONG SPEAR

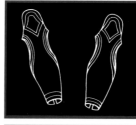

Keep your foe at bay with our extra long spear. Tested up to 100 thrusts, these should be part of every red-blooded soldier's kit. Can also be leaned on when you're a bit worn-out.

ITEMS CAN BE PURCHASED INDIVIDUALLY. BUT FOR COMPLETE KILLING CHIC WE OFFER THE WHOLE RANGE AT 30% DISCOUNT.

Send SAE plus one iron bar for our brochure. (No fancy coins accepted.)
SPARTAN SPECIALS, 10c Gymnasticum Lane, Sparta City, Sparta 103474.

KING PHIL'S
MACEDONIAN MASH-UP

BOONDOCK BOYS HIT BIG TIME

🔲 338 BC 🔲

Whoops! Maybe those city-states aren't so hot after all. Athens and Thebes have just been smashed at the battle of Chaeronea by a bunch of bumpkin northerners called the Macedonians.

"We're gutted," said an Athenian spokesman. "We'd always thought the Macedonians were useless. They speak such bad Greek you can only just understand them. In fact, we're not really sure they ARE Greeks. Until 20 years ago they hardly had an army because so many of them had been killed in civil wars. I don't know how they suddenly got so powerful. **It's probably something to do with that King Phil.**"

Philip II, as he prefers to be called, revealed all to the *Gazette*.

"When I came to the throne in 360 BC, Macedonia was a mess. But I soon put things in order. I built up the army and conquered all the locals to make an empire three times as big as all the southern city-states put together. After this latest victory I'm sure the Peloponnesians will recognize who's boss. **And my name's not Phil it's Philip.**"

Phil's bright ideas include giving his hoplites gigantic spears so they can walk the enemy off the field without even having to get near them. He's also invented two elite units –

King Phil – Macedonia's man of the moment.

the Companion Cavalry and Companion Infantry – for hand-to-hand fighting.

The spears and Companions are a clear winner. And soothsayers predict this is only the start.

Mystic Mag of Megara says: "Using the latest divination methods, I have observed the flight of birds and recorded the last few lightning strikes. The portents suggest Greece will unite to fight the Persians. The Greeks will call themselves the *Hellenes* and create one of the **biggest empires ever**.

"Yet wait! What do I see in my magic mirror? The leader of this empire will not be Philip. It will be another. The words are hard to make out but... yes, it is one called **Rednaxela**!"

YOUR GUIDE TO KING PHIL'S TOPPEST TROOPS
THERE'S NOTHING LIKE A PAL!

"Posh and pugnacious?" ask King Philip and his son Alexander, "then join The Companions!"

Phil and Alex are seeking fit young men of noble stock to join their close-knit team of elite battle executives. If you are a thrusting, get-ahead infantryman with a persuasive fighting manner then you're just the man for the job.

If you become a Companion you'll travel the known world, and be in with a big chance to **annihilate** Asia Minor*, **pillage** Palestine, petrify Persia, **intimidate** India and **exterminate** Egypt! What more could a rough-and-tumble, jabbing-and-stabbing kind of a guy ask for!

*That's Turkey, geography fans!

A Companion contemplating combat with the Persians.

Nine Muses
M U S I C

7 Kithara Way
Athens

The very latest musical instruments

Tinkle! HARPS

Thonk! TIMPANON

Plink! LYRES

Tootle tootle! PAN PIPES

Tish! CYMBALS

GORDIANS IN KNOT FIASCO

"MONEY FOR OLD ROPE," SAYS HUNKY NEW KING

 **333 BC**

It's Empire Time folks! He's been fighting the Persians for only a year, but already Macedonia's King Alexander looks set to become Asia's next No. 1.

The vibrant young king showed his style at the town of Gordium in Turkey today when he solved their famous wagon-and-pole puzzle. The knot which joined the wagon to the pole was so complicated that an oracle declared that **whoever untangled it would become Lord of all Asia**.

His brainy Majesty, who studied under Aristotle, one of the greatest philosophers of all time, gave the knot the benefit of his education. **He took out his sword and cut it in half**.

"This is divine proof that I am going to wipe those Persian scum from the face of the earth," crowed Alex to cries of "Cheat!" from the crowd.

But if Alexander's happy the Gordians aren't. "It's a great blow to the tourist industry," said a town spokesman. "Our knot was all we had. What'll we do now? I suppose we'll have to highlight one of our other features. But between you and me the **Gordian Dusty Market Place** doesn't have quite the same ring as the **Gordian Knot**."

Alexander. "To be or knot to be," he quipped before slicing.

STOP PRESS...
The oracle was right!!! Reports are reaching the *Gazette* that Alexander's army have just smashed King Darius's troops at the Battle of Issus!!!

SWING LOW, SWEET CHARIOT

Mired down by enemies? Not if you fit our "Darius Demons" to your chariot. Based on an original model used by King Darius of Persia, these super-sharp, long-lasting axle blades are at the cutting edge of technology. They'll make mincemeat of any opposition. Simply snap 'em on and let your chariot do the work. The faster you go the more mayhem you'll create! You'll cut a dash on any battlefield – GUARANTEED!

Can be used in peacetime too! With a pair of "Darius Demons" it's GOODBYE to parking problems and inner-city congestion. People lining the street? No hassle! You pull in, they pull out – and if they don't they'll wish they had!

CHARIOTS OF FIRE

The Freeway, Alexandria.
"The One-Stop Shop For All Your Charioteering Requirements."

WARNING: Despite their potential for thrills, particularly when cornering, "Darius Demons" have not been approved for speed testing or competitive use. Regretfully we must advise racing owners not to attach this equipment to stadium chariots.

IMPORTANT! Battle performance can be adversely affected if the enemy simply parts ranks and pelts you with stones as you drive through. In such situations Chariots of Fire Products takes no responsibility for any adverse outcome.

LION MAN BUILDS CITY

 **332 BC**

A PHAROS DAY'S PAY FOR A PHAROS DAY'S WORK

Thrusting young architect Dinocrates finally got the break he wanted. Having trailed Alexander's army all over Persia he got miffed at the way nobody took any notice of him. So he dressed up in a lion skin and walked around carrying a big club. They noticed him then!

"This is the kind of get-ahead attitude I like to see," Alexander told him.

"Build me a new capital for Egypt. Put it here, just where the Nile stops and the sea starts. Let's really push the boat out, youngster. No expense spared. I want people to be talking about this city for centuries."

"It was a hard commission," said jubilant Dino. "But I got it under control. I laid the city out on a grid plan, gave it an agora, a tree-lined park and a big double quay. But what it still needs is a lighthouse. Nobody's ever thought of that before! The city council are currently considering ideas.

"The only problem with the city was the name. The boss said it should be called Alexandria. Well, there are at least 15 other Alexandrias dotted around the Middle East by now, and most of them are grungy little villages. I thought since this was something special we could call it something different – like Dinocrates City, or Dino-on-sea, or Dinor Regis. But he put his foot down. And you don't argue with a foot that's conquered half the known world, do you? No sir!

"Still, beats going around in a lion skin for a living."

According to the *Gazette*'s oracle, Alexandria has a big future. She says,

"I predict it will be a hub of Greek civilization with the most famous library in the world, a population of at least half a million and a building called The Museum which will be a magnet for Greek scientists."

A wonder in the making? Architect sketch for the Pharos lighthouse, soon to be built in Alexandria.

NO MORE WAR!

Map alert, strategy fans! The red part with arrows on it is where Alexander and his army went. The gold part on top of the yellow shows how much of the world he actually conquered. Not bad eh?!? And all before he was 32!

Asia Minor 334 BC
Battle of Issus 333 BC
Afghanistan 326 BC
Alexandria 332 BC
Syria 332 BC
Persia 330 BC
Babylon 323 BC (Watch out for mosquitoes around here, say oracles.)
Egypt 332 BC
India 325 BC

LAHORE'S A BORE

325 BC

It's all over! After ten years of successful campaigning Alexander's men have told him "We want to go home now!"

The surprise announcement followed a wipe-out victory in India, when Alex's army thrashed the King of Lahore and sent his 200 war elephants packing. But this time the troops weren't satisfied with victory. After another week's march into India they refused to go any further.

"We don't like Lahore and we're fed up with fighting," said an army rep. "We think we've done far too much already. In the last ten years we've...

• walloped the Persians.
• occupied Palestine.
• grabbed Egypt.
• walked over Afghanistan.
• trampled the Indians into the ground.
• created the biggest empire the world has ever seen.

• shown everyone who's boss.
• left squiggly lines all over the map of Asia.

Isn't that enough? We think it is."

RELUCTANT

Alexander has given in reluctantly to his troops' demands. Or at least he says he's reluctant. We think he's secretly relieved.

Not only has he married the beautiful Roxane, daughter of an Afghan chieftain, but camp gossip says he plans to marry a second wife when he gets to Persia.

AMOROUS

Our social correspondent writes: "Alexander obviously has his mind on other things. There is no doubt that a long campaign puts a man in an amorous mood. He and Roxane face a long journey through hot deserts.

"But once he's cooled down Alex will want to get into the Persian swing, and what better way to do that than marry a Persian wife? Nothing odd in that, particularly if you're an emperor.

DRAINS

"But I'd advise his wives to watch him vigilantly. They should be particularly careful not to let him inspect a Babylonian drainage project in 323 BC. The portents suggest he will be bitten by an infected mosquito and die a few days later. And after that things will really go down hill."

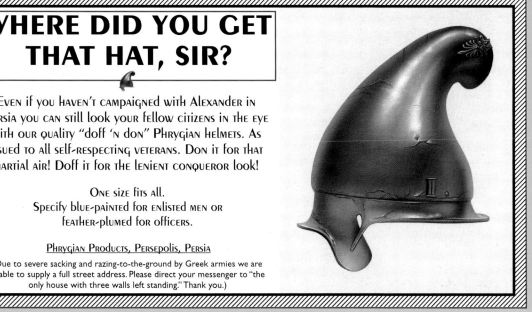

QUADRUPLE ROYAL MURDER SENSATION

THE PRIME SUSPECTS

1. Mr. Ptolemy of Egypt.

2. Mr. Antigonas of Greece.

3. Mr. Seleucus of All-The-Rest.

---

301 BC

"Not us," say benefactors as Alexander's empire collapses

In the 22 years since Alexander's death, his generals have divided his empire among themselves, and his court has become a foaming, swirling whirlpool of blind ambition, deadly intrigue and even deadlier murder. His mother Olympias, wife Roxane, son Alexander and half-brother Philip Arrideus have all died in mysterious circumstances – almost certainly killed. His main general is also dead. The once great Alexandrian Empire has fractured into three rival factions.

Nobody knows who committed the ghastly crimes. But three men are sitting pretty at the head of each faction as a result. We interviewed them on your behalf.

"I was nowhere near anywhere where the murders occurred. I was having a nice glass of wine with my friends in Alexandria on all possible occasions. When the news came through I was shocked. Send my condolences to the relatives and tell them I've taken the precaution of making myself Pharaoh of Egypt."

"Isn't it awful? And all of them within such a short space of time! I was just a small child at the time of the murders, so it wasn't anything to do with me. But if it's any consolation I'd like to announce that I plan to take over Greece in 276 BC, and control the country by keeping garrisons in all major cities."

"Those two have got it easy. They're running self-contained countries. Me? I've got to handle an empire stretching from Palestine to India. It'll break up at any minute! And they're going on about condolences? Get a life! Sorry I didn't send any flowers. Alex was a great guy. OK? End of interview. **I'm busy.**"

Our political correspondent writes: "I'm afraid the end is nigh. Whoever did the dirty deed, it's obvious that Alexander's empire is on its last legs. It's only a matter of time before everything falls to pieces. I'd give Greece about 150 years then it'll all be over."

ONE FOR THE WOAD

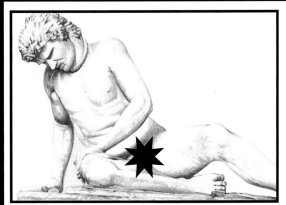
A dying Celt. He's blue really, but the *Gazette*'s resident sculptor told us: "I'm not ruining a perfectly good piece of marble with blue paint. Be off with you!"

297 BC

Celts give last orders in Greece

Invading Celts have decided to get out of Greece after enduring a horror-packed night of fear.

The woady wuffians – trademark: spiky yellow hair and a blue skin dye called woad – have rampaged throughout northern Greece. But they withdrew from an all-out assault on Delphi following a **stunning series of natural disasters**.

General Brennus of Gaul, the Celtic leader, was angry at the way things turned out.

"First we had an earthquake. Then there was lightning and thunder followed by a fierce storm. Then there was a night of frost and snow. And in the morning we were hit by rockfalls.

"We like a fight as much as the next man but this just isn't fair. We're going to leave Greece and set up a small colony in Turkey instead."

Reports say that the Celts were so afraid of the weather that they jumped up and tried to kill it with their swords. Result: a lot of wounded Celts.

The *Gazette* is worried. If a load of heavy-drinking barbarians can get this far, who's next? **There's lots of them out there and they all want a slice of our civilization. Be on guard, citizens!**

IT'S CURTAINS FOR CORINTH

These coarse little men are Romans. Ugh!

CITY CRUSHED IN ROMAN RAMPAGE

146 BC

"Vulgar" newcomers set the agenda

Wow! What an extremely unpleasant surprise! The Romans have burned Corinth to the ground and crushed Greek independence.

"No one will live in this city for 100 years," bragged Roman consul Lucius Mummius as he strode through the smoking ruins of Corinth followed by thousands of crack Roman legionaries and a convoy of siege weapons stretching to the horizon.

"This is fighting talk!" said an Athenian onlooker. "But we'll let it pass for now."

SNEAKS

The Romans have been sneakily conquering Greek territory for some time. First it was the colonies, then it was parts of western Greece, then it was Macedonia. Now it's the city-state heartland – the Peloponnese.

"What they do," explained a singed Corinthian, "is conquer next door and tell you

that you can remain free so long as you behave yourself. Then if you do the slightest thing wrong they're on top of you like a ton of coals."

The Romans have taken everyone by surprise. Until recently they were a bunch of nobodies with a low-grade democratic political system. Now they run the whole Mediterranean. What's more, they've stolen Greek architecture and Greek gods and are trying to pass them off as their own.

FRIGHT

"We are well acquainted with Romans," said Lady Helen of Thebes. "They often come to visit and are very polite and respectful, with a lot of cash to flash around. You can tell they admire us. They shower the oracles with gold. And they're building temples just like ours, back in Rome. **But between you and me, they're frightfully vulgar!**"

THE ORACLE SPEAKS

Live from Delphi, Madame Pythia is poised on her tripod to solve any query you put to her. In a mystic smog, produced by a brazier-full of aromatic herbs, the finest oracle in Greece offers uncanny insights into your personal problems. Love? Health? Family? Business? War? Plumbing? You ask it, she'll answer.

BAD OMEN

Q Dear Oracle, I went up to the Pnyx to have a debate – i.e. yell at all the speakers – when I felt a few drops of rain. To my astonishment everyone went home. They even left their barbecue behind. What's going on?

A *You silly citizen. Obviously this is your first time at an Assembly. Any fool knows that no debate can take place when it rains because rain is a bad omen. Besides which it makes people wet. And the so-called barbecue is in fact a burned sacrifice to the gods.*

JUST SUPPOSING

Q Dear Oracle, I am a Greek peasant. But supposing I wasn't, could you tell me the best time to invade Greece?

A *I divine that you are a Persian king and will therefore give you no answer save, "Don't even think of it!"*

LETTER OF THE WEEK

Q Dear Oracle, I went to the gym because I was feeling flabby. To my horror it was full of men dancing about stark naked. I was so aghast I did not even bother to open my Adidos bag, and went straight home. Have any other readers had this problem?

A *You must be from out of town. Greek men are not renowned for their shyness. Particularly in the gym. In fact, the word "gymnos" means naked. So a "gymnasium" is a place you go in order to be naked. Get on down there and tone up those muscles!*

LOW WATER TABLE

Q Dear Oracle, What is an Archimedes Screw? How can I get one? I am a 70-year-old farmer with a low water table who is constantly searching for new ways of getting it up.

A *You must be referring to the method of raising water through a tube from a lower level to a higher level, by means of an ingenious screw-like device, as invented by the scientist Archimedes.*
These can be obtained in most agoras for a few drachmas.

KEEN

Q Dear Oracle, I am a Spartan veteran who takes a keen interest in military holidays. Could you tell me when Greek armies are most commonly off duty and thus unable to repel invasions?

A *You are a transparent Persian king. But since your letter included several gold coins I can tell you that nobody does any fighting when they're bringing in the harvest.*

MISSING MRS.

Q Dear Oracle, I haven't been able to locate my wife for several weeks. Do you know where she is?

A *No probs. She's in the women's part of your house. You know, the gynaeceum, where all wives have to stay because they're not considered decent enough for everyday society. Why not knock on the door? See who's in there. You might also find a lot of daughters and nieces.*

BURNED

Q Dear Oracle, Isn't it lucky that our country doesn't have a tradition of pie-making? Imagine what would happen if Aristotle's wife said, "Your pie is in the oven." The poor man wouldn't know if it was a pie or the similarly sounding Pi, meaning the ratio of the circumference of a circle to its diameter, which he first calculated. Every mealtime he would fear his life's work had gone up in flames!

A *Yes. Next?*

SMARTY-PANTS

Q Dear Oracle, I am a young girl and I have so many toys I don't know what to do with them. I'm going to throw them away. This isn't a question. I just wanted to share this simple solution with you so you know you don't have to be a smarty-pants on a tripod to solve everyday problems.

A *Don't do it! Keep those toys intact! You'll need to sacrifice them to the goddess Artemis on your wedding day as a sign that your childhood is over. Great Colossus of Rhodes! I only hope it's not too late.*

NO KIDDING

Q Dear Oracle, Every night I walk along a remote path which is always lined with little babies. When I look in the morning they're gone. Are my friends playing a surreal trick on me? Or am I going mad?

A *You might well be going mad. More likely, you're walking along the path where poor people leave the kids they can't afford to bring up. Not to worry, though. These children will be removed by better-off families and trained as slaves. More important is your paranoia. Got any other problems? I can counsel privately too, you know.*

NOT YOU AGAIN

Q Dear Oracle, Where did I leave my sandals?

A *Under the bed as usual.*

PATTERNS

Q Dear Oracle, I am a student studying invasion patterns over the centuries. I'd like to pinpoint Greece's weakest areas. Can you tell me where they are?

A *Begone, you pernicious Persian fool.*

NO DILEMMA TOO THORNY! OUR GIRL IN THE GROTTO WILL PRONOUNCE ON ANYTHING!

PHILOSOPHY

It's philosophy week in the Gazette and we're marking the occasion with a double-page brain bonanza! What's life all about? Consult the Gazette guide to the Greeks with the greatest grey matter, and find out!

WHICH PHILOSOPHER?

Gathered around for a serious think, Plato (left), fails to amuse his fellow philosophers when he pronounces "I'm pink therefore I'm spam".

We took a consumer survey of eight great thinkers and asked our "schoolmaster" to award them marks.

He's given them between 1 to 3 brains for intelligence 🧠 and 1 to 3 yawns for tedium 🥱. Aristotle came out tops with 3 brains but didn't make it into the best buy category because he also clocked up 2 yawns. We suggest you look for the mid-range thinkers who offer brain cells AND entertainment.

Thales
624-546 BC

The first philosopher ever! Said the world began as water. The original absent-minded professor – fell into a well while watching the stars. **Verdict:** a likely thale.

Anaximander
611-546 BC

Like Thales (but didn't fall down a well), and said men came from slime and were originally fish. **Verdict:** much more like it. Making good progress.

Pythagoras
580-500 BC

Bit of a weirdo. Ran a religious colony in Italy and didn't eat beans. Believed in the importance of numbers and revered triangles. Also believed in reincarnation and remembered all his previous lives. **Verdict:** takes all sorts. Good at numbers, but still hasn't learned to write.

Anaxagoras
500-428 BC

Another stargazer. Announced that the sun was a flaming mass, explained eclipses, and revealed the moon was a moon. Wrote a book about nature as a result. **Verdict:** innovative. But should spend less time looking out the window.

Socrates
470-399 BC

The man who stood still for days on end pondering life (when he wasn't partying!) Spent ages trying to work out how society should be run. His answer: everyone should be good. Ugliest man in Athens and too clever by half. **Verdict:** soc it to me. Excellent work.

Plato
427-347 BC

Popular man, popular books. Thought Pythagoras was tops. Thought Socrates was even more tops. Founded Academy school in Athens and developed idea of perfect society based on virtue. **Verdict:** typical schoolmaster despot. A word after class, please.

Diogenes
412-323 BC

Lived in a barrel and said everyone should have no possessions and live as close to nature as possible. Was picked on because he got on everyone's nerves. The original drop-out. **Verdict:** nothing in the lost-property cupboard. Good effort! (Bonus brain for entertainment.)

Aristotle
384-323 BC

Towering but impenetrable intellect. Told us all about nature, humans and Artemis-knows-what. Taught Alexander the Great. Invented logic. Here's a quote: "Man is mortal. Aristotle is a man. Aristotle is mortal." May look obvious but wasn't then. **Verdict:** Bright but dull! Definitely room for improvement.

Zeno
336-264 BC

Nice, quiet, wine-and-pastries sort of guy. Said everyone should put up with the bad things that happen because that's life. **Verdict:** sloppy thinking. Well-meaning but must try harder. See me in my study.

Best Buy!

Plato. He's written more than any of the others. His ideas are a little dull but he's easy to understand.

Worth Considering Socrates – because that's where Plato got his ideas from – and Diogenes because he's way ahead of his time. We would have chosen Aristotle but he's just too tedious.

84

WATCH

Here are some cuttings from our archives which just go to prove that brains and common sense aren't necessarily natural bed-fellows!!

399 BC Greek Gazette

CHOP SHOCK FOR SOC

"Hemlock? Make mine a double."

Party-loving philosopher Socrates was told to change his tipple yesterday when a trial jury ordered him to drink poison!

The shock sentence came after Athens's top egghead was accused of corrupting his students.

"It's a stitch-up!" said a pal. "All he said was that it was important to find the truth and to live by it because the soul was immortal. He was very big on right and wrong and didn't approve of corruption. The only thing he did was annoy the authorities by being too clever."

When the jury found him guilty they gave him a choice: go into exile or think up another suitable punishment. Soc suggested that he be maintained at public expense for the rest of his life. The court was so outraged they ordered him to take deadly hemlock.

"He's putting on a brave face," said his friend, "but he's obviously quite shaken. He feels they didn't give the matter enough thought. What it boils down to is that he'd made a lot of important people look stupid."

The *Gazette* says "Call that clever? Not in <u>our</u> scroll it isn't!"

360 BC Greek Gazette

D.PHIL V.DULL
SAY ATHENIANS

The brightest brain in town hit a flat note when he put forward his revolutionary theory – virtue is all.

Dr. Plato was greeted with massed yawns as he unveiled his new lifestyle plan. According to him, democracy should be abolished, Athens should be ruled by philosophers and everybody should be virtuous.

By virtuous he means:
- *Compulsory religious lessons in school*
- *The death sentence if you're bad*
- *Believing that the gods are incorruptible*
- *Read my books*

341 BC Greek Gazette

"STONED AGAIN"
SAYS MAN IN BARREL

Diogenes, the philosopher who lives in an old barrel, despises material possessions, and attacks dishonesty and wealth, got rough justice when he went on a stroll around Athens.

"We love dishonesty and wealth," said an Athenian, "so he's very unpopular here. Just the other day he was plodding through the streets with a lantern saying he was trying to find an honest citizen. Well, we threw a lot of stones at him. That taught him a lesson. Ran back to his tub quick as lightning, he did. Cocky beggar."

520 BC Greek Gazette

THAGS SLAMS RUDE FOOD

Colonists Knocked Sideways By Philosopher's Bean Blast

"Thags" Pythagoras has got his finger on the pulse. He's decided the soul is made of wind and so he's telling everyone: "Lay off the beans! They can damage your spiritual health."

This is the latest loony order issued in Croton, southern Italy, where the mathematician-turned-philosopher runs a cult colony.

The no-beans edict is No. 1 on a list of ridiculous rules which settlers have to obey. Others include:
- *Don't wear rings*
- *Don't look in a mirror beside a lamp*
- *Don't leave your bed unmade in the morning*
- *Don't help a man unloading freight - but do help him if he's loading*
- *Don't stand on nail clippings*
- *Don't touch a white rooster*

"Thags" is a bit of a mystery. He never writes anything down and only confides in a small circle of pals, so nobody really knows what he's saying. But his supporters claim he's still top-dog.

"His methods may be difficult to follow," said a Croton spokesman, "but they've got a purpose.

"He believes that the soul can be reborn and his rules are designed to ensure you come out well in the next life. Here at Croton we all hope to be reincarnated as kings or emperors. You other guys will probably end up as snails or beetles, and we will tread on you."

POT BLACK

NEW HUE TO-DO

500 BC

The art world is up in arms over the latest development from Athens. For decades Greek pots have been orange with black and white figures painted on them. But the Athenians have given tradition the thumbs-down. In an astonishing flight of fancy they've started producing black pots with orange and white figures on them.

"This is one of the most provocative and innovative concepts we have seen in years," said an Athenian critic. "There can be no doubt that we are entering a period of mind-boggling creativity. Centuries from now art lovers will be gazing in rapture at our pots and saying 'Truly, this was their finest hour!'"

Others disagree.

FLASH IN PAN

Peri Style, editor of *Pots and Potmen*, pointed out that, "It makes much more sense if pots have an orange background because the clay they're made of is orange. If you have a black background you merely increase your workload. In my opinion this new style is just a flash in the pan. Things will soon get back to normal."

The ordinary pot-user is baffled by the whole business. "What I don't understand," said house-wife Nelly Savalas, "is why they don't broaden their spectrum. After all, it's not as if orange, white and black are the only paints available. Why can't we have purple pots? Or yellow pots? Personally, I've always wanted a magenta one with lime-green figures. Why aren't there any of those in the shops?"

Why not indeed? Let's say NO to the stuck-up so-called experts who won't use anything but black, white and orange. Here at the *Gazette* we like to encourage variety. We're offering 50 drachmas to the reader who comes up with the brightest design by next Thursday.

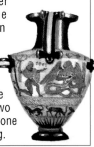

Arts INSIGHT

THOSE SEVEN WONDERS!

YOUR GAZETTE GUIDE TO ALL THAT'S GREAT

— *270 BC* —

We sent the *Gazette* architecture correspondent on a trip around the Seven Wonders of the World. He reckons Greece tops the Google League for sheer eyes-out-of-sockets stupendosity. Here's his report.

THE COLOSSUS OF RHODES

• See this if it's the only thing you see this year. More zip than a hoplite's quickstep! A wonder in the best GREEK tradition! This one will run and run!

THE PYRAMIDS OF EGYPT

• OK if you're passing.

Otherwise three big, dull, pointless pointy type buildings. Don't get out of bed.

THE TOMB OF MAUSOLUS

• Stupendous is the only word. This GREEK marvel has to be seen at all costs. Superb! Magnificent!

The Hanging Gardens of Babylon. Consistently voted "best wonder" by readers of *Slug Week* magazine.

THE TEMPLE OF ARTEMIS

• One of the best temples I have seen anywhere at anytime! Phenomenal example of GREEK architecture! Stunning! A must-must-see!

THE HANGING GARDENS OF BABYLON

• Cruddy load of pot plants. Typical Babylonian junk. Not wonderful at all. Stay at home.

THE STATUE OF ZEUS

• Massive! A towering achievement! Monumental masterpiece by GREEK sculptor, the fabulous Phidias! Beg, borrow, steal, sell your children into slavery – whatever it takes – JUST GO!!

THE PHAROS OF ALEXANDRIA

• There is no way to describe this magnificent GREEK-built lighthouse! But I'll try. Fantastic! Incredible! Left me breathless! Wonderful! Something for all the family! A tour de force! Utterly delightful! Sheer magic! Unforgettable!

BUMS ON SEATS!

CITIZENS GO STAGE CRAZY

Talk about Full House! Athens has done it again! The city that invented drama has come up with a new way of pulling the crowds – discount seating for the poor! The state has decided drama is so essential to everyday life that it's willing to pay for down-and-outs to get a slice of culture.

"It's a wonderful idea," beamed one of Athens's top drama bosses. "The tickets weren't that expensive to begin with – only two obols apiece (an obol is one-sixth of a drachma, finance freaks!). But now everyone can enjoy a good afternoon out at the theatre."

A packed theatre near you, yesterday.

"Some people are confused about drama. They say what's a comedy? What's a tragedy? Well, it's simple. A tragedy's about heroes and death and everybody cries. And a comedy's about posh people who slip on banana skins and everybody laughs. Anyway. I tell them: go and see for yourselves."

WHAT YOU THINK OF THE THEATRE

HERE'S A SELECTION OF COMMENTS BY GREEK GAZETTE THEATRE-GOERS...

• "Fantastic! I really liked the chorus line, dancing and singing in front of the stage. Some of the comments they made!"

• "I loved the skene, that wall behind the stage where they paint the scenery. What lifelike forests, palaces and temples!"

• "The stone seats were very uncomfortable. No one told me I had to bring a cushion. But the acoustics were amazing. You could hear a pin drop. Very helpful for actors who've brought their darning."

• "The best part was when they hoisted that guy up with a crane and had him flying through the air to look like a god."

• "Great show! Great action! Great stunts! But how about a few more laughs?" (Try a comedy next time. Ed.)

Like it or loathe it, the theatre's here to stay. And with every town boasting an auditorium – some seat up to 14,000! – attendance has never been easier!

COMING SOON

to a theatre near you:

The Oresteia

Aeschylus's doom-laden trilogy about life after the siege of Troy.

Bacchae

Euripides's tragic account of rural passions under the influence of Dionysus, the god of wine and fertility. Explicit mother-tearing-son-to-pieces scenes.

Lysistrata

Aristophanes's naughty romp in which women go on strike to prevent men going to war. (What won't they do, eh?!?)

Entertainment

BROWSERS' CORNER

MAKING A JOURNEY?

Looking for a present for Gran? Or simply lost for words? Look no further. Here's the *Gazette's* Top Ten bestsellers. Certified to stand you in good stead for thousands of years.

1. *The Republic,* **Plato** – how to run the ideal state with only a small elite of brainboxes. Vibrant arguments, vivid imagery and practical examples.

2. *History of Animals,* **Aristotle** – what does an elephant do with its trunk? Wait and see! This is the ideal gift for nature lovers or for people you want to shut up for a while. Perfect for the beach.

3. *History of the Peloponnesian War,* **Thucydides** – eight volumes of fact-packed history. The ostracized Athenian general gives us the info on... wait for it... the Peloponnesian War! A long-journey special.

4. *History,* **Herodotus** – known as the Father of History, but some people call him the Father of Lies. Here he plies his spellbinding pen to tell us everything about everywhere. Want to know about Fiery Phoenixes and jewel-encrusted crocodiles? Then turn straight to his chapter on Egypt. A nugget of nonsense on every page!

5. *The Anabasis,* **Xenophon** – hard-hitting stuff by the one-time mercenary for Sparta and Persia, Xenophon knows what he's talking about. In this gripping adventure he relives his time as a rebel commander in the Persian army. He's better known for his previous bestsellers about farming, horses and finance, but fans won't be disappointed.

6. *The Iliad,* **Homer** – THE tale of the Siege of Troy. You'll love the bit where Achilles kills Trojan hero Hector and drags him past the city walls. A sizzling cocktail of love, heroism and revenge in the best epic tradition.

7. *The Odyssey,* **Homer** – Part II of Homer's gripping Trojan saga. Odysseus makes his way home from Troy.

8. *Elements,* **Euclid** – latest offering from the world-famous expert on maths and geometry. Popular with some.

9. *The Frogs,* **Aristophanes** – text of the belly-achingest play, from the master of comedy. Author of 40 other side-splitters.

10. *Oedipus Rex,* **Sophocles** – a heart-rending tragedy from a genius playwright. Grimace as Oedipus puts his eyes out when he realizes he's married his mother. **Urch!** Makes the best of Sophocles's most revolutionary concept – more than two characters in a plot.

DOC FROM KOS IS BOSS

"HE KNOWS BEST"

It's cat-among-the-pigeons time as Hippocrates, a doctor from the island of Kos, turns medicine on its head. His radical two-point proposal says:

• Illness isn't a punishment from the gods.
• Doctors can cure people.

"Before I came along," explained Hippocrates, "the medical scene was a mess. People used to worship Aesclepius, the god of healing. They'd do all kinds of stupid things, like burn sacrifices to him and sleep in his temple, so that he could visit them in their dreams and tell them how to get better. I thought, 'Nonsense! Surely there's a better way than this!' And there is."

His scientific approach to healing has made Hippocrates the main medicine man in Greece.

"My advice to doctors is this: feel 'em all over; find where it hurts; and then do something about it. Or don't, as the case may be, because most minor ailments cure themselves without interference. A lot of it's got to do with diet, so you could invent some pithy statement like, 'An apple a day keeps the doctor away.' And if none of that works, tell 'em to pray to Aesclepius.

"Most important of all, a doctor's first duty is to his patients rather than to himself. That'll be two drachmas, thank you."

"Rest the arm for a couple of days, son, and you'll soon be as right as rain." A doctor, yesterday.

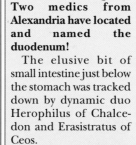
GOTCHA!
DUODENUM "FOUND"

It's here! The news we've been waiting for! Two medics from Alexandria have located and named the duodenum!

The elusive bit of small intestine just below the stomach was tracked down by dynamic duo Herophilus of Chalcedon and Erasistratus of Ceos.

"It was nothing really," said Herophilus, whose initial research led to the breakthrough. "The thing was there all the time. All we had to do was get to it."

But how did they do it? An internal memo, leaked to the *Gazette*, revealed that the pair have developed a ground-breaking technique called cutting-people-open-and-seeing-what's-inside.

"We've discovered many important things using this method," said Erasistratus. "We've investigated the nervous system, for instance, and we've found the difference between sensory and motor nerves. Also, we're pretty sure that blood circulates around the body."

Alexandria is proud of the two docs – and not just because of their medical discoveries. Thanks to H. & E. the crime rate is plummeting. Why? Because the knife-wielding docs only work on the bodies of criminals. And some of those criminals are STILL ALIVE!

ACHILLES:
HIT OR MYTH?

NOT A BLISTER SAY EXPERTS

The autopsy is through! Mythical hero Achilles died because he was hit in the heel by a poisoned arrow.

The coroner told us:

"It appears that when the deceased was an infant his mother, a goddess, dipped him in the River Styx. (That's in the underworld, mythology fans!) The treatment was supposed to keep him safe from all injuries. In this unfortunate case, however, the mother had held onto his heel and the magic waters did not reach that part. This was only discovered during the Trojan Wars when a cunning archer twanged a poisoned arrow into his foot."

STYLE

The *Gazette* guide to what the well-dressed man and woman are wearing in the Hellenistic Period

HIM

Stylish tunic: let it all hang down if you're a senior citizen. Otherwise keep it up for maximum WOW! Lads: those legs have to be in perfect trim!

Girdle: keeps the tunic neat. Also holds in stomach if you're getting a philosopher's paunch.

Cloak: long for oldies, short for sporty, fighting types.

Hair: short and snappy does it. You don't want to have that shaggy, Archaic Period look do you?

Beard: clean chins are in! No more dithering over what length to grow your beard. Shave that face NOW!

HER

Himation: the indispensable all-over item. Two rectangular pieces of cloth joined at the shoulders by buttons or brooches, will keep you nice and warm. Make it patterned for added style.

Hair: waves and curls are IN! Pile it up. Headbands are OK but no tiaras, nets or scarves. That's old stuff!

Wrap: as fine as you can bear it. And don't forget the gold ornaments! You're after the clinging, see-through, spangled look! Forget what your mother told you about heavy materials and drab dyes. That's the Classical Period!

Jewels: stack 'em high. Bracelets, necklaces, rings – lots of gold essential.

COLONIST IN CORNISH CONTROVERSY

— *320 BC* —

"I sailed around Britain – but nobody believes me!"

Wildcat explorer Pytheas of Marseilles has set the Mediterranean buzzing with an astounding story.

In his newly-released book he reveals how he sailed through the Straits of Gibraltar and circumnavigated Britain!

"What nonsense," said an Athenian admiral. "The mark of a true explorer is if he comes back with news of a fantastically profitable trade venture. If you ask me, this excitable fellow sailed into the Atlantic, hung around for a while, then came back and pretended he'd been somewhere new. If he discovered what he said he did, we want proof."

"It's true," insisted Pytheas. "I landed in Cornwall then I sailed

Pytheas approaches Britain. He told the *Gazette*, "Oracles say this land will become famous for appalling football hooligans, disgusting meat pies and world-class pop groups, whatever they are?!?"

around Britain for six days. What's more I saw an island which might well be Ireland. In fact, I went so far north that the nights were only two hours long. Using the principles of latitude and longitude – invented recently by my friend Dicearchus of Messenia – that places me at 65° north.

"And what does that admiral mean by suggesting I didn't find a source of trade? Cornwall has got tin coming out of its ears.

Within a few years it'll be supplying the entire ancient world or my name's not Pytheas."

While Greeks mull over Pytheas's controversial book, others are jubilant at its publication.

"We're very glad to have been discovered," said one Irish citizen. "We always thought we were here and we're delighted that an independent authority has finally recognized our existence."

YOUR POLIS

ORGANIZATION

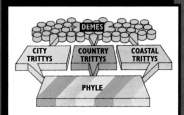

DEME

Let's start at the bottom. The deme is the basic unit of democratic administration. **This is where you fit in**. Your deme organizes local festivals, runs your affairs and raises money. Ideal starter for the ambitious politician!

TRITTY

Lots of demes make a tritty. There are 30 trittys, ten each from the city, the coast and the country. Trittys don't do that much. But they get a say in choosing who goes into the navy. Good if you want to play a trick on a landlubber friend.

PHYLE

Three trittys make a phyle. So if your mathematics isn't too shaky you'll realize that there are ten phyles altogether. **Phyles are important stuff**. They elect generals, pick teams for games and festivals, form the army, say who's going to be a council member and basically have lots of scope for pushing people around.

DITCH THAT DOLT!

Yes you can! Every year you get the chance to depose the politician you love to hate. Just scratch his name on a piece of pottery called an ostracon and put it in the voting box. If more than 6,000 of you vote against a candidate then he's ostracized. That means he has to leave the city for ten years. Hurrah!

EVERYTHING YOU ALWAYS WANTED TO KNOW ABOUT DEMOCRACY

But were too idle to ask

The Gazette's step-by-step guide to what we think you ought to be told about Athenian democracy.

Start at the top left, and let's have a look at how it all works...

IT'S A LOTTERY

Don't ever get the idea that Athens is TOTALLY democratic. You don't vote for the ruling council, it gets chosen by lot annually. There are 50 members from each phyle with a leader being selected at random every day. (FACT: one in three Athenians will run the city at some point in their lives no matter how incompetent they are.) The only elected officials in Athens are the generals.

THE ASSEMBLY

Clamber up to the top of a hill called the Pynx, where the Assembly debates council proposals every ten days. Membership is open to male citizens aged 18 or over. You get the chance to vote on all major decisions, tell officials off if they're doing something wrong, and have top-notch, shrink-in-your-sandals debates.

Just stick up your hand to vote yes or no. Or drop a token in the ballot box. But don't be late! There must be at least 6,000 citizens before a meeting can take place. If there aren't enough, the police will come and round you up!

EMERGENCY!!!

Are you a council member who wants an emergency debate? Then come to the Tholos. This building is where 50 duty council men spend the night ready for anything — anything that the other 450 council members don't mind missing, that is.

TALKING SHOP

Make new laws at the Bouleuterion. Here's where the 500 phyle council members spend the day yakking about how life could be improved. That means they make a lot of proposals and ask the Assembly if it'll approve them.

NEEDS YOU

BALLS IN LINE? WATER CLOCKS SYNCHRONIZED? GO, GO, GO!

Or: How to work the legal system

WHO'S ON THE JURY?

Every citizen is eligible for jury service. In fact, if you're over 30 you have to volunteer. But don't worry, the trials will never last more than a day. **Plus you get paid!** Not bad for a bit of sitting around. And, since there are 200 jurors to every trial, you're guaranteed to meet some of your mates. (They say there's so many jurors to stop them from being bribed or intimidated, but we know better, don't we party lovers!)

HOW DO THEY CHOOSE?

Everybody's name is put on a card which is then slotted into a machine called a kleroteria (right). Next to the

slots is a tube down which they pour little black or white balls. If there's a black ball next to your name then you get to be a juror. Simple!

WHERE'S THE TRIAL?

It's in the agora! This is where the fun starts. True, there's an official who tries to keep order, but nobody pays much attention to him. It's all up to you!

WHAT HAPPENS NEXT?

• First, a few prayers. Gabble, gabble, gabble.

• Then choose a judge from among yourselves and get on with the mayhem.

• A few witnesses will say something. (No interruptions allowed, so chat among yourselves).

• Next, the defendant will get up and make a speech. Shout him down! He's guilty! And even if he continues he only gets as long as the water clock allows him (see below). This is a device to give him a reasonable time to speak. He gets as long as it takes for the water to pour from a higher urn into a lower urn. But one of you watches the water clock, so if you're cunning you can make his speech snappy by secretly scooping water out of the top urn.

DELIVERING A VERDICT

Nothing could be easier. Each of you is given two bronze tokens. One's got a hole in the middle, the other hasn't. If you think he's guilty, drop the token with a hole into the box. If you think he's innocent drop the other one in. But keep your thumb over the middle so nobody knows how you've voted!

THEN WHAT?

Four of you count the votes. Once you've found him guilty you have to sentence him. Loadsa fun this! Choose from a wide range of penalties. For really serious violations exile is standard. But if he kicks up a fuss, tell him to drink poison. Amuse yourself by telling jay-walkers to "Drink a pint of..." (fake a coughing fit and watch them sweat!) "...rancid goat's milk!"

The information contained in this article has been selected by a show of hands among the *Gazette*'s employees in the full knowledge that the editor will fire them if they don't democratically choose what he wants.

SITS VAC

Experienced rowers required for war trireme. Sense of rhythm essential. Must enjoy teamwork. Own oar an advantage. (Ref. GG04)

Top oracle needs quick-witted assistant to invent pithy prophecies. Successful applicant will have good whispering voice and experience of standing motionless behind curtain for hours on end. (Ref.GG07)

Prestigious city Assembly is looking for competent speakers, able to sway crowds and with good knowledge of local issues. No ranting demagogues, please. (Ref. GG08)

Vacancies exist for sports groundsmen. We're not very fussy. So long as you can rake sand and roll clay that'll do. Ability to drag dead boxers out of ring a help. Contact Olympic Systems. (Ref.GG09)

Athens Odeon has part-time opportunity for rear half of stage centaur. (Ref.GG13)

Research assistant required by compilers of The Seven Wonders of the Ancient World. Should have good sense of awe and the ability to gape. Travel allowance. (Ref.GG30)

Halicarnassus Hoplites are always on the lookout for capable right-wingers. If you're willing to shield the man on your left while leaving yourself totally unprotected you're the soldier we want. Naive, innocent applicants welcome. (Ref.GG37)

KOJAK REAL ESTATE

We'll sell anything. No property too small. Central Greece preferred but colonies also catered for. Small commission. Nice staff. What more do you want?

Managing-Director Ronnie Kojak, says, "If you don't snap up these unbeatable offers you'll look sillier than a Spartan in silk stockings!"

NEW ON THE MARKET

SMALL THOLOS
This elegant little building would make ideal meeting place for city-state. Offers?

MANSION
Politician's luxury mansion. All facilities. Ostracized owner going abroad hence low price for quick sale. A snip.

STOA
Fully colonnaded, with 20 shops. Vacant Possession except for one stubborn old cobbler – but they promise he'll be gone come the next dark night.

ACROPOLIS
Pillaged by Persians so decoration isn't what it used to be (neither are the buildings, to be frank). Delightful prospects. Offers also sought on surrounding area of rubble which once housed 2,000.

FOUNDATIONS
Nice set of foundations in Corinth. Lord knows what happened to the rest of it. Perfect starter home.

FARM
Delightful farm outside Syracuse. Yours for a tasty consideration.
Plenty of sheep, goats cows, grain, grapes – all the usual. All this and a sea view too. How can you resist?!?

BARREL
Freehold barrel in fashionable area of Athens. Suit Cynic or similar philosopher. All fixtures and fittings. Bargain.

These properties are correctly described at time of going to press. So buy them before things change.

KOJAK REAL ESTATE,
22 The Cypresses, Athens. Sole Proprietor: R.Kojak

CLASSIFIED

SLAVES SLAVES SLAVES!!!
For all your household needs. Top quality specimens from the Mediterranean and beyond. Write for our super-silly price list. **Fantastic discounts on ugly old men.**

"The face that launched a thousand ships." Our lovely models of Princess Helen will look perfect on your sideboard. Only three drachmas apiece, or twelve drachmas for five. **Pericles Pots**

MARBLE
Ex-sack of Corinth. Columns, pediments, capitals etc. Daft prices. Free delivery in Peloponnese area. Otherwise two drachmas per item.
Roman Salvage and Reclamation Co.

FOR SALE
Three wrinkly olives and an old cheese. No time-wasters

Delos Deli is taking orders for the Feast of Dionysus. Hellespont mackerel, Thessaly puddings, Rhodes raisins plus all our festive usuals. Hurry while they're fresh.

PERSONAL

Helen. Come home. All is forgiven. Menelaus. *LH03*

Want the perfect partner? Try Carbon Dating. Our unique introduction service covers all Ancient Greece. We have literally thousands of customers on our books. Call now. *LH07*

Share my barrel! Bearded philosopher seeks slim stunner to explore life's mysteries. *LH08*

I'm just an ordinary guy. I want a wife who'll stay at home all day and not say anything. Is that <u>too much</u> to ask? *LH09*

Have you got good ears? Tall, handsome, orator-type is looking for a wife. I talk. You listen. *LH14*

Bunnykins. Your lonely tyrant misses you. *LH28*

I know you are out there. Lady oracle would like to meet Mr. Kreosote of 10 Lymph Lane, Athens. *LH47*

You are a beautiful young girl with a massive dowry. I am a has-been Olympic athlete who once came fifth in a race. Let's meet. *LH53*

Eureka! I reeka too. Successful goatherd, own flock, seeks like-smelling soulmate for love and affection. *LH58*

Light my fire! Colossos of Rhodes would like to meet petite Egyptian effigy of Isis. *LH63*

Me Ares, you Aphrodite. Can we make the earth move? *LH68*

Comic playwright needs someone to tickle his ribs. I am author of "Why did the chicken cross the road?" and other mega-gags. You are? Send full details and a pot with your portrait on. *LH70*

Personal crisis? Contact Oedipus Introductions. We'll turn it into a drama with five acts. *LH73*

Whimsical hoplite seeks cuddly camp follower for snug winter campaigns. *LH77*

Got what it takes to make a new dynasty? Ex-Lord Of All Asia would like to meet nice Persian girl for friendship and more. *LH83*

Theban potter, 32, non-smoker, requires wife from large family of wealthy, pot-collecting aristocrats. *LH92*

Let me stamp your ticket! Elderly librarian would like to renew an overdue spinster. Alexandria-based but can travel (not very far). *LH97*

Send your replies to the **Greek Gazette P.O. BOX 278**

SPORTS SPECIAL

GREECE IN GAMES DISPUTE

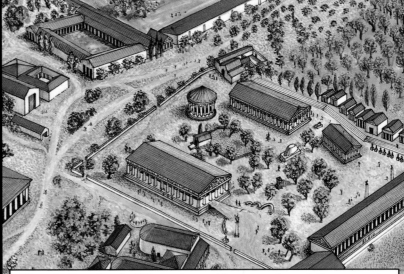

Olympia. Top-class facilities and a world-renowned reputation may not be enough to ensure the city keeps its monopoly on the Olympic Games.

NUDE ATHLETES CONFUSED

—— *580BC* ——

The Pan-Hellenic games are in turmoil. Ever since 776 BC sportsmen have been meeting in Olympia at four-year intervals to see who's the best. The Olympic Games have become such a part of Greek culture that everybody takes a month or two off fighting to give their men the chance to compete.

All over the Greek-speaking world, from the Black Sea to Italy, athletes have made the effort to be there.

But now there's competition. Three other cities are muscling in on the act. Delphi, Nemea and Corinth have set up rival games and officials are worried.

"This is a very serious business," said an Olympic spokesman. "The Olympic games have always set the standard. For example, ever since Orsippos's pants fell down in 720 BC and he lost the race, all athletes have competed in the buff. We've defined every single event, from long jump to discus. But now these others are trying to copy us. It's disgraceful."

CORNER

But the new games-hosts are holding their own.

"We resent the way Olympia is trying to corner the market," one Corinth senator told the *Gazette*. "We reckon that if they're going to hold games every four years that leaves three years free for us, Delphi and Nemea to stage our own events."

Each city has the backing of a top deity. Olympia and Nemea have Zeus, Delphi has Apollo and Corinth has Poseidon. So if any athlete asks "Who's going to hold it?" we say **"It's in the hands of the gods!"**

GO FOR GOLD IN THE CHICKEN RUN

THE COWARD'S GUIDE TO VICTORY

Want to win the games? Course you do. But how do you go about it if you've got a yellow streak the size of the Hellespont? Everybody knows the games are based on military skills and this makes it very difficult – to say the least – for confirmed milksops to win anything at all.

Don't abandon hope! The *Gazette* has listed the key sporting categories and has come up with some handy hints for the intrepidly-disadvantaged.

Wrestling – quite leisurely. A popular aristo-cratic pastime, so little danger of having your arm/leg ripped off. Still, can be quite upsetting for highly-strung types, especially if your opponent makes scary faces.

Pankration – called wrestling. BUT NOT WRESTLING AT ALL. BE WARNED. All-out, anything-goes, legalized assault. One step short of manslaughter. For psychopaths and hardened head-bangers only. Even the referee is dangerous. An event to be avoided at all costs.

Boxing – steer clear of this one, too. No gloves used. Instead you wrap your fists with hard leather straps and beat six kinds of stuffing out of each other. Ouch!

Running – no physical contact, which is a good start. If you already have experience of running away this could be the one for you. Those who usually desert with all their weapons etc. will enjoy the Sprint-in-breastplate, greaves and helmet.

Pentathlon – combines sprint, javelin, discus, long jump and wrestling. Not a bad choice. All you have to do is win three of them. Running and long jump will come easy. Of the others, javelin-throwing will best suit your battlefield experience – i.e. being as far away from the enemy as possible.

Chariot racing – perfect! Twelve hair-raising laps, 180° turns, multiple collisions, maximum casualties, dust, blood, shrieking crowds – and you don't have to do a thing! No sir! As the horse owner all you have to do is collect your prize and enjoy the adulation. (Whatever you do, don't make the mistake of entering as a charioteer.)

ATHLETES TO GO PROFESSIONAL?

"CELERY STINKS" SAYS WRESTLER

— 570 BC —

Winning doesn't count! It's money that matters! That's the opinion of many competitors in the Pan-Hellenic Games.

"These games can be really tough," said a disgruntled wrestler. "There's one wrestling event, for example, in which you're allowed to do anything except gouge each other's eyes out. If you do anything wrong, the ref. belts you with a stick. Then there's the chariot races. You wouldn't believe the carnage. I remember once at Delphi there was only one survivor out of a 41-chariot line-up.

"And what do you get? An olive wreath at Olympia, a laurel one at Delphi, a pine one at the Isthmian Games, and at Nemea they give you a **wreath of celery** – for goodness sakes!

"If you're a Spartan winner your 'prize' is to go in the front line at the next battle! Unbelievable!"

But sports chiefs were unimpressed. "All this glory has gone to their heads," said one.

"It's good for our city-state to come first," he continued. "It shows what a brave, warlike bunch we are and that makes everybody respect us. True, we don't pay sportsmen as such, but we do give them certain inducements to win – like rich, beautiful wives of their own choice, freedom from taxes, statues of themselves in a public place, free meals and so on. That sounds pretty good to me, so personally, I don't understand what they're whining about."

"Celery and olive wreaths are for suckers," says "Ramrod" Themistocles (right). "We want steaks and beer, and a fat bundle of cash."

KNICKERS OF FIRE

Hen-Games For Gals

— 480 BC —

At last women have the chance they've been waiting for – a Games of their own.

"That's right!" said a Spartan housewife.

"Women aren't allow-ed to compete in the men's games. We're not even allowed to watch. In fact, we can't get anywhere NEAR Olympia when the Games are on."

The new festival is called the Heraia, after the goddess Hera, and it will be held every four years at Olympia.

But established athletes are already pooh-poohing it. Thirty-times-champion wrestler "Mangler" Milon of Croton said, "I suppose it's something for them to do. But it doesn't compare with the real thing. There's only one track race with three classes for women of different ages! Well, it's hardly worth making the journey, is it? They'd be better off staying at home secluded from male company, which is how all right-thinking Greek women should behave."

THE ROMAN RECORD
HOT NEWS FROM THE SWIRLING MISTS OF TIME

ATTENTION
CITIZENS

Welcome to your empire-building, slave-driving, barbarian-bashing, lion-feeding, ROMAN RECORD. What we've got here is 1200 years of Roman history in 32 pages of blood-letting entertainment!!!

TROUBLE

We start with the NEWS, and the **founding of Rome** in 753BC by wolf-boy twins Romulus and Remus.

What next? From 510-31BC we report on the **Roman Republic** when we're ruled by consuls and senators, and start to take over the entire Mediterranean.

After that, from 31BC to 500AD, we look at the **Roman Empire** at the height of its powers, when we rule most of the known world, until we're knocked off our perch by a pick-and-mix assortment of barbarians.

It's not just battles and bloodshed. We've got 13 pages of FEATURES – all those daily-life kind of things that make us Romans so intriguing.

CURIOUS

We're a curious bunch. We're so civilized we've got central heating, roads, apartment buildings and fast food eateries. Our temples, aqueducts and amphitheatres are so well built that many of them will still be standing in the 21st century.

We conquered the entire Mediterranean, and most of western Europe. Yet we don't really care what race you are as long as you're a loyal citizen. Some of our Emperors even come from Africa or Spain.

But we've got a darker side too. Our idea of heaven is a packet of salted nuts, a front seat at the amphitheatre and a sunny afternoon of gladiator fights and executions for entertainment. (Find out about these on page 30, gore-fans!) And if you get on the wrong side of us, we'll raze your cities to the ground, sow salt into the earth to stop anything from growing, and kill YOU, **and your pets**, with chilling efficiency.

Happy reading!!!

Catullus the Elder

**Catullus the Elder
Editor,
The Roman Record**

THE ROMAN RECORD

was written by
Paul Dowswell

and designed by
Karen Tomlins

Historical consultant
Charles Freeman

With thanks to Fergus Fleming (Text), Laura Fearn (Design) and Guy Smith (Illustrations).

ROMAN RECORD
ON OTHER PAGES

NEWS

Double trouble with Romulus and Remus 753BC	98
Rome not built in a day 264BC	99
Punic War special 146BC	100-1
Colonies shock 133BC	102
Who's tops with Ops v. Pops? 59BC	103
Julius Caesar – a nation mourns 44BC	104
An Empire is born AD14	105
Mad, bad and dangerous to know? Who's Rome's maddest Mr. Mad? AD68	107
Trajan tops the lot AD117	108
Emperors cause concern 235AD	110
God-man Dio goes for glory AD305	111
Know your barbarian AD370	112
Rome ransacked AD410	113
Oh no, it's Odoacer! AD476	114
Remember us this way AD500	115

FEATURES

Rome – eternal city or fleshpot cesspool?	116-7
Are you a senator or a slave?	118
Foretelling the future	119
Property page	120
Women's page	121
God shop	122
Entertainment extra	123
The *Record* salutes the Greeks	124
Senula's slave spot	125
Sports special – Riot at Circus Maximus & Colosseum report	126-7
Adverts	128

DOUBLE TROUBLE!!
WOLF BOY KILLS TWIN THEN FOUNDS CITY

The twins pictured with their mother. Such adoptions almost always end in tears.

753BC

Here's the good news: Rome has been founded by Romulus. And here's the bad news: he's killed his twin brother Remus in an argument over where the city should be.

The troublesome twosome have been in the papers ever since it was sensationally revealed that they had been brought up by a wolf. Welfare workers are concerned that they may not have a stable enough background to found a major capital. Recent events have only increased their doubts.

SPOT

Romulus spoke to our reporter. "What are you all moaning about? I've given you a world-class city, in a beautiful spot on seven hills by the River Tiber. It's far enough upstream to be safe from pirates, and it's bang on all the major trade routes so it's going to become phenomenally wealthy. What else do you want me to do? Build it in a day?"

SQUEEZE

When pressed about the slaying, he replied: "This town wasn't big enough for the two of us. Anyway, I was fed up being a twin, all those people going 'Are you you, or your brother?' and 'when you were

naughty at school did the other one get the blame?' Well this is certainly one murder I won't be able to blame on Remus!"

The twins are well known local celebrities. Sons of Rhea Silvia, a vestal virgin, and Mars, the god of war, they were adopted by the wolf after a wicked uncle threw them in the Tiber.

RARE

Attempts by the *Record* to trace the twins' wolf mother have not been successful. However we did speak to city social service chiefs who issued this statement. "The twins' mother is believed to be living in a forest just south of the city, and does not wish to speak to the

press. However, we would like to take this opportunity to point out that animal/human adoption is not encouraged. Experience shows that most adopters eat the children in their care rather than suckle them. Romulus and Remus were an exceptionally rare success."

TARQ'S A GONER

KING THROWN OUT AS CONSULS TAKE CONTROL

509BC

It's ALL CHANGE in today's hurly-burly modern Rome,

Blazing saddles! A couple of consuls lead the way.

as citizens say GOOD RIDDANCE to kings and A BIG HELLO to consuls.

KING SIZE

Ever since wolf-boy Romulus declared himself king, Rome has been run by a bunch of snooty royals. This hasn't gone down well with your man in the street, especially as some of those kings haven't even been Roman

– they've been Etruscan! So who are they? They're the bunch who've ruled most of Italy for the last three centuries, that's who. True, we've learned a lot from them. We've taken up their alphabet, copied their drainage systems and started wearing their funny toga outfits. In fact, thanks to them we've established ourselves as the Numero Uno city in Italy.

BOOT

But now we've had enough. Current king Tarquin the Proud, also an Etruscan, has been such a twerp that top citizens launched a *Boot-out Tarq* campaign and **EXPELLED** him.

Now instead of a king this is what we've got:
• **Two consuls.** The top men in government.

They're elected every year for one year only, to lead the senate, command the army, and keep an eye on each other.
• **Senators.** A group of 100 or so people selected from Rome's poshest families. They've got the job for life. Senators meet together in the **senate**. Top government jobs such as judges, tax collectors and financial controllers are all filled by ambitious citizens, but they have to be elected to these posts. All citizens are allowed to vote, and competition is FIERCE! **The Record says: A Roman "nose" best. If we want to be a Republic, that's what we'll be. Consuls and senators will do us very nicely for at least the next 400 years!**

OUFF! BLAT! POW! OUCH!

PLEB REVOLT SPARKS CHANGE AT TOP

PATRICIANS V PLEBEIANS

366BC

Class warfare has erupted in Rome. In the blue corner – *the Patricians*, the heavyweight people who run everything. In the red corner – *the Plebeians*, flyweight ordinary folk. SECONDS AWAY!

ROUND ONE
509BC
Ding, ding!

Patricians fill the Senate and govern Rome. It's almost impossible for anyone else to get into politics. THUNK!

ROUND TWO
494BC
Ding, ding!

Plebeians hold violent political demonstrations and strikes. They're protesting against such bottom-of-the-heap ailments as starvation, debts and no land to farm. They also demand more of a say in how Rome is ruled. When this is refused, Plebeians withdraw from the city to set up their own **Popular Assembly**, and elect representatives called **Tribunes** to look after their interests. BOP!

ROUND THREE
450BC
Ding, ding!

Plebeians insist that a full list of laws be written down by the Senate. These are published as the so-called **Twelve Tables**. This stops senators interpreting the law as they please, to suit themselves. WALLOP!

ROUND FOUR
449BC
Ding, ding!

Patricians give the Pleb Assembly the power to stop any law passed by the Senate. SMASH!

ROUND FIVE
367BC
Ding, ding!

Plebs win the right to stand for official government positions, and the first plebeian consul is elected. BLATT!

ROUND SIX
287BC
Ding, ding!

The Popular Assembly is allowed to pass laws, as well as block laws passed by the Senate. OOUFF!

KNOCKOUT!

Political correspondent Servius Sleazus writes: What a match! The Patricians were up against the ropes and they just couldn't bounce back.

The result throws the old system out of the window. The Patricians have learned that it's easier to give the Plebs a say in government than waste energy trying to batter them down. From now on, the best men can rise to the top no matter where they come from.

ROME NOT BUILT IN A DAY – IT'S OFFICIAL

264BC

What a scorcher! The past 200 years have been red-hot as we've sizzled our way to success and taken over THE WHOLE OF ITALY.

Mind you, it's not been easy. First we had to show the locals who was who. Then we had to trample all over the Etruscans and their central-Italian allies the Samnites. And what with seeing off a few Celts (*Surely "paying them off to go away before they utterly destroy you?" – History Ed.*) then crushing Greek colonists and some other raga-muffins in southern Italy, we've had our work cut out.

So why are we the best? Two reasons...

• **We're the dirtiest fighters**. Our army is the most disciplined, largest, and the most

Here we are, spreading like ivy! (We're red, our allies are green.)

unpleasantly ferocious in the world. When we ransack a city, we even cut the DOGS into pieces, never mind the population.

• **We're generous**. After we've conquered anyone, we offer them an alliance. They supply us with soldiers, in exchange for our protection and the fruits of any further conquest. Not a bad deal!

Now that we've defeated our rivals in Italy, you'd think we'd feel like a rest. Not a bit. The *Record* says **LOOK OUT, THE ROMANS ARE COMING!!!**

ROME MAULS

CITY RAVAGED AS TOP-DOG GRUDGE MATCH GRINDS TO GRISLY HALT

146 BC

The Punic* Wars are finally over. At long last Rome has beaten chief Mediterranean rival Carthage. Top general Scipio Aemilianus has made the following announcement: "During hostilities in the Third Punic War, Carthage has been destroyed. This means that WE ARE NOW TOP DOGS AROUND HERE AND ANYONE WHO DISAGREES IS IN BIG TROUBLE.

"To show that we mean business we've burned Carthage to the ground, slaughtered most of the population, and sold the remaining 50,000 still alive into slavery.

"Even as I speak soothsayers are wandering among the ruins, howling and muttering curses to prevent the city rising from the ashes. And just to make sure, we're tilling the

Carthage gets toasted.

rubble into the ground and sowing the furrows with salt. In fact we're doing such a thoroughly horrible job, even I, supreme destroyer of Rome's greatest enemy, feel just a little guilty about it."

END

Scipio's statement ends a 120 year, three-round struggle between Rome and Carthage. To mark the occasion we've gathered together a collection of cuttings from our archives so you can relive those glory, gory days of the FIRST AND SECOND PUNIC WARS once more. Happy reminiscing, readers!

* Punicus is our word for Carthaginian, Latin fans.

**Next week: Scipio – "I did it my way"
First hand accounts from the front.**

FIRST PUNIC WAR 264-241BC

MESSANA MAMERTINES SPARK CLASH WITH CARTHAGE

264BC

The Mamertines – a bunch of Italian bully-boy mercenaries – have seized the Greek settlement of Messana in Sicily. AND THEY'RE NOT GOING TO GIVE IT BACK.

The Greeks have appealed to their pals in Carthage to help them. The Mamertines in turn, have asked Rome to support them. **Add it all up and you've got the start of the First Punic War!**

THAT'S RICH

So who are the Carthaginians? The *Record*'s foreign correspondent Travellus Chequio explains: "Carthage is this very rich city in North Africa. It's been there for 600 years, has a massive navy, and is at the heart of a thriving empire which goes all along the North African coast, and includes parts of Sicily, Sardinia, Corsica, and the tip of Spain. Stop falling asleep at the back there!!"

COPYCAT CLAIM LEAVES ROMANS UNRUFFLED

256BC

Rome has made a shock breakthrough in the First Punic War with a series of stunning naval victories. After eight years of deadlock where we were better at fighting on land, but the Carthaginians ruled the sea, military bosses in Rome hit on the bright idea of building some ships.

"We didn't have a navy," one sailor told us, "in fact we didn't even know how to build a warship.

Luckily, the Carthaginians stranded one of theirs on a beach, so we found out how it was made, then built 100 identical copies in 60 days, and added a new feature of our own. It's called a *corvus* and it's a big spiked gangway which you drop onto the enemy ship. Then your soldiers can pour aboard and thrash the crew. Works a treat!

"Our navy has remained completely unruffled by sourpuss Carthaginian taunts of "Copycat! Copycat!", and the stage is now set for a knockout blow to Carthage."

Our boys in action.

ROUND-ONE TO ROME AS CARTS LICK WOUNDS

241BC

The curtain's come down on the first Punic War and it's splints and bandages all round.

Our expected massacre of Carthage turned into a series of thousands-feared-dead defeats, in which our brand new navy was wiped out.

REELING

But the Carts took a battering too. We built a new navy which soon sank theirs. And Roman troops have captured Sicily.

Analysts predict a return bout when both sides have stopped reeling.

PUNIC WAR SPECIAL • PUNIC WAR SPECIAL

CARTHAGE

SECOND PUNIC WAR 218-201BC

RECORD COMMENT

WATCH OUT WORLD!

Those Punic Wars! Dontcha hate 'em? All we wanted to do was capture some land outside Italy and look what happened – the longest, nastiest, bloodiest battles in history so far.

But we say they were worth every last warship and Roman soldier.

Why? Well first of all because we won, dummy. (Honestly, some days I despair.) And we didn't just win. We won with style and a considerable amount of pluck and gusto.

RICHES TO RUBBLE

The Carthaginians may have been bigger, stronger and better equipped. But we taught ourselves how to build ships, and we learned a lesson from every battle we fought whether it was on land or sea, victory or defeat.

Result: Carthage is now a heap of rubble and we're on the road to creating a world-class empire.

Our success in the Punic Wars has taught us a thing or two. We've realized that:

1) The more we fight, the more territory we capture and the richer we become.
2) A successful war makes a successful politician.
3) Every politician now wants to wage war.

The Record's verdict is – WATCH OUT WORLD! WE'RE ON A ROLL. And if you live in Greece or Pergamum you'd better get your running shoes on because YOU'RE NEXT!

ELEPHANT MAN IN MOUNTAIN BREAK OUT

218BC

Carthage is on the warpath and tough-guy Hannibal is at the helm! Since their defeat in the First Punic War, the Carts have taken over most of gold-and-silver-rich Spain. Now, following a rumpus with Rome over their occupation of **even more of it**, they're all set for a **full-scale ding-dong battle.**

Hannibal is reported to have sworn an oath of vengeance on the Romans. If he keeps

Jumbo trouble for Rome

going at this rate, we're all mincemeat. So far he's...

• Gathered together an army of hardened mercenaries from Spain and Africa.
• Obtained three dozen war elephants. Each one is equipped with **four huge stomping feet and two razor sharp tusks.**
• Taken the whole lot

of them and crossed over the mighty Alps. Inhospitable, craggy, snow-bound, ferocious – and that's just the savage tribes that are witless enough to live there, never mind the terrain itself.

Now he's in the Po valley in northern Italy – mere days away from Rome, and **Round Two of the Punic Wars is about to commence**. Please fasten your seat belts, spit out that chewing gum, and HOLD ON TIGHT!

"Cunc" does a bunk

217BC

Rome's military dictator, Quintus Fabius Maximus – (known as *Cunctator,* the delayer) has **again** refused to let our boys fight the Carthaginians. Quintus told the *Record*: "Hannibal is a military genius, and he'd love to take us on. But he's decided Rome's too well defended to attack directly, so he's trying to cut us off from the rest of the country.

"My policy is to let him flounder around Italy. History will prove me right, you'll see."

UN-PLEASANT UN-EDIFYING UN-CANNAE

216BC

Hot-head Romans have dismissed *Cunctator* Quint from his dictator job and ordered our legions to attack Hannibal. 86,000 soldiers, the largest army ever assembled in Roman history, met the Carthaginians at Cannae in the south of Italy. The result – **THE WORST DEFEAT EVER IN THE HISTORY OF OUR ROMAN CIVILIZATION.**

SO-AND-SO

"That Hannibal's a clever so-and-so," says Barracksus Brawlus, the *Record*'s military correspondent. "He's familiar with our tactics and knew we'd launch an all-out attack at his weakest point – the middle of his ranks of soldiers.

"So he put his best cavalry on his left and right wings, and when we did attack him in the middle he just encircled us. Our troops were so tightly packed in they didn't even have space to swing their swords. We've had 50,000 men killed and 10,000 taken prisoner. It's all a little upsetting."

Zama-wamma! Scipio wallops Carts

204BC

News is reaching the *Record* of a major Roman victory in Northern Africa.

Following our crushing defeat at Cannae, the army bosses realized that *Cunctator* Quint was correct, and let Hannibal flounder around in Italy for another thirteen years.

Meanwhile hot-shot Roman general Publius Cornelius Scipio invaded Carthaginian territory in Spain. Then he attacked North Africa.

Carthaginian army chiefs, correctly fearing for their safety, called back Hannibal to defend their city. Scipio clashed with Hannibal at the battle of Zama and beat him fair and square.

Peace negotiations are currently taking place, and Rome is expected to demand a **vast sum of money** (around 10,000 talents) and **no small amount of territory** (at least Spain) as compensation.

COLONIES ARE GIVING US INDIGESTION

133BC

Burrrp! That's the state of Rome today. It's stuffed full of bloated citizens who've gobbled up too much territory.

Since the Punic Wars we've set up colonies all over the place – Carthage, Greece and Pergamum, to name just a few.

But some people are claiming that our new colonies are actually a BAD THING – especially if you're a peasant farmer.

This is what they're saying...

RUIN

• Peasant farmers, who made up most of the army, have spent so much of their time fighting, their farms are *overgrown and ruined*.

• Rich senators and businessmen have made *masses of money* from our conquests. They're spending it on buying up LAND from the poorer farmers, and creating huge farms worked by slaves brought in from conquered territories. Some politicians are even *swiping* land to give to their own soldiers as a reward for loyal service.

• The poorer farmers who have kept going, are being *forced out of business* by the big farms who can sell goods cheaper, and also by cheap food coming in from our new colonies.

FLOCK

• The poor farmers are flocking to the big cities – especially Rome – to look for work. But there are few jobs in the cities, because there are so many slaves to do them.

Our political correspondent Servius Sleazus II writes: This all adds up to a **really big problem**. These colonies have made a lot of money for a few rich people, and the rest of us are getting poorer. With Egypt to the south and Gaul to the north just **ripe** for conquest I predict **more** land-grabbing Empire building, and a **great deal of trouble and strife here in Rome.**

No future? Some poor people hanging around in Rome, yesterday.

A big farm, yesterday. Social unrest not pictured.

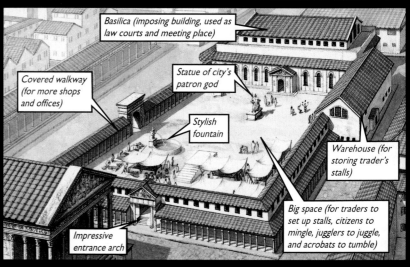

WHO'S TOPS WITH
OPS V. POPS?
OPTIMATES AND POPULARES CLASH

YOUR 10 POINT COUNTDOWN TO THE COLLAPSE OF THE REPUBLIC

59BC

Your *Record* is always right! We predicted stormy weather way back in 133BC and we were absolutely <u>on the button</u>! The richer and more successful we get, the more we're tearing ourselves apart. Now it looks like the Republic is about to collapse, and we're in for centuries of military dictatorship. The *Record* Countdown starts here....

10 In 133BC tribune Tiberius Gracchus proposes that some land owned by the VERY WEALTHY should be given to the VERY POOR. This ridiculous suggestion results in him and 300 of his supporters being **clubbed to death** by a mob led by land-owning senators.

9 In 123BC Gracchus's brother Gaius, also a tribune, initiates more land reforms. He and 3,000 of his supporters are **SEIZED AND KILLED**. The murder of the two brothers marks the end of political disagreements being settled by a nice chat, and the beginning of even more violence.

8 By 120BC two factions have emerged:
The Optimates – they say: We're all right Jack. Keep things as they are, and beat anyone who steps out of line with a big stick.
The Populares – they say: let's make things pleasanter for the poor by giving them more land to farm, and hand out grain to the starving.
After the slaying of the Gracchus brothers the *Optimates* have the upper hand.

7 107BC. The pendulum swings. Military campaigns led by *Optimates* go badly. Backlash results in election to consul of top *Popularis* General Marius. He defeats a bunch of foreigners and becomes even more popular.
However, he gets himself re-elected **six times in a row**, in direct defiance of Roman convention that consuls serve for one year only. Marius dominates Roman politics in a way **one man is not supposed to**.

6 88BC. Marius squabbles with Sulla – a consul, *Optimate*, and rising star. Sulla, with his own army in tow, marches on Rome to confront Marius. **Clear message to all *Record* Readers – If you thought an army was there to defend the state, YOU'RE COMPLETELY OUT OF DATE!!**

5 Marius flees and Sulla hops over to Asia to do some successful smiting and laying waste of King Mithradates of Pontus.
Rome collapses into rioting, assassinations, and all sorts of anarchy. Marius returns to restore order, kills any Sulla supporters he can find, and declares himself consul.

4 83BC. Marius dies of old age. Top *Optimate* Sulla returns to Rome and executes 6,000 *Populares* supporters of Marius. He is **declared dictator for as long as he wants the job.** (Previously, dictators only held office for six months during a dire emergency.) However, Sulla gets bored after four years, and retires to the country to write awful poetry.

3 70BC. Top soldier Pompey the Great takes a leaf out of Sulla's book, and turns **military success** abroad into **political popularity** at home. He is elected consul. Joining him at the top of the greasy political pole is fantastically wealthy land-owner Marcus Crassus.

2 61BC. Their pal Julius Caesar also becomes a **big noise** in Rome. Military genius, charismatic rabble rouser and top class brain, Caesar is blindingly brilliant, and almost too good to be true.

1 59BC. Cheesed off by the Senate's refusal to let them have their own way on everything they want, Pompey, Crassus and Caesar form the **First Triumvirate**, and arrange for Caesar to be elected consul. Roman politics reaches the stage where a few individuals are more powerful than the senate itself.

WARNING WARNING!!! BEEEP!!! BEEEEP!!! BRRRRRRRR RRINNGGG!!!

These men are about to trigger events which will topple 400 years worth of Roman Republic and bring about 500 years of military dictatorship. STAND CLEAR!!!!

JULIUS CAESAR
A NATION MOURNS

KNIFE-FIGHT WIPEOUT ENDS BRILLIANT CAREER

44BC

Julius Caesar is dead – fatally stabbed by a gaggle of senators. His murder brings to an end the career of Rome's greatest soldier. He was 55.

Caesar was born into a posh patrician family in 100BC and went to the best schools in Rome and Rhodes. Always ambitious, he soon gained a reputation as a brilliant speaker, and rose quickly to the top in politics, siding with the *Populares*.

RAMPAGE

Palling up with fellow fat cats Pompey and Crassus, he took the job of consul in 59BC. His year as top man in Rome was followed by a nine year rampage through Gaul (that's France to our younger readers), which he added to the Empire. During his campaign, Caesar's troops blitzed a record-breaking, rampart-storming 800 towns! He also invaded Britain a couple of times, although he didn't stay.

OO-ER

But back in Rome his two allies Crassus and Pompey were having mixed fortunes. In 53BC

Crassus went off to Asia to fight the Parthians. They completely wiped the floor with his army. AND his severed head was gleefully tossed at the feet of the Parthian king. (How embarrassing!)

Pompey had done better. Envious of Caesar's success he plotted with the senate (who were mostly *Optimates*) to bring Julius down a peg. In 52BC the senate declared Pompey sole consul and ordered Caesar to give up his army and come back to Rome.

Caesar sensed that returning home might well involve having **his** head tossed at *Pompey*'s feet. He came back to Rome, but sensibly took his army with him. So began a CIVIL WAR.

MURDER!

Caesar overran Italy, wiped out seven of Pompey's legions, and then chased him to Greece where he pulverized Pompey's army at Pharsalus. Pompey fled to Egypt, which was unwise. He was murdered the moment he stepped ashore, on the orders of a King anxious to keep on the right side of Caesar.

There followed a

stopover in Egypt, where Caesar was presented with Pompey's embalmed head. He also found time to woo top local, Cleopatra, the dishiest queen in ancient history.

He returned to Rome in 46BC, and declared himself dictator for 10 years. Sensing they were thoroughly beaten, the senators nodded meekly.

PURPLE

Earlier **this year** he made himself dictator for life. He kept himself busy, giving land to 80,000 soldiers, reducing debts, improving the government, and commissioning some fine new buildings.

But many senators fear-

Remembered chiefly by the salad that was named after him, Caesar was the greatest man of his era.

ed that power was going to his head. He rarely consulted the Senate, who had run Rome for the past 500 years. Senators thought he was acting like one of those kings they'd ousted in 510BC. He even appeared in public in a gilded chair, wearing a purple toga.

Fearing he was actually going to declare himself king, 60 senators attacked him during a political meeting, and stabbed him

23 times. (A strike rate of only slightly more than one senator in three – not very impressive.)

But the murder has not been greeted with much enthusiasm. Senators expecting to be applauded for their actions were greeted with stunned silence, and have fled to the hills.

The *Record* says: Watch this space for more edge-of-seat political high jinks!!!

7 THINGS YOU NEVER KNEW ABOUT CAESAR

★ The month of July is named after him.

★ The German and Russian words for king – Kaiser and Czar – are based on his name.

★ Caesar first met Cleopatra when she smuggled herself into his palace, wrapped in a carpet. Their red-hot romance held up the

civil war for seven months!

★ Shortly afterward she had a son called Caesarion.

★ Caesar introduced a new 365-day calendar, which (give or take the odd tweak and extra day) is still in use today.

★ His daughter Julia

was married to ally and then enemy Pompey. She died in childbirth shortly before the two men fell out.

★ He was elected chief of the Roman priesthood aged just 37 – an amazing feat, as the job always went to someone who was considerably wrinklier, and sage-like.

AN EMPIRE IS BORN!!

HOW SON OF CAESAR SEIZED CONTROL

Octavian, a.k.a Augustus, looking revered.

AD14

Welcome to the hottest series in history: the birth of the Roman Empire! After Caesar's murder there've been more twists and turns than a soap opera. So, for those of you who haven't been paying attention every week, HERE IS WHAT'S BEEN GOING ON...

CAST

MARK ANTONY

Caesar's dashing, handsome pal. Twinkle-eyed M.A. (as he's known to his friends) is a ladies' man from the top of his tousled black locks to the bottom of his dusty marching boots.

LEPIDUS

Caesar's second in command, and a dreary nonentity. Almost certain to be written out before we're halfway through.

OCTAVIAN

Caesar's steely 18 year-old nephew. He may be a callow student, but he's sharp as a razor!

CLEOPATRA

Queen of Egypt, femme fatale, and a real minx, by all accounts.

A cast of thousands of assorted legionaries, slaves, senators, dancing girls, armies, navies, flunkeys and mobs with burning torches.

EPISODE ONE

Hearing his Uncle Caesar has declared him son and heir in his will, teenager Octavian hurries home from Athens University in Greece, to claim his inheritance. He learns that Mark Antony and Lepidus are after his job.

EPISODE TWO

Octavian leads an army against Mark Antony. He beats him, and then marches to Rome to demand a consulship – and all before he's 20. There's precocious!

EPISODE THREE

Consul Octavian meets with Mark Antony and Lepidus, and the three agree to rule Rome together. They have 45 legions between them, which adds up to a lot of soldiers to reward for their loyalty. The three draw up a list of 2,300 powerful enemies, have them executed, and divide their land and wealth between the troops. Ratings go sky high – especially with the execution scenes. We like that sort of thing in Rome.

EPISODE FOUR

Ructions at the top. Octavian and M.A. squabble over who does what, and almost come to blows. Octavian takes over the west of the Empire. Antony takes the east. Lepidus becomes increasingly irrelevant. Ratings drop. Spectators switch off in droves.

EPISODE FIVE

Lepidus turns on Octavian, but his troops desert him. He's such a wimp, Octavian doesn't even kill him. Meanwhile Mark Antony, who's based in Turkey, summons sultry Queen Cleopatra of Egypt to see him. She floats up to his doorstep wearing a gold-plated barge, and 19 gallons of exotic perfume. M.A.'s tongue hits the floor, and they return to Egypt together. The pitter patter of three pairs of tiny feet follow on. Ratings soar.

EPISODE SIX

Deliriously in love, M.A. starts handing out Roman territory to Cleo and their children. Octavian goes BALLISTIC.

EPISODE SEVEN

No-expense-spared showdown in Greece, as Mark Antony and Octavian clash in a thousand-ship sea battle at Actium. M.A. and Cleo are beaten and flee to Egypt, pursued by Octavian. In a shock double suicide, M.A. stabs himself in the stomach (very nasty) and Cleo has an elegant encounter with a poisonous asp. (Such style – and so like her.) Ratings go through ceiling!

EPISODE EIGHT

Octavian takes over the entire Empire, is declared supreme ruler and renamed Augustus – "the revered one". He is Rome's first Emperor. He halves the size of the army, and pays off his old troops with the riches he's gained from his various conquests. He also works closely with the senate, orders the construction of many wonderful buildings in Rome, and officially adds Egypt to the Empire. He is a great success for 45 years, and Rome prospers. By the time he dies, everyone accepts that one strong man will run the Empire, and **the idea of a republic is dead.**

105

SPECIAL *IN FOCUS* REPORT ON "OUR BOYS" IN THE ARMY

TOUGHER
THAN THE REST

AD14

There's tough, there's tougher, then there's the Roman army. This week's IN FOCUS looks at what makes our boys in breastplates so world-beatingly great.

UNPOPULAR

Once, our army was a shambles. You could only join it if you owned property. You hardly ever got paid. And it was such an unpopular job that sometimes we had to enlist slaves just to keep the number up.

That's all changed. Now any citizen can join and our soldiers are full-time professionals who get a much better salary than the average worker.

What's more, a good war record carries major political clout if you're from the ruling class. Guess who's going to look most impressive in the Senate – Mr. Ploddus, dried-fish magnate from Ostia; or General Julius, heroic conqueror of Thrace and Segovia? No prize for the right answer!

POPULAR

So. The army's a Number One career choice for high and low alike. But can it deliver the goods? You bet! When it comes to battle capability we know no equal! We've got:
• State-of-the-art weaponry and training.
• Masses of soldiers (we're the biggest army in the world – stick that in your factfile, military buffs!)
• Streamlined organization.
• Fiendish discipline. Soldiers are flogged for the tiniest misdemeanours. As for mutiny or not fighting hard enough – well, any sign of that and we kill one in ten men as a warning to the others.

JOB

What are the retirement prospects? Plenty!! Having spent half your time learning how to build roads, towns and aqueducts, you'll never be at a loss for a job.

The *Record* says: ISN'T WARFARE WONDERFUL?

TOP GEAR

We invest in the best. The Roman army offers its soldiers the latest military technology.

❶ Scarf to stop breast-plate from scratching neck.

❷ Wool cloak to make your neck itchy instead.

❸ Lightweight chain mail vest – doesn't keep out the cold, but useful for keeping out arrows.

❹ Wood/leather shield, with inlayed iron bands, for in-battle, peace-of-mind, extra protection.

❻ Hat with plume. Chic or what??!!

❼ Your everyday, whistle-while-you-work big sword.

❽ "Stealth" boots with extra-thick hob nail soles. Just what you need for those lightning-strike 30km (20 mile) route marches.

❾ Metal-tipped javelin. These can pierce chain mail, but if you miss, the soft iron tip bends on contact with the ground, so the enemy can't use it against you. Clever, eh?

WHO'S WHO IN THE ROMAN ARMY?

LEGIONARY

The sharp end of the army. He joins for 20 years, as part of a legion of around 5000 soldiers. He gets to see most of the known world. If he fights well and behaves himself, when he retires the army gives him a plot of land, or a cash bonus of 12 years pay.

CENTURION

He's in charge of a century – that's 80 men to you civilians. There are 60 centuries in a legion.

The centurion gets his own tent , whereas a legionary has to share with eight others – phoooey – all those stinking feet!

SIGNIFIER

He carries the century's emblem into battle. He also runs a funeral club, to make sure soldiers get a proper burial if they're killed in battle. Now there's a comforting thought.

TRIBUNUS MILITUM

He's a junior officer, in charge of around 500 men. Look out for him – he's very ambitious.

LEGATUS

He's top man in the legion, and a friend of the Emperor. He won't know most of his troops from Adam, as there are 5,000 men under his command.

AQUILIFER

He carries the legion's standard – an eagle made of silver. If this is captured the legion is disbanded, and everyone is in **serious disgrace**.

AUXILIA

This bunch are non-citizens from our Empire. They get paid less, and can be a bit of a rabble. However, if they behave themselves they get to become Roman citizens when they leave the army after 20 years service.

MAD, BAD AND DANGEROUS TO KNOW!

WHO'S ROME'S MADDEST MR. MAD???

AD68

Emperors come and go. Sometimes we get lucky and sometimes we don't. Following the death of Augustus in AD14, we've had some of the most headbanging loony-tunes this side of a SPITTING COBRA. But who *is* the **maddest and, baddest**? READ ON...

	TIBERIUS AD14-37	CALIGULA AD37-41	CLAUDIUS AD41-54	NERO AD54-68
WHO WAS HE?	Stepson of Augustus. Top soldier and pretty good at ruling. Strengthened frontiers of Empire, and saved up lots of money.	Great-nephew of Tiberius. Never quite right, even as a child. Got a lot worse once he became Emperor. Extremely extravagant – mainly with the money Tiberius had saved.	Nephew of Tiberius. Became Emperor at 50, having been plucked from obscurity by Palace guard following assassination of Caligula. Disabled, frail and nervous, he was far brighter than he looked.	Stepson of Claudius. Started off well, but power went to his head. Built a lot, including one of Rome's finest public baths, and a luxurious palace called the Golden House.
MAD?	Nope, but not unreasonable fear of assassination and unpleasant skin disease made him very edgy – not to mention rather unforgiving.	Built temple to himself, and appeared in it dressed as a goddess. Married sister. When she died he declared weeks of public mourning, when no one was allowed to laugh. Tried to have his horse declared consul. Assembled massive army to invade Britain, but forgot to provide ships for them to cross channel. Had them gather seashells instead.	Not remotely. Devoted his rule to improving the civil service, and involving the provinces more directly in government. He also added territory to the Empire. (Particularly Britain, and more of Greece.)	Artistic temperament – he thought the Greeks were wonderful and imagined himself as a poet, musician, charioteer and actor. When he performed NO ONE was allowed to leave the theatre, not even women to give birth. When he was really on form he had himself crowned five times a day.
BAD?	Not so much bad as hard to deal with. Moved from Rome to the remote isle of Capri, where he felt safer and ruled by post. Hit and miss nature of Roman postal service caused loss of patience in the capital, and prompted assassination attempts.	Told his girlfriends while kissing them on the neck, "You'll lose this beautiful head whenever I decide." The silver-tongued charmer! Alas, many of Caligula's activities are unsuitable for a family newspaper.	Not really. Main failing – a weakness for scheming wives, especially his fourth, Agrippina. (See below)	Blamed Christians for a great fire in Rome (AD64) and persecuted them mercilessly. Some were even tarred, staked and torched to provide illumination in his private gardens.
DANGEROUS TO KNOW?	Plots to depose him dealt with in starkly brutal fashion, and led to reign of terror in Rome, which cast long shadow over his final years as Emperor.	Usual executions of rivals and plotters against him. Had a courtier executed for being too well-groomed. Insisted the victim's father come to the execution, and then invited him to dinner.	Only if you wanted to kill him. Despite being good at his job, he lacked support of Rome's ruling class. Various assassination attempts resulted in execution of 35 senators during his reign.	Murdered mother, wife, brother, stepbrother, and forced tutor Seneca (the greatest philosopher of his age) to commit suicide. Also did away with scores more real and imagined rivals.
THEN WHAT?	He died of old age.	Assassinated by his own soldiers, and not a moment too soon.	Agrippina poisoned his mushroom soup to make way for her son Nero.	Committed suicide, shortly before his own soldiers came along to bump him off.

IMPERIAL LATHER

Emperor comes clean on succession

AD98

Too much ruling can damage your health! That's the message from top lifestyle magazine *Which Emperor*.

According to their survey, being Emperor carries a major risk of assassnation.

Our political correspondent Servius Sleazus III explains: "Since Nero killed himself, it's been a real white knuckle ride. The year after his death there were four Emperors (the first three murdered each other). That left Vespasian who was in for a decade. He made a good job of it, built the Colosseum, and left his two sons in charge. The first one captured Jerusalem. The second was a royal pain, so he was assassinated.

WHAT A NERVA!

"Now we've got Nerva. He's been chosen by the Senate, and seems like a sensible fellow. He's come up with a wonderful idea. At the moment when the Emperor dies the job goes to his son, or nearest male relative. This seems to be leaving too much to chance. Just because you're good at the job doesn't mean your son or nephew will be.

"What Nerva's suggesting is that the Emperor picks a suitable successor from the best people available, and makes <u>him</u> his son and heir. He's picked a brilliant soldier called Trajan. We're all sure he's going to do a great job."

TRAJAN
TOPS THE LOT

Empire peaks at 100 million people

AD117

WE'RE BIGGER THAN EVER – AND THAT'S OFFICIAL! Emperor Trajan has captured large parts of the Middle East and Eastern Europe, and the Roman Empire is at its glowing, triumphant peak. You can walk from the frosty border of Britannia to the baking desert of Babylonia, and it's ALL OURS!!!

Mind you, a word of warning. Capturing a country isn't always sound business sense. We took over Britannia a hundred years ago, and it's proved to be a very poor investment. It costs far more in legionaries and the like to be there, than we ever get out of it. Still, never mind. Check out the map!! How do we do it? – See our special feature on page 109.

Some barbarians get the wrong side of our boys!

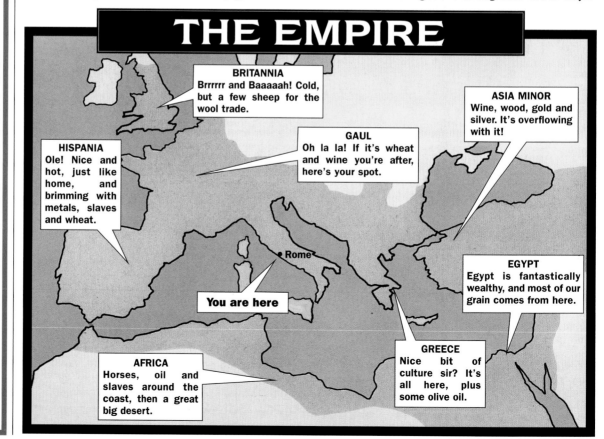

THE EMPIRE

BRITANNIA
Brrrrrr and Baaaaah! Cold, but a few sheep for the wool trade.

ASIA MINOR
Wine, wood, gold and silver. It's overflowing with it!

GAUL
Oh la la! If it's wheat and wine you're after, here's your spot.

HISPANIA
Ole! Nice and hot, just like home, and brimming with metals, slaves and wheat.

Rome

You are here

EGYPT
Egypt is fantastically wealthy, and most of our grain comes from here.

AFRICA
Horses, oil and slaves around the coast, then a great big desert.

GREECE
Nice bit of culture sir? It's all here, plus some olive oil.

SMASH AND GRAB

Here's how we do it

Attention all conquered territories! Once we've got the nasty business of defeating you out of the way, this is what your country could look like. Nice, isn't it!

YOUR NINE STEP GUIDE TO ACQUIRING A NEW COUNTRY

It all started with Sicily and Spain. Now look where we've ended up! But how <u>do</u> we go about adding to our Empire? Follow this nine-step guide, and you can't go wrong.

❶ Pick a country on our border with something in it worth stealing (Wheat, sheep, wine, silver, we're not fussy). If the tribes there are a threat to Rome, so much the better. If you conquer them, all the more glory for YOU!

❷ Invade it with our large, extremely disciplined and ferociously unpleasant army (see page 106).

❸ Pick on a few towns and raze them to the ground, killing everything that moves inside them. (This lets the locals know we really mean business.)

❹ Charge them an *indemnity* – a fine imposed on all newly conquered peoples to cover the expense of fighting them.

❺ Build some roads. These let us move troops around to crush rebellions very quickly. What's more, a messenger can travel 80km (50 miles) a day on a Roman road. Who needs to invent the telephone!

❻ Establish some towns. They don't really have these in western Europe (although the eastern side of the Empire is well acquainted with urban life). Towns are beacons in a dark mist of barbarity. Their fine civic buildings, baths, aqueducts and amphitheatres can't fail to impress the locals, who don't really stretch to anything more than a few mud huts and rickety rope bridges.

❼ Are there any local top dogs around who we didn't kill when we conquered the place? Get them to run the towns. They'll soon see it's in their interests to keep everyone sweet. Reward them with Roman citizenship if they're good.

❽ Respect the local religion and customs if they're not a threat to Rome. After all, we don't want any needless aggravation over something silly like wearing a braided beard, stone worship, or sacrificing a couple of maidens every spring.

❾ Make sure our frontiers are secure by building a big wall, or a ditch at the very least.

If we've played our cards right, we'll be able to get the locals to defend it, especially if we pay them well.

WALL MAN BACKS DOWN

HADRIAN CALLS A HALT

AD130

Frostius Breechus, your Edge of Empire correspondent, shivering to death on the outer limits of Britannia, sends this report from the River Tyne.

Here I stand neck-deep in cold, damp fog. It's not difficult to see why Emperor Hadrian has chosen this spot to mark the most northerly extent of the Roman Empire. It's a barren wasteland, and farther north are tribes of untameable barbarians, not to mention the odd dragon and packs of ferocious three-headed dogs with very big teeth.

RAMPART

The wall here combines good old-fashioned Roman grit and determination with the very latest in rampart technology. It's been built in just seven years by the Roman army, and stretches an uninterrupted 130km (80 miles) across the width of this country.

NAIL

It's a clear message to the barbarian Picts and Scots who live on the other side. It says "We're extremely well organized and efficient, and if you come over looking for trouble we'll nail your ears to the floor."

ENOUGH

With frontiers in Germany, along the Danube, and down in the east, Hadrian has decided that we've conquered about as much territory as we can hold on to. And that's good news for Rome, and good news for the Roman Empire.

Hadrian's very own out-on-the-edge wall. Not a popular army posting.

CALAMITY CLAIM

CAUSES CONCERN

IS FUTURE BLEAK???

AD235

We know we're the greatest civilization on Earth, after all WE'VE GOT A MASSIVE EMPIRE TO PROVE IT. But they say pride comes before a fall, and according to a soothsayer's report commissioned by the *Record*, THAT might well be the fall of the Roman Empire! Our team of top entrail dabblers say:

• We're becoming too complacent for our own good.

• We've gone from being tough guys to nerds who complain if our orgies aren't disgusting enough.

• The future looks greedy, brutal, corrupt and incompetent.

• That'll be 500 denarii, please.

HOPELESS

The Record blames the men at the top. Since AD180 we've been saddled with a succession of sometimes hopeless, fly-by-night Emperors, just when we needed **some good men for the job.** (Check out our **Who was who** guide to Rome's most recent rulers, right.)

But hard-line Senator Whackus Maximus disagrees with our forecast. He told the *Record*: "Any talk about the fall of the Empire is just drivel. Just wander around the dazzling metropolis of Rome, then wonder at the roads and aqueducts we've built from Britannia to Egypt, and you can see that. D'you know we can trade from Spain to Syria and they'll accept our Roman money? **We're as safe as houses!"**

Some concerned soothsayers. Politicians have dismissed their report as "drivel".

WHO WAS WHO?

EMPERORS WHO CAME AND WENT

AD180-235

Commodus AD180-192

Made peace with invading barbarians, killed vast numbers of political opponents (but only after they tried to kill him first). Thought he was mythical Roman superman Hercules. **Murdered** while having a nice relaxing soak in the bath.

Pertinax AD192

Not very interesting. **Murdered.**

Septimius Severus AD193-211

Introduced taxation of Roman citizens to help pay for vast cost of defending Empire. Came from Africa and spoke Latin with funny accent, which he never lost.

Had terrible temper, but this is not surprising, as he spent half of time on throne fighting off rivals. Had some success restoring peace and order to the Empire, and held on to his job for an admirably long time.

Reformed justice system to give poor a better deal. **Died** at York, in Britain, after successful but exhausting campaign against invading Picts from Scotland. Left Empire to two sons – Caracalla and Geta.

Caracalla AD211-217

Killed brother and (allegedly) 20,000 other rivals for throne. Raised army pay, bribed barbarians to stay away from borders, granted citizenship to all free males in Empire, but only so he could tax them. Idolized Greek supremo Alexander the Great, and planned massive conquest of East. **Murdered.**

Macrinus AD217-218

Murderer of Caracalla. **Deposed.**

Elagabalus AD218-222

Despotic, pimply youth, who was fanatically dedicated to the worship of some obscure Syrian sun-god. **Murdered.**

Severus Alexander AD222-235

More like it. Became Emperor at rather precocious age of 13, so his mother Julia ruled for him. She made sure the army behaved itself, and let some powerful senators look after the Empire.

Improved life for the lowly, with hand-outs for teachers and scholars, and landlords who repaired their properties.

However, he failed to deal with barbarian threat to Empire in north, so mother and son both **murdered.**

God-Man Dio Goes For Glory

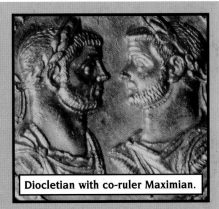
Diocletian with co-ruler Maximian.

AD305

What's that clacking sound? Is it castanets? Nope. That's our teeth rattling as Emperor Diocletian grabs the Empire by the scruff of the neck and shakes some life into it.

Strong Man Dio, formerly a peasant from Dalmatia, has launched a series of shock reforms in a last minute attempt to avert catastrophe. Here's what he's done so far...

DIO'S DOINGS

• He's clamped down on tax dodgers. Extra revenue gained pays for improving and enlarging the army, so we can defend our Empire better.
• He's claimed he's top god Jupiter's agent on Earth, which means that Dio's almost a god himself. Not only that, but he insists on being addressed as 'Your Majesty', wears snazzy purple and gold robes, and demands that everyone kiss the hem of his robe when they see him. ("It's not for me," he insists. "It's to bring back respect for the tarnished office of Emperor.")
• He's tried to tackle runaway inflation by freezing prices on everything from bread and salt to hare's fur underwear and fattened goldfinch snacks.
• He's introduced an annual budget for his government, so that provincial governors will know in advance how much tax to raise.
• He's mercilessly persecuting Christians. "What's

wrong with the old gods, that's what I say," he told the *Record*. "I like conformity and obedience, and these Christians are a bad influence."
AND MOST IMPORTANT OF ALL...
• He's split the Empire into two parts – East and West. He says it's too big, and two Emperors working together with two governments will make it easier to control. He's appointed fellow big wig Maximian to look after the West while he looks after the East.

TRUCK

Diocletian has been quick to defend his controversial reforms. "Desperate times demand desperate measures. When I came to power it was anarchy. Between 235 and 284 we had 18 Emperors in less than 50 years, money all but lost its value, and our economy fell into ruins. Instead of working the farms, peasants were fleeing to the cities, or turning bandit. The Empire was falling to pieces. I said to myself, 'there's life in the old dog yet,' and d'you know, **I was right.**"

IT'S CAPITAL!!

Constantinople is Empire's number one city

Constantine shows his pals a model of Constantinople.

AD330

Emperor Constantine has made an epic bid for immortality. He's already made a massive mark on the world by officially ending the Roman persecution of Christians, leaving the way open for Christianity to become the Empire's top religion. Now he's founded a new capital for the eastern part of the Empire, and named it after **himself**.

SEEDY

Constantine told the *Record*. "Rome's become a bit seedy lately. Besides, the eastern side of the Empire is a lot more stable and prosperous than the west, so it makes sense to run things from here. The old Greek city of Byzantium is well placed for trade, and is very well defended. **So we're launching a massive building project, and renaming it after me**.

HIPPO

"Architects have been summoned from all over the Empire to build prestigious city buildings, such as a hippodrome, forum and senate house. Statues and treasure from Rome, Athens and anywhere else that's got any, are also being transferred here.

"It's time to turn over a new leaf. Rome's washed out. It's pagan, and rooted in the past. Constantinople stands for everything that's fresh about the Empire. We're mainly Christian, most of us speak Greek, and we intend to be a beacon for the civilized world for a thousand years to come."

CRUMBLE

But critics say the foundation of the city will further hasten the decline of the Empire. By taking power and wealth from Rome, it leaves the western half of the crumbling Empire vulnerable to barbarian hordes massing on the borders. (See page 112 for the latest news on THEM.)

BARBARIANS

Your Record guide to all that's uncivilized and looking for a scrap

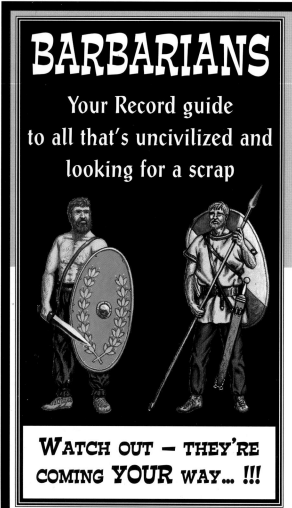

WATCH OUT – THEY'RE COMING YOUR WAY... !!!

I MAGINE THE SCENE. YOU'RE SITTING IN YOUR VILLA ENJOYING A LEISURELY BREAKFAST OF BAKED FLAMINGO TONGUES. SUDDENLY A HUGE HAIRY FELLOW WITH A FUNNY HELMET AND A BIG AXE POKES HIS HEAD THROUGH THE WINDOW AND BELLOWS SOMETHING OBSCENE. WHAT DO YOU DO, PAT HIM ON THE HEAD OR RUN LIKE MAD? READ OUR GUIDE AND FIND OUT!

GOTH

Habitat: *Europe, Western Russia*

Most prominent of all barbarians. Species can be found in various forms throughout Europe, with much individual variation. Natural enemy of Vandal and Hun. Big, beardy, long-haired types who like a fight and can drink beer for days without falling over. Generally recognizable by broad physique, round shield, short sword, and dog-like obedience to chief.

Distinctive feature:
Most of them have one of these.

OSTROGOTH

Habitat*: Western Russia.*

Type of Goth. Can walk naked through snow storms. Eats grass and roots. Despite hard-as-nails reputation, have recently been crushed by Huns.

Distinctive feature:
They like to wave these around.

VISIGOTH

Habitat: *Eastern Europe*

Yet another species of Goth. Semi-tame, but liable to turn nasty if over-taxed by greedy officials, and generally treated with contempt. Spitting, swearing types, and rather vulgar, so watch your step.

Distinctive feature:
Lots of them have reddish-blond hair.

GAUL

Habitat: *France and parts of Belgium*

This Celtic species can be fairly tame and cooperative, but is prone to occasional revolts. However, if treated with respect, a Gaul will repay you with loyalty and devotion.

Distinctive feature:
Nifty little chain-mail tunic.

SAXON

Habitat: *Coastal Northern Europe*

Voracious predator, eager to migrate to Gaul and Britannia. Skilled in piracy. Has worst table manners this side of frenzied Tyrannosaurus. Avoid if possible.

Distinctive feature:
Their heavy axes are a serious health hazard.

FRANK

Habitat: *Lower Rhine*

Leaner and swarthier than most other species. Has characteristic shaved back of head, with rest of hair gathered in fetching "top-knot". Natural enemy of Gauls. Quite dangerous when provoked. Usually fights on foot without helmet or other body protection. Prominent weapons – small throwing axe, javelin and short sword.

Distinctive feature:
Nice, bright striped wool tunic.

VANDAL

Habitat: *Hungary*

All too common these days. Nomadic species and fiercely predatory. Guaranteed to

HUN

Habitat: *Eurasian plains*

Smallest of all barbarians. Feared foes of Goths and Vandals, ferocious warrior nomads and frighteningly efficient archers. Other barbarians running away from this bunch are spilling into OUR TERRITORY and causing no end of problems.

Has prominent and sinister ritual scarring on face, and always fights on horse-back. Voted all time winners of annual *Gut-wrenchingly-terrifying-foe-we-would-least-like-to-fight* competition in *Roman Soldier Monthly*. Dour in appearance. Lives on diet of baked babies and tree bark gnawed straight from branch. Also reported to wear shrunken human heads as earrings, and smell worse than a beached whale.

If encountered, remain very still and hope they don't spot you. If contact unavoidable, do not attempt to engage in conversation, especially regarding relative merits of Greek or Roman poetry. Approach with extreme caution carrying long spear, and toss over some raw meat on end of a stick.

Distinctive feature:
Absolutely lethal with a bow and arrow.

smash up any form of public transportation, and carve name on park benches. Enemy of Visigoths, and dedicated to erasure of Roman culture.

Distinctive feature:
None: Look pretty much the same as the others.

BRITON

Habitat: *British Isles*

Usually harmless. Similar to Gaul, but habitat more inhospitable. Watch out for Picts and Scots branch of species in north of the Island.

Distinctive feature:
None worth mentioning.

SASSANID

Habitat: *Persia*

Treacherous, and thriving in east of Empire. Disappointingly civilized for barbarians. If encountered is more likely to discuss supremacy of Sassanid architecture over Roman, than flay you alive over snake pit. Caution: Still very dangerous and acquisitive.

Distinctive feature:
Great helmets! They obviously like a joke!

ROMAN RECORD DISCLAIMER

Some of these illustrations are based on very rare sightings, so we cannot guarantee their accuracy.

ROME RANSACKED BY RAMPAGING GOTHS

WAAAAAGH! THEY'RE HEEEERE!!

AD410

Never mind "The barbarians are at the gates" – the barbarians are INSIDE the Empire's most famous city, AND THEY'RE LOOTING ROME LIKE THERE'S NO TOMORROW!!!

Eyewitnesses say that anything that isn't nailed down or too heavy to lift is being loaded onto carts and horses and driven away. AND WHAT'S MORE, THERE'S NOTHING WE CAN DO ABOUT IT.

OH DEAR

It's been downhill all the way since Constantine died in AD337. The usual squabbles and civil wars occurred over his successor. Then we dithered about, wondering whether to be Pagans or Christians. While all this was going on, no one noticed the barbarians had really got themselves organized.

By the time they invaded the Empire in AD378 and beat one of our armies at Adrianople, it was too late to complain. We were too weak to kick them out, so we made treaties with them and got them to work on our farms and in our army.

BUNCH

But in AD402 a bunch of Goths led by Alaric INVADED Italy itself, and now they've even occupied Rome. Fortunately Emperor Honorius moved his Imperial court from Rome in AD402, and made Ravenna the capital of the Western half of the Empire. But Rome hasn't been knocked about like this since it was sacked by Gauls nearly 800 years ago, **so it's still a terrible blow.**

In the last year alone Spain has been invaded and overrun by Vandals, AND we've had to abandon Britain. Disease and famine are sweeping through the population. **The** *Record* **says:**
WE'RE HANGING ON BY OUR FINGER-NAILS...

Plenty of looting, but no fiddling. Rome burning, yesterday.

Exploding Brain Kills

Honeymoon Hun

BEDROOM CATASTROPHE FOR ATTILA THE KILLER

Attila, heading for a disappointing honeymoon.

AD453

Top Hun Attila "the Hun" kissed his bride Ildeco goodnight, then dropped dead! Blond, buxom Ildeco, a German princess, told the *Record*: "Instead of whispering sweet nothings in my ear he said "I've got a headache." Some headache that turned out to be! A blood vessel in his brain burst and it was over and out before you could say donner und blitzen!"

SMIRK

The news is sure to bring a smirk to the face of Roman soldiers everywhere. Newlywed Attila, formidable leader of Rome's most feared foes, has terrorized the Empire for 10 years.

Half-beast mongol horsemen, the Huns were Rome's one-time allies, and helped us keep other barbarians in order. But their successes against various assorted Alans, Visigoths, Ostrogoths and Burgundians **went to their heads**.

Attila decided that the smart money lay in attacking the Empire itself, rather than a rag-tag assortment of peripheral barbarians. The wily head Hun has:
- **Laid waste** the Balkans in AD443 and headed for Constantinople, only turning back when petrified city bosses gave him a golden handshake of 2,750kg (6,000lb) of gold.
- **Came back** to Constantinople in AD447 anyway, defeating a Roman army en route, and demanded another MASSIVE handout to go away.
- **Invaded** Gaul in AD451 with a mighty army of barbarian allies, and fought an enormous Roman army to a stalemate at the battle of Troyes.

OH NO!

IT'S ODOACER!!

"MY BARBARIAN SHAME" BY EMPEROR AUGUSTULUS

"Hi, I'm a Vandal, and I've come to loot and pillage the Roman Empire like there's no tomorrow. Have a nice day now, and mind how you go."

AD476

Emperor Romulus Augustulus has spoken for the first time about his deposition by barbarian chief Odoacer. Safe in exile in a snug provincial castle in Naples, he spoke exclusively to the *Record*'s political correspondent Servius Sleazus IV.

Servius. So what's happened to your job then?

Augustulus. From what they tell me, after we fought Attila to a stalemate in 451, there were the usual squabbles about who was going to be Emperor. Meanwhile, various barbarians took over our territory in Spain, Africa, and Gaul. Then this Goth fellow, Odoacer, comes along to Ravenna where I was having a turn at being Emperor, and tells me to pack my bags and head as far south as possible. Then he said he was going to be King of Italy. And bingo, that was that – the end of the Roman Empire – or at least the western half of it.

S. So how do you feel about the fact that you weren't executed? Odoacer obviously doesn't see you as much of a threat.

A. Well, in some ways it's quite an insult. I'm the last ruler in a line of nearly 500 years worth of Emperors, and you'd think he'd have had me strangled or something – just to mark the magnitude of the occasion. But between you and me, the sun is shining, there's a roast pig on the spit, a gallon of cooled wine in the cellar, and I'm quite glad to be alive really.

S. And do you have a message for the citizens of the Empire who now face a life of barbarian discomfort, the prospect of watching their running water tail off to a trickle, and their temples get choked with weeds?

A. I do. It's "That's all, folks. No refunds are available."

CONSTANTINOPLE
IS OH SO PRETTY

AD500

It's not all doom and gloom in the Roman Empire. We may be sitting in the ruins of a crumbling civilization here in Rome, but the eastern territories around Constantinople are still sitting pretty. If you're looking for that fast-fading Roman way of life, then get on the next boat out there!

In the next 50 years we'll become so prosperous we'll be able to build churches like this.

What have they got? A stable Roman-style government and army, Christian religion, and a fantastic chariot racing stadium at Constantinople (complete with all the usual modern conveniences), that's what!

HORDES

As the western half of the Empire has declined, so the east has grown richer. How's that?
• Far fewer hordes of barbarians invading them.
• They've had the good sense to talk their way into a settlement with their greatest enemy, the Persians.
• Far fewer Emperors, who usually stay in power a lot longer than ours have done in the west. And they usually rule well. Their current Emperor, Anastasius, is balancing his budgets and even cutting taxes.

PERCH

And what's more, their main city, Constantinople, is perched right on the crossroads of Europe and Asia. It's in a perfect spot for trade, and is all set to become powerful and immensely wealthy. Our business correspondent Lunchus Accountus says:
The West may have collapsed, but in the East they've got enough to keep them going for another thousand years.

REMEMBER US THIS WAY

WE SAY THERE'S MORE TO US ROMANS THAN LION FEEDING, EMPEROR KILLING AND SLAVERY.

With all this mayhem going on, and the world collapsing around our ears, it's about time we had something positive to say about ourselves. We were smart enough to get a lot of our ideas from the Greeks. (See our special report on page 124.) But what have we given the world? Read on...

LATIN for a start. For almost two thousand years, the language of science, law, medicine and diplomacy will be Latin, and anyone who wants to get along in the world will have to learn it.

Not only that but French, Spanish, Portuguese, Italian and Romanian will all become languages directly based on Latin. Even English will have at least 12,000 words that come from Latin.

CITIES. Most of western Europe had no cities before we came along. We founded such great cities as London, Paris, Lyon, Cologne, Milan and countless smaller towns and settlements. We didn't build New York, but it's streets are directly based on our grid system.

Our BUILDINGS. With their elegant arches, domes and concrete construction, people will still be copying our buildings in 1500 years' time. Famous generals like Napoleon, and Frederick the Great of Prussia, will build triumphal arches just like ours to celebrate great victories. Even United States President Thomas Jefferson will base his government buildings in Washington on ours. (Their government will even have senators and a senate!)

Our LEGAL SYSTEM. Six massive volumes of our statutes, decisions and commentaries will be incorporated into the laws of Church and Medieval courts in Europe, and become part of legal systems throughout the world.

THE GREEKS. People will know about Greek writing and art because we preserved and copied it. What we did will survive, where-as most of the original Greek versions won't.

And that's just a slice of what we've given to the world. Our ideas for government and empire, politics and philosophy, painting and sculptures, plays and poetry (some fellow called Shakespeare will take a lot of his plots from Roman stories, for example), will all be copied, and influence the way the world is run for thousands of years into the future.

EDITORIAL

WHY THE END IS NIGH

AD500

SO WHAT'S IT ALL ABOUT THEN, THIS FALL OF THE ROMAN EMPIRE?

It's not difficult to see how we rose from being a bolshie little city to rulers of Western Europe and the entire Mediterranean. The fact that a lot of our opponents were declining old empires or disorganized rabbles obviously helped. But we had a fair few fights on our hands too – especially with that Hannibal.

WELL

We did so well because we were the best. Having the most ruthless and determined army was a major advantage. But having the best roads, and the best planned towns and cities didn't go amiss. We also had a system of government that encouraged Empire building by rewarding successful generals with political power. AND we had the good sense to let the people we conquered become citizens of our Empire. Some even rose to become Emperor!

WATER

Why it all fell apart is a lot more complicated. There are several theories around, and none of them hold much water. Some say we lost our will to fight when we adopted kindly, merciful Christian values. This doesn't explain why the Eastern Empire – which was far more thoroughly Christian – continues to thrive. Others say we got too fat and flabby with our appalling amphitheatres and slaves and alley cat morals. But they were saying stuff like that in 200BC, and that was 700 years ago.

MARBLES

Another theory goes that many of our leaders got brain damage after drinking water that had too much lead in it. (This got into the supply from lead pipes used to transport water to our cities.) This doesn't stand up either. We use clay pipes wherever possible, and drink very little lead-piped water.

WONDER

So what is it that's caused the collapse of such a monumental Empire? The Record says the wonder is that we've lasted so long, not that we've finally collapsed.

With an Empire and culture stretching 16,000km (10,000 miles) from Britain to the Caspian Sea it was bound to be vulnerable to attack. We fought off invasions for 200 years. But when the cost of defending our frontiers from hoards of barbarians became too great, our Empire collapsed like a deck of cards.

ROME

THE OUT-OF-TOWNER'S GUIDE TO THE WORLD'S

No.1 CITY!

AD100

Okay. You've made a little money in Britannia or Gaul, and now you want to SPEND IT. Or maybe you're a poor carpenter from Ravenna who wants to make his fortune in the big city. Where better to go than ROME? Grander than Mount Olympus. More beautiful than Venus. More zing than one of Jupiter's thunderbolts. A glittering whirlpool of power, corruption, and crazy, crazy people – that's Rome. And what's more – all roads lead to it.

But be careful. Your wildest dreams could turn into your worst nightmares. When you visit Rome you're putting your head in the lion's mouth. It might just get bitten off!

ROME FACTS

We may have copied a lot of our architecture from the Greeks, but Rome makes Greek cities like Athens look like a provincial horse and cart station. Check out these Rome facts:

One MILLION Romans make this the biggest city in the world, and 400,000 of them are slaves! That means most of the other 600,000 of them get to sit on their fat behinds a lot, and bellow for more WINE and ENTERTAINMENT, especially when it's one of the city's 100 annual feast days.

Fortune tellers say there won't be a European city this big again until Nineteenth century London.

Nineteen stone aqueducts keep those thirsty, dirty Romans supplied with constant fresh water.

ETERNAL CITY OR FLESHPOT CESSPOOL???

THEATRE OF MARCELLUS

THE CIRCUS MAXIMUS

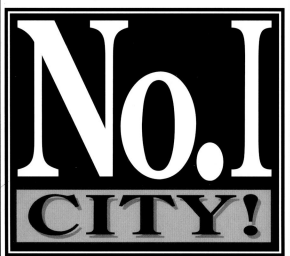

Parades. We like a parade. When one of our Emperors wins a big battle he marches through the city with his troops and captives and booty. The troops hurl insults at him (it's considered good luck) and everyone else cheers and throws flowers. Then the captives are strangled or sold as slaves, and everyone has a big feast.

LOOK AT THIS LOT!

Every Emperor wants to be remembered forever, and what better way than by ordering the construction of one of the most spectacular buildings in the world.
Temples, public baths, theatres, ornamental gardens, race tracks. Take your pick, we've got THE BEST.

THE CIRCUS MAXIMUS

Maximus thrills and spills at the chariot racetrack with the highest death rate in the city. Room for 200,000 inside.

THEATRE OF MARCELLUS

We like a little culture too, you know. It's not just chariot races and gladiators here.

BATHS OF TRAJAN

Just one of the city's 11 public baths. Lollop in the hot pool. Shiver in the

FORUM OF AUGUSTUS

Basilica. No, not a type of plant, but a public building used as a law court or government office. Plenty of these in Rome.

Statues, we got THOUSANDS of 'em! This one was built by madcap Emperor Nero, as a likeness of himself. When he was assassinated they lopped the head off, and replaced it with Apollo the sun god.

BATHS OF TRAJAN

THE COLOSSEUM

AQUEDUCT OF NERO

Arch. (See Parades). When an Emperor wins a battle he builds one of these to show how wonderful he is. Then he and his soldiers march under it.

Temple of the Divine Claudius. Rome has so many temples it's easy to get blasé about them. This one's quite nice though, with its gardens and everything.

TOP TIPS FOR TOURISTS

They say when in Rome do as the Romans do, so here's what you have to do to avoid standing out like the straw-chewing bumpkin you actually are...

WHEELS

Anything with wheels on is BANNED during the day. You can only bring your horse and cart into the city at night, and it's almost gridlock even then.

LITTER

If you can afford it, get yourself carried around in a litter, so you won't have to walk in the mud and sewage that coats the pavement. You can also look down on all the beggars, drunks, thieves and peddlers that will see you as EASY PREY if you're on their level.

WASTE

Try and avoid the narrowest streets. They're uncomfortably crowded AND people throw their waste out of windows. If you do get drenched by the contents of a chamber pot, just feel lucky it wasn't a brick or concrete beam. Plenty of them fall off the tops of buildings every day.

FERRETS

If you must go out at night, DO take some bodyguards. As well as ferrety bottom-of-the-heap poor people, who'll rob tourists like you quicker than you can say *Tempus fugit*, there are also gangs of posh kids, who think it's fun to go out and give an unsuspecting passer-by a good kicking.

---

cold pool. Wander in the cool shade of the ornamental gardens. Watch a boxing or wrestling match.

AQUEDUCT OF NERO

He may have been mad, bad and dangerous to know, but Emperor Nero did make himself useful by building this aqueduct to carry water from the countryside into the city.

THE COLOSSEUM

50,000 can cram in here to witness the most degrading, disgusting, deplorable spectacles money can buy. See Gladiators fight to the death in their thousands! (Frankly, it gets boring after the first ten or eleven.) See the senseless slaughter of wild and exotic animals on the very brink of extinction! See Christians being fed to the lions! **Sounds great doesn't it?** But it gets better – it's absolutely **FREE!!**

FORUM OF AUGUSTUS

Stuffed with temples and law courts. Emperor Augustus turned Rome from shoddy bricks to gleaming marble, and this forum is one of his many building projects. Most cities have one forum, Rome has at least three.

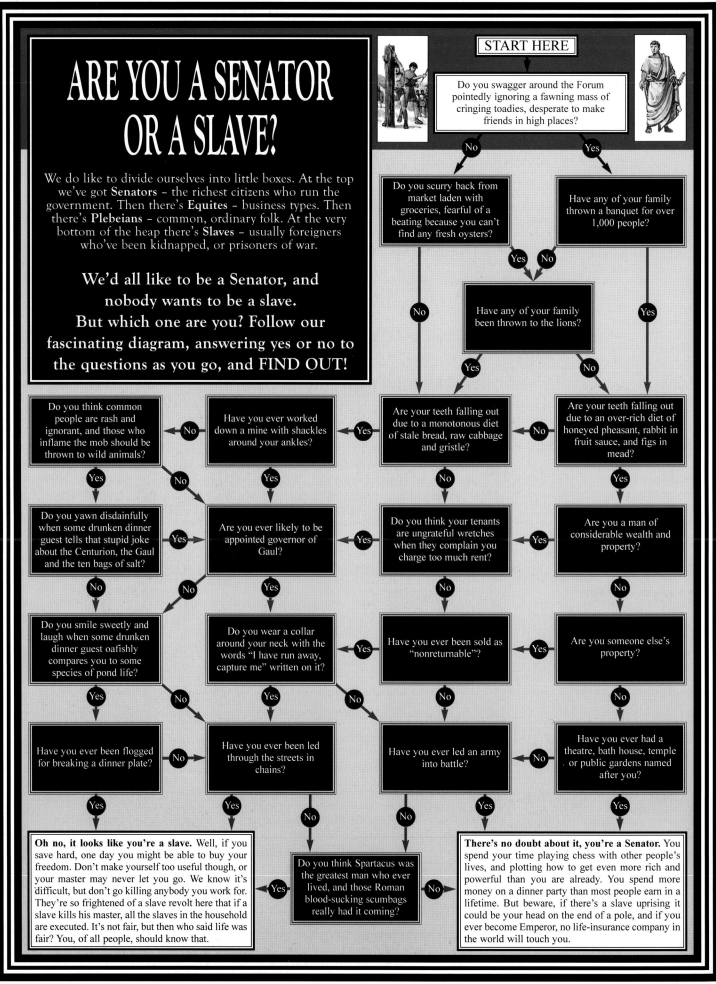

ARE YOU A SENATOR OR A SLAVE?

We do like to divide ourselves into little boxes. At the top we've got **Senators** – the richest citizens who run the government. Then there's **Equites** – business types. Then there's **Plebeians** – common, ordinary folk. At the very bottom of the heap there's **Slaves** – usually foreigners who've been kidnapped, or prisoners of war.

We'd all like to be a Senator, and nobody wants to be a slave. But which one are you? Follow our fascinating diagram, answering yes or no to the questions as you go, and FIND OUT!

START HERE

Do you swagger around the Forum pointedly ignoring a fawning mass of cringing toadies, desperate to make friends in high places?

No → Do you scurry back from market laden with groceries, fearful of a beating because you can't find any fresh oysters?

Yes → Have any of your family thrown a banquet for over 1,000 people?

Have any of your family been thrown to the lions?

Are your teeth falling out due to a monotonous diet of stale bread, raw cabbage and gristle?

Are your teeth falling out due to an over-rich diet of honeyed pheasant, rabbit in fruit sauce, and figs in mead?

Do you think common people are rash and ignorant, and those who inflame the mob should be thrown to wild animals?

Have you ever worked down a mine with shackles around your ankles?

Do you think your tenants are ungrateful wretches when they complain you charge too much rent?

Are you a man of considerable wealth and property?

Do you yawn disdainfully when some drunken dinner guest tells that stupid joke about the Centurion, the Gaul and the ten bags of salt?

Are you ever likely to be appointed governor of Gaul?

Do you smile sweetly and laugh when some drunken dinner guest oafishly compares you to some species of pond life?

Do you wear a collar around your neck with the words "I have run away, capture me" written on it?

Have you ever been sold as "nonreturnable"?

Are you someone else's property?

Have you ever been flogged for breaking a dinner plate?

Have you ever been led through the streets in chains?

Have you ever led an army into battle?

Have you ever had a theatre, bath house, temple or public gardens named after you?

Do you think Spartacus was the greatest man who ever lived, and those Roman blood-sucking scumbags really had it coming?

Oh no, it looks like you're a slave. Well, if you save hard, one day you might be able to buy your freedom. Don't make yourself too useful though, or your master may never let you go. We know it's difficult, but don't go killing anybody you work for. They're so frightened of a slave revolt here that if a slave kills his master, all the slaves in the household are executed. It's not fair, but then who said life was fair? You, of all people, should know that.

There's no doubt about it, you're a Senator. You spend your time playing chess with other people's lives, and plotting how to get even more rich and powerful than you are already. You spend more money on a dinner party than most people earn in a lifetime. But beware, if there's a slave uprising it could be your head on the end of a pole, and if you ever become Emperor, no life-insurance company in the world will touch you.

Roman Record

PEER INTO THE MISTY REALMS OF TOMORROW WITH THE ROMAN RECORD

Watching the sky

16 ancient sages in Rome called augers peer at the sky. Then they make predictions based on the shapes of flocks of birds, clouds and lightning. This is the most ancient divination technique known to Romans.

What they said to Bibulous:
"The conjugation of a dark thundercloud, and the hooting of an owl in the east at sunset, quite clearly suggests that the gods will visit an adverse foreign exchange rate on this business venture."

Pros
Venerable, respected, sanctioned by tradition.

Cons
They could say ANYTHING, couldn't they?

FORETELLING THE FUTURE

Let's face it, who WOULDN'T like to know what the future holds in store? But with so many different ways of predicting the will of the gods, which one <u>do</u> you go for? All of the methods we currently use go in and out of fashion as much as the cut of your tunic. And all of them are so old we've forgotten why they work and even where they came from.

WE'VE GONE CRITICAL

Here at the *Record* we thought it was about time we turned a critical eye on the prediction industry. So when businessman Bibulous Unctuous wrote to us recently asking whether he should invest in the Armenian slave trade we put our top divination techniques to the test.

We've picked five of the most well known, and asked their practitioners whether the gods would look aimiably on Bibulous's investment. Here's what they said, followed by what WE think about it.

Our verdict: There's a sucker born every minute!

The Sibylline books

These are a set of prophesies by the prophetess Sibyl who lived in a cave near Naples around 750BC.

They're kept in the Temple of Apollo in Rome and, following authorization by the Senate, are consulted by seers at times of extreme national crisis.

What they said to Bibulous:
"Whether you should invest in the Armenian slave trade is NOT what WE would consider an EXTREME NATIONAL CRISIS. Now be off with you, and don't show your face here again.

Pros
Nice walk up to the temple.

Cons
Crotchety staff. No prediction.

Palm reading

Some old lady looks at the lines on your palm and makes predictions based on them.

What she said to Bibulous:
"The broken lifeline in the mount of Venus suggests you will soon be run over by a chariot while crossing the road, and therefore will be unable to enjoy any adequate return on your investment."

Pros
Dramatic increase in road-safety drill for Bibulous.

Cons
Reply limited only by palm-reader's imagination.

Animal innards

A special priest called a haruspice slits open a sacrificial animal and examines its liver. Then he makes predictions about the gods' attitude to your special problem, according to whether the liver's the wrong shape, or blotchy, or the right shape and clear.

He also pronounces on weeping statues and talking cows.

What he said to Bibulous:
"Well, this oddly bulbous vein here is a clear indicator that the gods are partial to low returns on your immediate investment. However, the slightly grey tinge to the upper lobe of the liver does suggest that, with other market indicators taken into account, returns should be good within a decade."

Pros
You and your family get to eat the sacrifice afterwards.

Cons
Messy, expensive, almost certainly unreliable.

Reading the stars

An astrologer examines the position of the stars and makes predictions based on whether or not Aries is rising in Capricorn, and what time of night the Moon comes up etc, etc...

What she said to Bibulous:
"You're a Virgo aren't you?" (He isn't.) "I can tell by your stern and scrubbed appearance. Hey, loosen up, man, you need to do some tantric yoga.

Your chart shows that Mercury rising in the house of Aquarius suggests that investing in the Armenian slave trade would be really far out."

Pros
Accepted three beads and a daisy as payment.

Cons
We wouldn't touch this with a barge pole. <u>AND</u> this stuff is **really** popular. We can't believe everyone takes it so seriously.

NEXT WEEK: HOW THROWING DICE CAN REALLY DECIDE YOUR FUTURE!

EMPIRE ESTATES

34 AQUEDUCT AVENUE, ROME

Luxury Town House

When only the best will do. A most elegant and centrally situated town house in Rome's choicest district. What more visible sign of authority could any senator, banker, businessman or general require?

• Impressive atrium for meeting and greeting guests.
• Decorative courtyard pool.
• Semi-transparent stone windows.
• Manageable walled garden.
• Most unusual and status-enhancing second floor, for family bedrooms.

• Shop at front of house, to rent out.
• Running water toilet.
• East facing study, giving bright morning light, and plenty of ventilation to prevent mildew occurring in paper and papyrus.

Potential buyers should note: This property has no bathroom, but there are public baths a short walk away.

RURAL PROPERTIES

VILLA

Only once in a century does a property as magnificent as this come on the market. "Dunrulin" in Etruria is the former home of a murdered and disgraced emperor, and Empire Estates is expecting a quick and competitive sale.

• Part of large estate producing olive oil and wine.
• Own baths, wine making area and granary.
• Beautifully decorated mosaics and murals.

ALSO ON THE MARKET

LARGE FARM
Maximize your profits with this magnificent farm in Apulia. Comes complete with staff and 300 slaves. Specializes in figs and wheat.

SMALL FARM
Every Roman dreams of a place away from the squalor and bustle of the city. What better place to start than this comfy three-room farm in Umbria.

EVEN SMALLER FARM
A property that's within reach of even the most humble buyer. Would suit extremely capable carpenter

---

BIG OLIVE APARTMENTS

ALL PRICES ON APPLICATION

The Forum Rome

APPLY WITHOUT DELAY

There's no place like Rome, and what better place to live than in a Big Olive apartment block. Rome has got 46,000 of these Insulae blocks, and we've just built another ten of them.

✦ **No kitchens!** Why cook when inns and bars are so cheap and convenient? (Besides, who wants to burn the block down? Imagine your shame!)

✦ **No private toilets!** But what better place to complain about the state of your bowels than the apartment's standard 12 seater, open-plan public toilet bench. Sympathy guaranteed!

✦ **No running water!** Get super-fit carrying buckets of water up five flights of stairs. A conveniently nearby fountain provides a constant supply.

✦ **No peace!** All apartments have shops or taverns on the ground floor.

THE CONSUL DELUXE
First floor, expansive, stone walls, luxurious, balcony (but watch out for refuse and sewage being thrown from upper floors.)

THE CENTURION
Second floor standard accommodation, wood-burning braziers, big windows.

THE TRADESMAN
Top floor, wooden living spaces, small easy-to-heat rooms.

Big Olive apartments take no responsibility for the upkeep and condition of their apartments, especially with regard to firehazard (extremely high), hygiene (extremely poor) and comfort (pretty chilly). Tenants are welcome on the understanding that their home may collapse at any moment.

RECORD WOMEN'S PAGE

WE'RE POTTY ABOUT THESE STANDS

KITCHEN NEWS

Those lucky few readers who are rich enough to have a kitchen will be interested in these new utensils.

Increase the life of your cooking pots with these pottery and iron stands. Place directly between your hot charcoal stove and the pot of your choice, and hey presto, all the heat, with none of the wear and tear.

Strain those sauces with the all-metal Stranulus Strainer. Sturdy construction means it will survive

Pot stands. So simple! So convenient!

the attentions of even the clumsiest slave.

WEDDING LATEST

• Most girls are waiting until they're 14 to get married now, although a few still take the plunge at 12 or even earlier. Medical chiefs are not happy with the trend. Death in childbirth is still all too common, and most experts agree that the younger the mother, the better chance of survival for both her and baby.

• Be sure to arrange your marriage for a good day on the calendar. Most weddings still take place in the second half of June, which is the luckiest time of the year.

• Our wedding day rituals are spreading! Placing the ring on the third finger, left hand, wearing a white wedding tunic, and having the groom carry the bride over the threshold of their new home, are all catching on throughout the Empire.

RECIPE OF THE DAY

ANCHOVY DELIGHT WITHOUT THE ANCHOVIES

It's happened to us all. You want to do a nice tangy anchovy dish, but there's none to be found at the market.
Your guests are waiting, **and they're getting impatient!**

What do you do? Here's what...

1. *Take a good size pan and gently heat a fish sauce with a dash of pepper, a butter and flour roux, and a little olive oil.*

2. *Add four fillets of grilled fish (any white fish will do) and stir.*

3. *Gently fold in raw eggs to bind the mixture together.*

4. *Now – the magic ingredient. Add a good quantity of small jellyfish. (Much easier to get hold of than anchovies, and half the price.)*

5. *Simmer until well cooked.*

6. *Serve with ground pepper. Not one of your guests will guess you've run out of anchovies!*

Today's recipe comes from Apicus's Cookbook, available in all good bookshops now

cut out and keep

FASHION UPDATE

SOFT TOUCH COSTS A BUNDLE

• **Fed up with that wool tunic?** Get hubby to trade in twenty slaves, and he can buy you the latest silk *stola* robe. Imported at great expense from faraway China, silk is so soft to the touch, and beautiful to look at. Buy silk and you'll soon appreciate why it costs three times its weight in gold.

• **Looking pale as a lily is still very fasionable**. Even if you spend the day at the market selling cabbages in the hot sun, you can still get that "I haven't done a day's work in my life" pampered look by rubbing powdered chalk on your visible extremities.

• **Ornate hairstyles are IN.** Get that piled high and curly look with heated metal tongs, and keep your hair in place with bone or ivory pins.

• **Longing to look different?** The answer to dull, dark, run-of-the-mill Mediterranean hair may be on your doorstep. Many slaves from our northern provinces have red or blonde hair. Such exotic plumage is wasted on them, so simply shave it off and have it made into a wig. If they complain, have them whipped and tell them it'll soon grow back.

BELLONA'S BAUBLES

We've come a long way since the days of the republic, when only the rich were allowed to wear gold rings. Having an empire means having the best choice in the world of precious stones and metals. Here's a selection of our latest wares...

"How delightfully unusual" – that's what they'll all say when they see your jet stone bangle, all the way from Britannia.

Gold ring with chic design cut into opal.

Gold snake bracelet. Looks great, and it's guaranteed to bring you a longer life.

Dangle with style with these gold earrings set with emeralds.

GOD SHOP

HELPING YOU DECIDE WHO'S WORTH A WORSHIP

VITAL FOR SURVIVAL

A standard-issue Roman temple. Remember, a sacrifice in time saves nine!

YOU'RE SPOILED FOR CHOICE!!!

Religion in Ancient Rome has always been a pick-and-mix affair. We've got our own Roman gods and goddesses, and keeping them sweet is vital for the survival of Rome. Then we've got all sorts of other ones from the people we've conquered over the centuries.

We don't mind who else you worship, as long as you pay due respect to our state gods and the Emperor!

THE STATE RELIGION

Rite or wrong? Of all our gods and goddesses are the state deities are the ones you've really got to watch out for. We've got temples dedicated to them all over Rome and if you don't say the occasional prayer, or offer the odd sacrifice, they won't protect you as you go about your daily business.

There are 14 or 15 really famous ones, and a whole bunch of lesser ones. (True, most of them have been adapted from the Greek models, but who cares? If the cap fits wear it!) Here's an overview of a few of the big cheeses to give you the general idea...

JUPITER

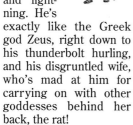

He's king of the gods, and the deity in charge of thunder and lightning. He's exactly like the Greek god Zeus, right down to his thunderbolt hurling, and his disgruntled wife, who's mad at him for carrying on with other goddesses behind her back, the rat!

NEPTUNE

God of the Sea, and identical to Poseidon in Greece. You pray to him if you are going on a voyage and don't want your ship to sink in a storm.

CERES

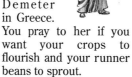

She's the goddess of agriculture, and the same as Demeter in Greece. You pray to her if you want your crops to flourish and your runner beans to sprout.

HOLIDAY TIME

As you know, each year there are over 100 public holidays and ceremonies here in Rome, devoted to venerating and celebrating these gods.

They're a great opportunity to let your hair down, get staggeringly drunk, and stuff your face with top quality nosh. Our fave festivals here at the *Record* are:

•**Anna Perenna** on March 15, which celebrates the goddess of the year. On this festival some Romans believe you'll live for as many years as you can drink glasses of wine.

•**Saturnalia** on December 17, which is devoted to the God Saturn. We celebrate this by swapping places with our slaves for a day, and waiting on them at the dinner table.

HOUSEHOLD GODS

These are a lot more affable than the state gods. Each family has its own personal guardian spirit – called the *genius* – and each part of the house has its own little domestic god. For example there's **Janus**, who's the god of the doorway, and **Vesta**, the god of the hearth. You keep these gods happy by praying to them and leaving small gifts of wine, bread or fruit at the family shrine. (Make sure you do too – otherwise the door will start to jam, and the fire will be impossible to light!)

EXOTIC FOREIGN STUFF

Many Romans find the state gods a bit too distant, and not terribly reliable. After all, if you sacrifice an expensive sheep to Neptune to keep you safe at sea, and then your ship gets ravaged by pirates and you spend 30 years as a galley slave, it somewhat undermines Neptune's credibility. So, many Romans are turning to a variety of foreign gods and religions. Here are a few of them...

CYBELE

The ladies' choice. Cybele comes from Asia Minor and she's most concerned about fertility, healing and nature. Ceremonies to worship her include wild music and dancing, which sounds quite entertaining, and definitely more fun than leaving an over-ripe apple on the family shrine for the god of the doorway. (Is it any wonder he never takes it...?)

MITHRAS

Top god with soldiers. Mithras comes from Persia and offers his followers life after death, which is quite a comfort when you're facing 20,000 fired-up barbarians all determined to hack your head off with a blunt axe. No women allowed in this religion.

JESUS

Popular with poor people, Jesus promised his followers life after death. **This religion only believes in one god.** It's not a good one for anyone seeking a quiet life, as it's unpopular with the Roman government which requires citizens to worship the Emperor and state gods. Expect a lot of persecution.

ISIS

This one comes from Egypt. Isis became really popular in Rome when devotee Cleopatra came here in 45BC.

This religion involves paying homage to goddess Isis who rules heaven and earth and wheat and barley.

Lots of elaborate and mysterious ceremonies to keep you wondering what it's all about.

ENTERTAINMENT EXTRA

NUDITY AND VIOLENCE NOT ENOUGH

CLAIMS THEATRE OWNER

The theatre has long been popular in Rome. We may not be as highbrow as the Greeks – but who really needs brow-furrowing metaphysical tragedies about man's relationship with the gods when you can have comedies stuffed to bursting with gratuitous nudity and violence!

STIFF

But recently, theatres have been facing stiff competition from fatalities-guaranteed chariot racing and mega-death gladiator tournaments. But fear not, culture lovers – theatre managers know just how to win back the customers!

PEP PLAN

"I've been in this business for 25 years, and I tell you, you can't go wrong with nudity and fighting," said theatre manager Andrius Ludicrous Wetulus. "But the problem with nudity is that once you're there, you can't go any further. After all you can't be any more naked than totally naked.

"However, violence is **different**, and that's where we intend to **pep things up**. Check out our forthcoming attractions. We've got plays coming up with **real live crucifixions**, and **hands being chopped off**. Best of all, for one night only, we've got a production of *The Death of Hercules* where the actor playing Hercules is **burned alive at the end of the play!**

RED HOT

"**Does he mind? I'm sure he does, but he's a convicted criminal and we've managed to persuade him that we'll do something FAR WORSE to him if he doesn't cooperate with this particular stunt!**"

In Roman theatre, when the actors say "I'm dying out here", they really mean it!

NEXT WEEK: INTERVAL SNACKS – SPECIAL REPORT

THE RECORD SALUTES
THE GREEKS!!!

The Greeks! What a classic bunch of fellows. As soon as we saw them we realized they deserved more than just conquest, exploitation and slavery.
So after we'd conquered them, exploited them and turned them into slaves, we COPIED their culture and ideas.
We're not daft, are we?
So join us in the *Record* guide to WHAT WE GOT FROM THE GREEKS!!!

CITY LAYOUT

When we build a new city we build it on a grid system. That means all the streets are at right angles. This was invented by Greek town planner Hippodamus in 450BC. When we occupied Greek cities we liked the idea and adopted it immediately.

CITY STYLE

OK, we admit it. WE LOVE GREEK BUILDINGS. That sense of proportion, harmony and balance gets us every time! Our temples are almost carbon copies of Greek ones – probably because they're built by Greek craftsmen and architects. We swiped the Greek column style wholesale, but we've added a few home-grown Roman touches of our own.

INTERIOR DECORATION

Sigh. Those Greeks, they really know how to paint a room. We love a nicely decorated house, and no one does it better than a Greek interior designer. Mosaics, wall painting, figurines, the Greeker the better!

COINS

Ker-ching! Yes, when we saw they used money we copied that too. The first Roman mint opened in 269BC. (Different face on the coins, of course – we do have some imagination.)

GODS

We've adopted Greek mythology lock, stock and barrel. We've given them different names, but apart from that our top gods are exactly the same as the Greeks, right down to the little details. For example, they have god of wine Dionysus, a portly fun guy who likes to get drunk and have a good time. Our god of wine is portly fun guy Bacchus, who likes to get drunk and have a good time.

MEDICINE

Say alpha!! Yup, practically all our medical knowledge comes from Greek physician Hippocrates. We've even adopted the transparently ridiculous Greek technique of sleeping in temples to try and cure ourselves.

ART

Ever since we first looted a Greek city we've been crazy about Greek art – those lovely engraved plates, that inlaid furniture, and especially those statues. We bet there won't be better statue makers until the Renaissance.

EDUCATION

Even though we're top nation, and anyone of any importance in the Empire has to speak Latin, all our brightest boys have to learn Greek at school. This is because all the best books are written in Greek, and Greek literature and philosophy is a MAJOR influence on our own culture.

The best universities are in Athens and Rhodes in Greece, and the richest Romans still send their kids there to finish their education.

AND THAT'S NOT NEARLY THE END OF IT. WE HAVEN'T EVEN MENTIONED PUBLIC SPEAKING, PHILOSOPHY, ATHLETIC GAMES, COMEDIES, MUSICALS AND POETRY. HOW DO THEY DO IT???

EXCLUSIVE RECORD SERVICE

What could be more everyday than a slave? They're as commonplace as togas and aqueducts. But unlike togas and aqueducts, slaves have minds of their own. How do you stop them from running away? What stops THEM from killing YOU? How should they be punished when they DO misbehave? Top slave dealer Senula Severus answers your queries...

SENULA'S SLAVE SPOT

STUPID

Dear Senula,
I know it's a stupid question, but where do slaves actually come from? They've always been around, but they must have come from SOMEWHERE in the first place.

Mr Honorius Constantius, Ravenna

I always say slaves are people that fate has given a second chance. Many are barbarian warriors. Our soldiers could have killed them, but no, out of kindness they turned them into slaves. Then there are the provincials who've rebelled against Rome. They could have been executed for their impertinence, but no – they're slaves too.

Then there are people sentenced to death by the courts, and children who were left to die in the street because their parents couldn't feed them... they were picked up by kindly slave dealers and given a new chance in life. Oh, and all the children of slaves are slaves too.

SUBSTANCE

Dear Senula,
I am a gentleman farmer from Britannia. We don't have many slaves out there. I'm passing through Rome and I'd like to know how I go about buying one.

Mr Iacus Bullus, Rome

Owning just one slave is rather vulgar. Anyone of any wealth and substance has at least eight. Many landowners have over 500.

You can buy slaves privately or from slave dealers. An established dealer is probably your best bet, unless you know the private individual you're buying from.

A dealer will guarantee that your investment is not a runaway, has no criminal record, and is in good health. Buying older slaves is cheaper, but I always say buy young, so you get more out of them.

Pick one that looks as well as can be expected. After all, you don't want to waste money on faulty goods.

Once you've bought, you'll be given a certificate of ownership. This can also prove that your slave is not a runaway.

Alternately you might like to consider renting. Rental slaves, though, are usually in much worse condition, and likely to offer a poorer service.

SURLY

Dear Senula,
These slaves are a surly bunch. I'm always having to hit them to get them to set the curls in my hair correctly. Why just the other day I had to have my cook whipped because he'd overdone the rabbit we were having for lunch. The look he gave me! What I'd like to know is, what stops these crabby beggars from killing us in our beds?

Mrs Callus Catillus, Verona

The main thing that keeps a slave in his place is FEAR, and there are a whole range of punishments available to the slave owner to make sure his property doesn't get out of hand. If your slave runs away you can have him whipped or thrown to the lions. A slave who murders his master is put to death. All the other slaves in that household are executed too. This encourages slaves to report any murder plots they hear about to their master.

BUY OUT

Dear Senula,
I'm a slave and I've heard that it's possible for me to BUY my freedom. Tell me more!

Name and address withheld, Rome

Yes it's true. It's not just whips and crucifixion that keeps a slave in his place. Many farsighted owners offer the prospect of freedom to slaves who serve their masters particularly well. It's quite an encouragement to be good. Some owners even free their slaves out of the goodness of their hearts. Others let their slaves BUY their freedom, from any tips and gifts they may have scraped together over the decades.

What happens is that you and your owner make a declaration in front of a magistrate, and then you're free.

LETTER OF THE WEEK

SEDITIOUS

Dear Senula,
I'm puzzled by this slavery business. My friend Stocksus Shario, who knows a fair bit about economics, says that keeping slaves is just as expensive as hiring workers to do the sort of jobs that most slaves do.

So why do people go to the expense of buying slaves which they then have to house, feed and clothe?

Mr L. Logicus, Venicia

In truth, I'm not often asked this question. What a seditious person your friend must be! People like to own slaves because it gives them a sense of power. What could be more deliciously powerful than having complete life-or-death control over another human being who's completely at the mercy of your whim and fancy? Having slaves also increases your status in the community. It's nice to look down on someone else too. It makes you feel better about yourself.

NEXT WEEK. SLAVES AND ALCOHOL - WHAT EVERY OWNER SHOULD KNOW

ROLL UP! ROLL UP!
FOR 123 DAYS OF
BLOOD, GUTS, AND CRUELTY
EEEEUUUGHHH, IT'S DISGUSTING!!!

Chomp! Slurp! Munch! The beast show gets bestial. And this isn't the worst of it.

Says the *Record*'s sports correspondent Soccerus Bungus.

Gladiators – they've been part of Roman culture since the days of the Republic. At first they only fought at funerals, as people believed the dead needed some bloodshed to see them on their way.

Then politicians started featuring gladiator fights as part of the public entertainment they laid on when they wanted to show off how wealthy they were. Now we've even got a special venue for gladiator matches – the Colosseum – with seating for 50,000.

Most Romans JUST LOVE these games, so I'm really flying in the face of fashion when I say it's all gone too far.

I've just been to day 11 of Emperor Trajan's 123-day Games, currently being held to celebrate our victory over the Dacians. Here I witnessed an unparalleled display of the most appalling savagery this side of a half-starved, rabid werewolf feeding frenzy.

JUGGLE

At 10:00am there was an **Opening Procession**. Everyone watched a host of gladiators, dancers, jugglers, priests and musicians as they trooped past the Emperor.

The horror really began at 11:00am with the **Beast shows.** The rarest, most powerful and beautiful species on Earth were brought into the arena and set against each other, or a ragged selection of unfortunate humans.

What was even more repulsive was the audience.

They were **thrilled** at the sight of starving bears as they battled to the death with terrified elephants. They **gasped** with excitement as bewildered panthers and bulls mauled each other. Then they **cheered** as Christians, criminals and assorted prisoners of war, were thrown to starving lions and **EATEN ALIVE.**

I was feeling quite queasy after that, so I was relieved to see in the schedule that the next section of the show was **comedy and light entertainment**.

I was expecting clowns, and musicians, but what I got was two blind, chained together gladiators fighting each other to the death. The audience roared with laughter as they swiped the air with their razor sharp swords. The clowns came after, but by then I wasn't in the mood for a laugh.

UNHINGED

At 2:00pm it was the **Gladiators.** This was where the audience got the chance to yell like unhinged lunatics. Each day 20 pairs of assorted gladiators fight in one-on-one contests. They're recruited from prisoners, slaves, and do-anything-for-money freemen.

During a bout, each pair of gladiators fought each other to a standstill, and the winner stood over the loser with his sword pointing into his vitals. The crowd and the Emperor then decided his fate... If the loser fought well, they cheered and he was dragged off to fight another day. If he'd not put his heart into it, they brayed and howled and he was killed on the spot.

And that wasn't the end of it. At 5:00pm there was a **Sea battle.** During a short intermission, the arena was flooded, and two fleets of a thousand men (picked from the meanest criminals and prisoners of war they could lay their hands on) engaged in a REALISTIC SEA BATTLE, with real swords, arrows and spears. Needless to say, most of them ended up getting killed.

STEAM

I know us Romans like to let off a little steam – especially the poor and unemployed ones with a lot of time on their hands. But isn't it time we stopped all this? I left that evening feeling like I'd spent the day in the company of the most repulsive, odious creatures on earth – and I work for a tabloid newspaper!!!

FLYING KICK SPARKS
RACING RIOT

GAIUS IN DEEP TROUBLE AGAIN

Gaius (on horse with red plumes on head) takes a corner three laps into his 39th win.

Rioting chariot racing fans tried to beat three shades of stuffing out of each other at Rome's 250,000 capacity Circus Maximus yesterday.

Stadium authorities were forced to call in security staff to restore order.

ABUSE

The trouble started around 3:00pm when fans of the Blue team* started to hurl abuse at the Red team's controversial star driver – hothead Gaius Brutulus Aquitanius – who had just won his 39th race, and was leaving the stadium in triumph.

As he passed by, Blue fan Scabius Scragulus Scrumulus shouted out "Gaius Brutulus Aquit-anius is a girly wimp who gives his horses lumps of sugar and puts pink ribbons on their tails."

SAVAGE

This was clearly too much for Gaius, a slave from Gaul, who leaped into the grandstand and replied with a savage flying head-kick. The incident ignited sections of the crowd, and a close quarters, hand-to-hand brawl erupted in various parts of the stadium. Racing was held up for half an hour while security staff attacked rioters with heavy wooden sticks, and cutting personal remarks.

ANGRY

Interviewed after the incident, Gaius's manager Ronus Ronulus admitted he was angry with his rider. "I didn't spend 30,000 sesterces buying him from the Greens in order to have him risk an injury attacking some cretin in the crowd. This sport is quite dangerous enough already. If he does it again he'll be whipped. Chariot racing is the nation's number one spectator sport, and this sort of conduct sets a very bad example. If fans want to see compet-itors behaving like bar-room brawlers they can go to a gladiator arena."

MOOD

But Gaius was in no mood to apologise. "Pah," he shrugged "what can they do. No one can balance on a flimsy wicker chariot quite like me, or take a corner so tightly without falling off, or control four wild horses with such finesse. My fans are the most loyal in the world, and if Ronulus has me whipped he'll have all the windows in his town house broken in the middle of the night...."

Note to foreign readers. Our racing teams are divided into four stables of drivers, trainers, and horses. They are called the Reds, Greens, Blues and Whites.

NEXT WEEK: THE SHOCKING TRUTH ABOUT BRIBES, TRAINERS, RIDERS AND HORSES...

WARM AS TOAST

THAT'S WHAT THEY'LL SAY WHEN YOU BUY A HOUSE WITH

HORATIUS CENTRAL HEATING

ECONOMICAL – Heat retaining pillars keep your house hot, even after the fires have gone out.

EASY – Just a few fires do all the work! Get your slave to keep them going.

SAFE – Say goodbye to the fire risk of an open grate and wooden floorboards.

Especially recommended for citizens in Britannia and Northern Gaul, where the sun doesn't shine quite like it does in good old Rome.

HOW TO MEET GIRLS

Do you pass your days drunk as a skunk, wondering why you're such a dud with the ladies? Do you spend long sleepless nights lost in torment, because Corinna at number 23 spurns your attentions with a haughty sneer? Suffer no longer. Join me, OVID, top poet, failed lawyer, and Roman literary genius, on a rollercoaster VOYAGE OF DISCOVERY with my book THE ART OF LOVE.

Just check out these tips from Chapter Three, "HOW TO MEET GIRLS AT CHARIOT RACES". You've spotted the gal of your dreams, so how do you get to speak to her? Here's how!

Step one. Stand behind her and listen for which team she follows. Immediately start cheering for the same team.

Step two. Try and get to sit down next to her. Then tell the dimwit behind to stop digging his knees in her back. Such courtesies are guaranteed to win over her simple female heart. (Top tip: Make sure he's not built like a seasoned gladiator, or it'll be HIM that's making an impression – on your skull.)

Step three. It's bound to be a hot day, so you can fan her with your racing program. If that doesn't get you well in there, then I'LL GIVE YOU YOUR MONEY BACK.

Yearn for love no longer. Write to me, OVID, right now, enclosing just 20 denarii, and I'll send you by return post THE ART OF LOVE. And remember, OLD DOGS **CAN** LEARN NEW TRICKS. WOOOF, WOOOF!!!!! (Box 48)

ANNOUNCEMENTS

Attention, citizens of Rome. A major misunderstanding has occurred. We believe it was Remus that murdered Romulus, and then went on to found the capital city – **not the other way around**. Rome should be renamed Reme at once! Send your missives of support to: Spotterus Crankius, President, The Remus Society, 24 Basilica Avenue, Reme. TOGETHER, WE CAN CHANGE THE WORLD. Box 29

JOBS

WE NEED MEN
Due to a high turnover of staff, the Roman Fire Brigade seeks NEW RECRUITS. Some skill with bucket of water and sponge would be useful, but not essential. With our hot climate, rickety wooden apartments and open fires, YOU'LL NEVER BE BORED!!! Box 31

FOR SALE

OLD GOAT
Hours of fun with the pet you can milk and fleece. Guaranteed never to bite or butt. Box 36

HAIR
Beautiful blond tresses – ideal for a wig. From recent consignment of freshly delivered Goths. (No more fun for them.) Box 39

"SLAVES! SLAVES! SLAVES!"
The one-stop shop, for all your slavery needs. Box 41

NET AND TRIDENT
Used once. Suit fisherman or gladiator. Box 88.

FIDDLE-DE-DEE!!!!

Forget Dungeons and Dragons. Re-enact the burning of Rome with FIDDLE-DE-DEE – the role-play game for Nero fans and city planners alike. Contains violin, "Easie-lite" arson kit, and full instructions. (Sheet music not included.) Box 91.

HONEST OCTAVIAN'S SECOND HAND FURNITURE EMPORIUM

HONEST OCTAVIAN'S, VII TRAJAN ROAD, ROME.

EXQUISITE MARBLE TABLE

Just the thing for a picnic in the garden. Seller has hernia. Buyer collects.

BARGAIN PRICES

BRASS LAMP

Genie free (or money back before you can say Abracadabra)

BIG CHEST

Sturdy wood construction. Ideal for togas and tunics.

DELIGHTFUL ARMLESS CHAIRS

Selection of armless chairs – guaranteed to fit even the largest bottom.

SALE ON

Index

Achilles, 90
Alexander the Great, 78-79
animals,
    farmyard, 15
    pets, 15, 61
    wild, 13, 19
architecture, 78, 87, 116-117, 124
armies,
    Egyptian, 41
    Greek, 71, 77-78, 83
    Roman, 106
Augustus, 105
Australia, discovery of, 9

barbarians, 39, 46, 80, 112-114
battles,
    Marathon, 72
    Thermopylae, 73
bronze, discovery of, 19
burial rituals, 30, 35, 46-47, 67

Caesar, Julius, 104
calendars, Egyptian, 49
Carthage, defeat of, 100
cave painting, 11
cities, growth of, 18-19, 69, 111,
    115-117, 124
coins,
    Greek, 71, 124
    Roman, 102
Constantinople, 111, 114
crime and punishment, 48, 70, 93

dreams, meaning of, 54

education,
    Egyptian, 37, 45
    Greek, 85, 124
emperors,
    Roman, 107-108, 110-111,
    114
empire,
    Egyptian, 41
    Greek, 69-70, 78-81, 92-93
    Roman, 99, 102, 105,
        108-110, 115

employment,
    Egyptian, 31, 41, 47, 63
    Greek, 93, 94
    Roman, 128
    Stone Age, 19
entertainment,
    dancing, 28, 57
    drinking, 58, 60
    feasting, 89
    parties, 58-59
evolution, 2-5, 8, 19, 24

farming, 14, 16, 102
fashion, 14, 22, 53-54, 58, 91, 121
    beauty, 22, 52
    hair, 52-53
    jewels, 39
fire, first use of, 6, 19
fishing, 27
food and cooking, 3, 26-27, 60,
    83, 89, 121
fortune-telling, 49, 83, 119

gladiators, 117, 126

Hadrian's Wall, 109
health, 16, 29, 55, 90
housing, 7, 42, 120
hunting, 3, 14, 19, 20-21, 64

irrigation, 16, 62

language,
    beginnings of speech,
    24-25
    Greek, 68
    Latin, 115
literature, 89, 91
love and marriage, 60, 83, 121

mathematics, 37
medicine, 29, 55, 90, 124
    Hippocrates, 90, 124
metal, invention of, 15
Minotaur, 66
mummies, 35, 46-47
music, 28, 57, 77

Mycenaeans, 67

Neanderthals, 10

painting and drawing, 10-11, 56
pharaohs, 40-41, 43, 45-46, 57
philosophers, Greek, 84-85
politics,
    Greek, 69, 73, 80
    Roman, 92-93, 98-99, 103,
        118
pottery, 12, 86-87
pyramids, 35

religion,
    Egyptian, 38, 43-44
    Greek, 82
    Roman, 122-124
    Stone Age, 31
Rome, 116-117
Romulus and Remus, 98

sculpture, 57, 81
slavery, 83, 118, 125
sport,
    Egyptian, 64
    Greek, 83, 95-96
    Roman, 126-127

theatre, 88, 123
tools, invention of, 3-4, 15, 32
travel, 17, 91
tribes, appearance of, 10

wars, 38, 40-41, 67, 74, 76, 79,
    100-101
    Peloponnesian, 76
    Punic, 100-101
    Trojan, 67
weapons, 15, 20-21, 75-76
    navies, 46, 75
wheel, invention of, 17
witch doctor, 29, 31
writing, 18, 36
    hieroglyphs, 36
    papyrus, 37

PHOTOGRAPHIC CREDITS

The Stone Age Sentinel
AKG Photo, London (pages 11, 12, 23); Ancient Art and Architecture Collection, London (page 20);
Robert Harding Photo Library/Rainbird, London (page 9).

The Egyptian Echo
All photos between pages 33 and 64 come from the
Werner Forman Archive, London, except page 53, bottom; which came from Bildarchiv Foto
Marburg. Credit is also due to: British Museum, London (52, 54 middle, 58, 59); Egyptian
Museum, Cairo (34, 38 bottom right, 40 top, 53); Louvre Museum, Paris (55); Musees Royaux du
Cinquantenaire, Brussels (49, 60); Staatlich Museum,
Berlin (47); E. Strouhal (36, 48, 54 top).

The Greek Gazette
Ancient Art and Architecture Collection, London (76, 78, 81, 90, 96); e.t. archive, London (74
(British Museum)); Museo Nationale, Naples (84).

The Roman Record
Ancient Art and Architecture Collection, Ltd (110, 111);
Barnaby's Picture Library (126); C.M.Dixon (104, 114); e.t. archive (113 – Pantheon, Paris); Werner
Forman Archive (108 – Museo Nazionale Romano, Rome).

Every effort has been made to trace the copyright holders of material in this book.
If any rights have been omitted, the publishers offer to rectify this in any subsequent
editions following notification.

First published in 1998 by Usborne Publishing Ltd,
83-85 Saffron Hill, London EC1N 8RT, England.
Copyright © Usborne Publishing Ltd, 1998.
The name Usborne and the device are Trade Marks of Usborne Publishing Ltd.

First published in America in 1999